# Schools of Opportunity

# Schools of Opportunity

## 10 Research-Based Models of Equity in Action

Edited by Adam York, Kevin Welner,
and Linda Molner Kelley

**TEACHERS COLLEGE PRESS**

**TEACHERS COLLEGE** | COLUMBIA UNIVERSITY

NEW YORK AND LONDON

Published by Teachers College Press,® 1234 Amsterdam Avenue, New York, NY 10027

*Library of Congress Cataloging-in-Publication Data is available at loc.gov*

ISBN 978-0-8077-6836-5 (paper)
ISBN 978-0-8077-6837-2 (hardcover)
ISBN 978-0-8077-8173-9 (ebook)

Printed on acid-free paper
Manufactured in the United States of America

# Contents

**Introduction: The Schools of Opportunity Project**     **1**
*Matt Garcia and Michelle Renée Valladares*

1. **A Challenging, Supported, and Engaging Curriculum for All**     **19**
   *Kevin Welner and John Murphy*

2. **A Multipronged and Equity-Oriented Approach to Transforming School Climate: The Story of Revere High School**     **35**
   *Kathryn E. Wiley and Lourenço Garcia*

3. **Authentic and Equitable Engagement in Learning at Pocomoke High School**     **49**
   *Kellie Rolstad and Jenifer Rayne*

4. **Authentic Assessment Embedded in Project-Based Learning**     **67**
   *Jeffrey Palladino and Lorrie A. Shepard*

5. **Preserving, Deepening, and Growing a Professional Teaching Culture: Lessons From Casco Bay High School**     **89**
   *Linda Molner Kelley and Derek Pierce*
   *(with Matt Bernstein, Susan McCray, and Rebecca Lynch Nichols)*

6. **Clark Street Community School: A Place for All Students to Live, Learn, and Create**     **109**
   *Jill Gurtner and Julie Mead*

7. **A Holistic Approach to Learning and Development: Shifting Paradigms One School at a Time**     **131**
   *Kristen P. Goessling, Kate Somerville, Adam York, and Kimberly Grayson*

8.  Student Organizing and Leadership for Education Justice:
    Curriculum as a Site for Healing and Wellness                    146
    *Kate Somerville, Kristen P. Goessling, Adam York, and
    Kimberly Grayson*

9.  The High School in the Middle of Everywhere: Nebraska's
    Lincoln High                                                     158
    *Edmund T. Hamann, Janet Eckerson, and Mark Larson*

10. "Like a Family": Sharing Leadership With Teachers, Students,
    Families, and Community at Rainier Beach High School             176
    *Ann M. Ishimaru and Dwane Chappelle*

Conclusion: From Schools of Opportunity to Systems
    of Opportunity                                                   193
    *Jeannie Oakes and Kevin Welner*


Index                                                                219

About the Contributors                                               230

# Introduction

## The Schools of Opportunity Project

*Matt Garcia and Michelle Renée Valladares*

This book's outlook on public schools is highly optimistic. In these pages, school leaders and researchers share stories of public high schools engaging in the long-term and demanding work of expanding educational opportunities for all their students. They provide evidence through their detailed examples that it is possible to create a safe and welcoming campus climate, provide all students with rich and rigorous curriculum, and treat teachers as professionals, among many other proven equity strategies. Volumes of past research document that the process of closing opportunity gaps is challenging (Darling-Hammond, 2015; Darling-Hammond et al., 2021; Oakes & Rogers, 2006; Welner, 2001). In contrast, this book shows that educators can successfully pursue equity despite immense obstacles such as educating students during a global pandemic, increasingly polarized political contexts, an educator shortage, and, in many cases, unsupportive policies and limited funding.

All of the schools described in these pages were recognized for expanding educational opportunities, and their perseverance charts a path forward that attends to multiple dimensions of student needs. These rich examples of schools expanding educational opportunities in challenging times can help us reimagine what schools and education systems could become if we fully resourced the innovative ideas and strategies developed by remarkable educators in less challenging times. We hope this book demonstrates how evidence-based, equity-focused change is possible. But our greater hope is that readers understand the importance of supporting these initiatives at multiple policy levels; that support is needed if we are to take these ideas to scale across the entire public education system.

The National Education Policy Center (NEPC; https://nepc.colorado.edu) launched the Schools of Opportunity Project (https://schoolsofopportunity .org) in 2014 to "recognize public high schools that demonstrate an extraordinary commitment to equity and excellence by giving every student the opportunity to succeed" (Welner & Burris, 2014). We asked, *What would happen if we recognized high schools not for the average test scores that are easily predictable in our unequal society but rather holistically for implementing research-proven strategies that expand educational opportunity?* We wondered what could be demonstrated by recognizing schools in this way and which audiences might pay attention. After several rounds of recognition, we now know that such measures allow schools to highlight some of their often-overlooked best work. We also now know that a broad audience of the public, school leaders, media, parents, and students are interested and inspired when we call attention to these exceptional schools. From 2015 through 2019 (when the pandemic forced a pause in the recognition project), 52 high schools were recognized as Schools of Opportunity.

Recognized Schools of Opportunity have a broad vision of success in both innovative practices and measured outcomes. They understand that standardized tests measure only a fraction of what students, parents, and society ask of our schools and seek for our children. Research has empirically established the limited causal role of schools in generating those test scores (Welner & LaCour, 2021). Less than a quarter of the test-score variance between schools can be attributed to measured differences in classroom teaching (Dobbie & Fryer, 2009). Since at least the time of the 1966 Coleman report (Coleman et al., 1966), researchers have understood the powerful role played by opportunity gaps that arise outside of school as a result of concentrated poverty and racism. This is especially true of schools serving students whose families face the harsh realities of inequities in all systems beyond schools, including the workforce, housing, health care, and the criminal justice system.

Although schools cannot fix the problems created by the stark inequities in our society, they can take them into account and then develop practices in response to student needs. Over the last several decades, replicable teaching and learning strategies have been developed for schools to address the inequalities caused by poverty and racism.

In 2013, Kevin Welner and Prudence Carter edited a book called *Closing the Opportunity Gap: What America Must Do to Give Every Child an Even Chance.* The book identified the opportunity gaps and offered research-based, within-school policies and practices to help close those gaps. Following the book's publication, Carol Burris, an NEPC Fellow and the principal of a high school that had been repeatedly recognized based on outcomes, proposed a Schools of Opportunity recognition project. Her idea was to take the ideas from the book and create a framework for measuring the presence of such policies and practices in schools, recognizing public high schools that do this work effectively.[1] The schools presented in this volume are among those recognized by the ensuing project.

To provide context for the following chapters, we first introduce you to the opportunity gap framework that guides the Schools of Opportunity Project. We then describe how that framework is operationalized as clear criteria. We move on to a brief description of how Schools of Opportunity are recognized. Throughout these descriptions, we introduce the schools discussed in this volume.

These schools and their stories embody important lessons for the future of education reform. We sincerely hope that parents, educators, school leaders, and policymakers find this book helpful as they develop their own strategies for closing opportunity gaps in schools across the country. By seeing what is possible even in the hardest of times, we also hope that this book supports the call for expanding support for public education as a whole so that these strategies become commonplace in schools around the nation.

## THE OPPORTUNITY GAP AND OPPORTUNITIES TO LEARN

We define the *opportunity gap* as unequal chances to learn resulting from systemic inequalities, such as poverty and racism. This simple concept shifts the focus from achievement on test scores, attributed to teachers and students, to a lens that foregrounds the opportunities schools and school systems (and larger societal systems) provide young people to learn over the course of their lives (Welner & Carter, 2013). Academic conversations about opportunities to learn date back to the 1960s and were becoming more common toward the end of the 1980s. For example, Oakes (1989) linked the concept of opportunity to learn to the development of educational indicators for understanding the contexts of learning environments in addition to learning outcomes. Most scholars of opportunity to learn standards reference Jennifer O'Day and Mike Smith (1993) as the moment when this academic concept entered the mainstream political conversation. O'Day and Smith (1993) were careful to include *opportunity to learn standards* as one of three core components of a systemic accountability system. Their idea was that practice standards should define the core curriculum, and resource standards or opportunity to learn standards should measure the effectiveness of elected officials, school system leaders, school administrators, and teachers in equitably delivering that curriculum. They explained that the third component, performance standards, could then be used to measure student learning of that curriculum.

Only two of the three proposed standards made it through the legislative process. Content standards became state curriculum standards and eventually Common Core curriculum standards, and state and national assessments were established to measure performance standards. The most equity-minded component of the O'Day and Smith (1993) proposal, the part that measured how well and how equitably adults deliver learning opportunities, was left behind in political negotiations. This was no surprise, as a significant body of research documents the difficulty of maintaining the equity intent of education policies (Welner, 2001), particularly when it comes with a substantial price tag (Welner & LaCour, 2021). It also comes as no surprise that implementing an incomplete accountability system did not close gaps in learning. Outcome demands are ineffective (and cruel) when leaders have not addressed the capacity to meet those demands.

It was in this context that Welner and Carter's 2013 book attempted to refocus the education debate back on systemic inequality. They presented an opportunity gap frame that calls into question the national overemphasis on student outcomes (standardized testing and the achievement gap), since those outcomes are so dependent on high-quality inputs—on opportunities to learn inside and outside of school. From this zoomed-out view, the book's contributors explained how systemic barriers are held in place by structures that unintentionally and intentionally marginalize students based on race, ethnicity, queerness, socioeconomic class, language, immigration status, disability, and many other identities. These barriers may be out-of-school conditions like lack of access to nutrition, health care, mental health, housing, and safety. They may also be in-school conditions like access to rigorous curriculum and highly qualified teachers or exclusionary discipline policies and a discriminatory school climate.

## THE SCHOOLS OF OPPORTUNITY CRITERIA AND APPLICATION PROCESS

One central challenge in creating the Schools of Opportunity Project (SOO) was synthesizing the vast academic literature on closing opportunity gaps and advancing education equity into clear criteria that can be used to assess applicant schools. It was also important to do so in a way that the application process would not consume too much time from school staff and leaders. We needed an overall framework that was simultaneously broad enough to represent the full spectrum of proven strategies, and specific and easy enough to measure at the level of each criterion. We also needed to ensure that we could effectively gather information about how schools are advancing in their work. We eventually landed on the 10 criteria shown in Figure I.1.

From the outset, we understood that the current public education context meant that it would be extremely unlikely for one school to make substantial progress across all 10 criteria. With this in mind, we designed flexibility into the application process, allowing schools to apply with evidence of their work in a limited set of criteria. As described below, we eventually concluded that all applications must address the first two criteria, concerning learning opportunities (e.g., tracking) and school culture (e.g., exclusionary discipline), with discretion then provided for applicants to choose four additional criteria that are most relevant to their given school.

**Figure I.1. Potential Schools of Opportunity apply to be evaluated on these 10 research-based criteria.**

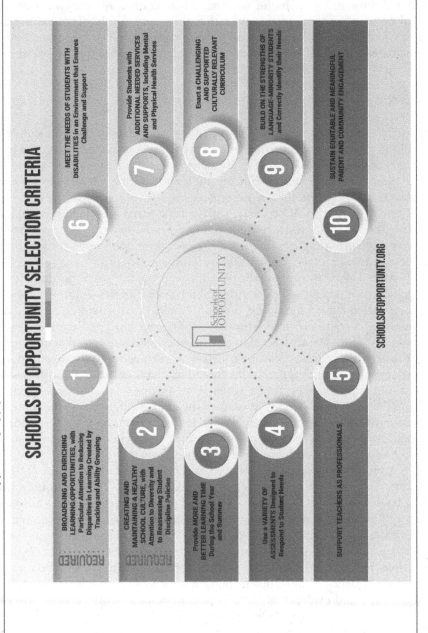

SCHOOLS OF OPPORTUNITY SELECTION CRITERIA

**REQUIRED**

1. BROADENING AND ENRICHING LEARNING OPPORTUNITIES, with Particular Attention to Reducing Disparities in Learning Created by Tracking and Ability Grouping

**REQUIRED**

2. CREATING AND MAINTAINING A HEALTHY SCHOOL CULTURE, with Attention to Diversity and to Reassessing Student Discipline Policies

3. Provide MORE AND BETTER LEARNING TIME During the School Year and Summer

4. Use a VARIETY OF ASSESSMENTS Designed to Respond to Student Needs

5. SUPPORT TEACHERS AS PROFESSIONALS

6. MEET THE NEEDS OF STUDENTS WITH DISABILITIES in an Environment that Ensures Challenge and Support

7. Provide Students with ADDITIONAL NEEDED SERVICES AND SUPPORTS, Including Mental and Physical Health Services

8. Enact a CHALLENGING AND SUPPORTED CULTURALLY RELEVANT CURRICULUM

9. BUILD ON THE STRENGTHS OF LANGUAGE-MINORITY STUDENTS and Correctly Identify their Needs

10. SUSTAIN EQUITABLE AND MEANINGFUL PARENT AND COMMUNITY ENGAGEMENT

Schools of OPPORTUNITY

SCHOOLSOFOPPORTUNITY.ORG

To be mindful of the scarce time and resources school leaders and educators have to prepare and submit an application, we decided to focus on readily available data. Moreover, a key part of the data collection is conducted through site visits for finalists, where trained researchers document and observe evidence of success rather than asking schools to collect and analyze qualitative data. We wanted the process to be simple enough to be replicated consistently and at scale, rather than just a boutique research idea that gets lost in the academy.

## The Nitty-Gritty of the Application Process

The Schools of Opportunity Project recognizes Schools of Opportunity as Gold or Silver. Using a scoring rubric, each criterion is evaluated on a four-point qualitative scale ranging from *early planning* (on the low end) to *exemplary implementation* (on the high end). Gold schools demonstrate *advanced implementation* or *exemplary implementation* practices on a total of five or more SOO criteria, with at least three assessed as exemplary. Silver schools demonstrate either *advanced implementation* or *exemplary implementation* practices on four or more criteria, with at least two criteria assessed as exemplary (http://SchoolsofOpportunity.org).

After 2 years of running the recognition program, we noticed that every applicant we recognized demonstrated advanced implementation or exemplary implementation progress on both Criterion 1 (providing a broad and enriching curriculum to all students) and Criterion 2 (creating a healthy school culture). We realized that these two criteria supported action across the other eight criteria and were necessary prerequisites to creating opportunity through other practices. This should not have come as a surprise, since a school stratifies opportunity when some groups of students are excluded from the school's environment or from the school's high-quality learning opportunities. Starting in year 3, we made Criteria 1 and 2 required for all applicants. Schools then choose what other four criteria, of the remaining eight, to submit as evidence for their application.

After an application is submitted, it is reviewed by experts for each criterion, followed by a site visit for selected finalists. The application asks for background information about the school composition and leadership, as well as specific information on each chosen criterion. For example, on Criterion 2, applicants are asked to submit the following documents for review: the school's code of conduct, documentation of their positive, non-exclusionary discipline plan (generally, but not always, using restorative justice), evidence of fair implementation of school discipline across student subgroups, and evidence of learning resources for suspended students. Two or more experts on this criterion would then review the full set of related materials using a research-based rubric.

Next, the individual criterion reviews are combined to create an overall set of scores across all criteria for a particular school and then reviewed again holistically by an additional school-level policy expert. Schools that meet advanced or exemplary practices on enough criteria are then eligible for a team site visit that provides an additional in-person assessment of that school's practices. Site visit data are added to the school's data portfolio. The Schools of Opportunity Project leadership then meet to make final decisions on recognition, with all schools who meet the required criteria standards receiving Gold or Silver awards.

Public recognition events are coordinated with each school, and each receives a physical banner to display on campus as well as digital badges for their website. To help other schools and educators learn from the recognized exemplars, the project has worked with *Washington Post* education reporter Valerie Strauss, who has a well-read and influential online column called *The Answer Sheet*. Each recognized school is profiled in the column. Media support toolkits are also provided to each school to support them in discussing the meaning of recognition with their own local and state public audiences. The project also publishes school profiles on the Schools of Opportunity website. (The Schools of Opportunity Application is available online in Appendix A, and rubrics for each criterion are available online in Appendix B. Both are downloadable from https://www.tcpress.com.)

## UNDERSTANDING THE SCHOOLS OF OPPORTUNITY CRITERIA

In this section, we explain each criterion using examples from the schools discussed in each chapter. While this book is primarily organized to highlight one School of Opportunity for each of the 10 criteria, this introduction helps demonstrate that the criteria are often overlapping and supportive of one another.

### Criterion 1: Broaden and Enrich Learning Opportunities, With Particular Attention to Reducing Disparities in Learning Created by Tracking and Ability Grouping

To close opportunity gaps, a school must provide universal access to a broad set of enriching, accelerated, and supported learning opportunities. The school must refuse to restrict or stratify student access to its best opportunities. This means that Schools of Opportunity must not track students into ability groups.

Grouping based on perceived ability is sometimes called *ability grouping*, sometimes called *streaming*, and sometimes called *tracking*. Most traditional public high schools across the country have lower-track classes called general, developmental, basic, remedial, or regular. Higher tracks are often called college prep, honors, Advanced Placement, and International Baccalaureate. These same labels are used for classes in each of the core subject areas: English Language Arts, math, science, and social studies. A large body of research, described by Jeannie Oakes (2005) in the second edition of *Keeping Track*, documents the harms done by stratifying opportunities in this way. As Kevin Welner and John Murphy point out in Chapter 1, "a school is not closing opportunity gaps when only higher-track students have access to the best opportunities."

The opportunity gaps described by Welner and Murphy fall into the same pattern across public education systems in the United States: lower-income and racially marginalized students disproportionately are enrolled in lower tracks, whereas wealthier, White students are enrolled into higher tracks (Welner, 2001). Schools of Opportunity avoid these inequitable processes and outcomes by increasing every student's access to high-quality learning opportunities through detracking—moving students into rigorous, mixed-ability classes where they can benefit from an enriched curriculum and engaging teaching practices (Welner et al., 2008).

South Side High School in New York provides a strong example of what this looks like in practice. As Welner and Murphy explain, "The overarching principles that govern each and every decision at South Side are straightforward: diversity is an opportunity every student deserves, class rosters should reflect the diversity of the student body wherever possible, and the success of one student should not and does not come at the expense of another." Their chapter describes how this explicit focus combined with focused work to build support among teachers and parents results in dramatically improved access and outcomes. For example, participation in the school's International Baccalaureate (IB) coursework increased from 30% to over 80% of students. All the school's demographic groups have shown greater success with these IB courses as well as the New York State Regents exam.

### Criterion 2: Create and Maintain a Healthy School Culture, With Attention to Diversity and to Reassessing Student Discipline Policies

Creating and maintaining a healthy school climate requires intentional relationships at all levels of a school community. The Schools of Opportunity framework embraces the view that every school can and should have an environment where students will have healthy and supportive relationships with one another, educators, parents, and community members. Moreover, healthy school climates present an alternative to the cradle-to-prison pipeline found in many schools located in marginalized communities (Wiley et al., 2018). There is evidence that creating strong school climates leads to improved test scores and student learning gains (Allensworth & Hart, 2018, p. 2). But this undertaking of working toward a healthy school culture and school discipline policy takes considerable effort. It is helpful to attend to three dimensions of school climate: the physical, social, and academic (Loukas, 2007). If we think about the school as a table, these three dimensions can each be thought of as a leg supporting the tabletop where school life takes place. A positive school climate, supported by the physical, social, and academic table legs, fosters youth development and the learning possibilities necessary for students to grow into their best selves (National School Climate Council, 2017).

As Kathryn E. Wiley and Lourenço Garcia tell us in Chapter 2, "Revere High School shows how creating and maintaining a positive school climate is possible through whole-school transformation over multiple years led with consistent equity-minded change and social justice leadership." Prior to their multiyear intentional reforms, Revere's school climate was a mix of deficit mindset and structural inequalities. The needed changes followed shifts in teacher mindsets, letting go of old ways of teaching and learning in favor of student-centered models, and transforming the school from a punitive model where students were not allowed to make mistakes to a restorative model where mistakes became a chance for students and the school community to improve. Notably, among these efforts, Revere severely limited exclusionary discipline (Skiba et al., 2014; Wiley, 2021)—expulsion and suspension—as one of many of its student-first remedies to the cradle-to-prison pipeline.

### Criterion 3: Provide More and Better Learning Time During the School Year and Summer

Experienced educators will readily explain that learning is not confined to the classroom. The SOO framework intentionally incorporates this reality by looking for examples of well-supported learning that goes beyond classroom teaching by providing students rich opportunities for more and better learning time (MBLT).

The effectiveness of the approach comes from an intentional treatment of each of its two components: more time and better time (Del Razo & Renée, 2013). More time can be created by increasing the amount of time (e.g., minutes/day, days/year) that students are in school, or by reorganizing the school day so that less time is lost (e.g., alternating shorter lunch periods that decrease time waiting in the lunch line, or minimizing the number of transition periods in a day) (Del Razo et al., 2014.) More time should not merely be used to replicate classroom activities to force more "time on task." Rather, as Jeannie Oakes writes, increases in learning time "must be used to leverage the other foundations of equitable, high-quality schooling—deeper learning strategies, effective teaching, adequate funding, and meaningful accountability" (Oakes, 2018).

Located in a rural area in Worcester County on Maryland's Eastern Shore, Pocomoke High School, profiled in Chapter 3, has an annual enrollment of about 400 students. As Kellie Rolstad and Jenifer Rayne describe, Pocomoke launched a plan to provide all of its students and the larger community with the tools and supports to meet the problems people face in their majority-minority, low-income community. According to Rolstad and Rayne, "Rather than thinking of learning as something that students do for discrete periods of time within tightly controlled settings (during class and while doing homework), Pocomoke has successfully created an environment that recognizes and promotes the notion that more and better learning occurs when every activity, every action, and every interaction holds the promise and possibility of authentic engagement." The school's educators view the role of broadening student lifelong opportunities as central to their mission, supported by programs like Project 100, which set the expectation for students to plan for life after high school beginning at their first step through the school's doors. Pocomoke also developed the Your60 program, which gives students 60 minutes each day to rest, do an activity, seek homework help, or focus on a project. Like all of Pocomoke's approaches, the Your60 program puts student learning in students' hands while maintaining a focus on relationships and support.

## Criterion 4: Use a Variety of Assessments Designed to Respond to Student Needs

Schools of Opportunity use multiple measures to assess student learning. This goes well beyond the annual requirement of standardized tests to include assessments about the learning happening on a given day or week or in a particular curriculum unit. Such assessments can inform a teacher's strategies to correct misconceptions and improve students' grasp of the material. For example, an informal assessment could help trigger a physics teacher to work more with one student on computational thinking and another student on memorization strategies of mathematical formulas.

Schools of Opportunity make excellent use of formative assessments to help each student move toward successfully achieving their learning goals. Formative assessments are made up of curriculum material, activities, supervision, and feedback (Sadler, 1989). Their use in teaching and learning creates a feedback loop where students engage with course material, demonstrate their mastery of the material through various activities, are supervised by the teacher, and reflect on their work before trying again. Examples of formative assessment could include any number of authentic activities and assignments, such as a spoken-word poem summarizing a novel, a dissection report with detailed anatomic drawings, a popsicle-stick tower-building competition in physics, an analytic essay on the connection between slavery and modern racism, or even a one-act play where certain acting skills need to be demonstrated. The point is for students to engage in an assessment process that will help them understand where they are meeting goals and where they have opportunities for growth and may need additional assistance. Advancements in assessment policy under the Every Student Succeeds Act (ESSA) allow for teachers and students to more deeply engage in such formative assessment practices (Shepard et al., 2017).

In Chapter 4, Jeffrey Palladino and Lorrie A. Shepard write about how Fannie Lou Hamer Freedom High School in the Bronx strategically uses assessment to support curriculum and instruction. The educators at Fannie Lou Hamer rely on formative assessment techniques as the core of their teaching and learning. Key to their strategy is the mutual understanding between teachers and students that assessment—like education—is about the journey, not the outcome. This careful framing reduces the stakes of tests and other assessments so that they can be used for learning rather than judging.

## Criterion 5: Support Teachers as Professionals

High-quality teachers are vital to closing opportunity gaps. For schools to cultivate teachers of the highest quality, teachers need access to meaningful, job-embedded professional development opportunities that are culturally responsive (Darling-Hammond & McLaughlin, 2011). This requires supportive working conditions, including a nourishing professional culture, inclusive and supportive leadership, and strong collegial relationships (Allensworth et al., 2009; Boyd et al., 2011; Bryk, 2010; Johnson, 2019). Schools of Opportunity also aim to create space for teachers to develop equitable practices and meaningfully engage students and local communities (Gorski, 2016; Sleeter, 2012).

In Chapter 5, authors Linda Molner Kelley, Derek Pierce, Matt Bernstein, Susan McCray, and Rebecca Lynch Nichols provide an in-depth view of how Casco Bay High School supports teachers as professionals, particularly within the context of their ongoing equity work. Casco Bay, in Portland, Maine, thoughtfully creates conditions in which teachers can thrive and turnover rates are low. This is possible due to seven guidelines followed by Casco Bay's leadership—including administrators, teachers, parents, and students. Casco Bay's seven guidelines are (1) adhere to a common vision of excellence and equity that encourages students and teachers to aim for greatness; (2) pay attention to the pace, process, and psychology of making change; (3) build clear and continuous processes for feedback, reflection, and learning for both individuals and the collective; (4) create structures that cultivate teacher interdependence and professional capacity; (5) empower and expect teachers to be leaders; (6) sustain excellence by attending to staff wellness; and (7) cultivate an adult culture that mirrors what you want to see in your students. School leadership anchors professional development and working conditions in these guidelines, creating a growth-focused professional environment.

### Criterion 6: Meet the Needs of Students With Disabilities in an Environment That Ensures Challenge and Support

More than 7 million public school students received special education services under the Individuals with Disabilities Education Act (IDEA; U.S. Department of Education, 2021a), and an additional 1.4 million students are supported through Section 504 plans (U.S. Department of Education, Office of Civil Rights, 2018). While these numbers vary by state, district, and school, the trends are steadily increasing (Riser-Kositsky, 2021). With the exception of some charter schools that actively avoid enrolling students with disabilities (Mommandi & Welner, 2021), on average 14% of enrolled students at a school have an Individualized Education Plan (IEP). But there is evidence that discrimination and structural inequalities result in inconsistent enrollment across schools and school districts. The Schools of Opportunity program recognizes schools that have developed strong supportive practices with this population of students at the center, rather than as an afterthought.

In Chapter 6, Jill Gurtner and Julie Mead write about how Clark Street Community School, a small charter school located near Madison, Wisconsin, uses an integrated comprehensive service model to meet the special needs of all students. Clark Street's full inclusion model relies on three pillars. The first emphasizes student voice and choice over as many aspects of their educational journey as possible. The second emphasizes a focus on the students' communities, both local and global, that are their real-world learning contexts. The third emphasizes student engagement in the process of creating and maintaining a school environment in which both individual and collective needs are honored. In this innovative, place-based learning community, students with special needs participate fully in the same rich learning opportunities as other students, with personalized support from teachers and staff.

### Criterion 7: Provide Students With Additional Needed Services and Supports, Including Mental and Physical Health Services

### Criterion 8: Enact a Challenging and Supported Culturally Relevant Curriculum

The Schools of Opportunity framework embraces schools that develop inclusive wraparound services, including mental health and physical health care supports. Here, as well as later in the book, we closely link those supports with initiatives to develop culturally sustaining curriculum, which attend to systemic trauma that may be perpetuated by classroom curricula. Schools can take proactive steps to mitigate the negative impacts of trauma and adverse experiences (Craig, 2016; Plumb et al., 2016; Terrasi & De Galarce, 2017). Schools can respond to trauma through mental health supports like on-campus counseling, by emphasizing socioemotional learning schoolwide, and by training teachers on how to notice, recognize, and intervene to prevent student crises. Physical health supports like a community-accessible campus clinic and an emphasis on physical wellness benefit students as well. While they are often discussed separately, an emphasis on well-being and culturally relevant curriculum can be intertwined to create a robust school experience that values the holistic needs of students. Empirical research on curriculum decisions finds linkages between culture, race, ethnicity, and achievement—schools must center the cultures of their students in order to promote well-being and achievement (Warikoo & Carter, 2009).

In Chapter 7 and Chapter 8, authors Kristen P. Goessling, Kate Somerville, Adam York, and Kimberly Grayson focus on Dr. Martin Luther King, Jr. Early College (DMLK), which is located in Denver, Colorado. DMLK's community has a people of color majority, and the school provides a social ecology that supports healthy student well-being through mental health programs. The school's educators build on positive relationships to re-examine the curriculum in collaboration with student leaders, to make it culturally sustaining and humanizing (Welner, 2020). The school's commitment to student wellness includes dedicated student-centered spaces, professional mental health, a therapy dog on campus multiple days a week, and a health clinic on-site for students to address physical wellness concerns. Likewise, the school supports students through culturally sustaining academic programs, rewriting curriculum to foreground authors of color, and creating assignments that situate learning in a challenging and accurate view of history. With student activists taking the lead, DMLK's educators have expanded their work to support this movement throughout the school district.

### Criterion 9: Build on the Strengths of Language-Minority Students and Correctly Identify Their Needs

The population of linguistic minority students in American schools is growing each year. From fall 2000 to fall 2019, the number of language-minority students attending public schools increased from 3.7 million to 10.4 million (U.S. Department of Education, 2021b). According to the National Center for Education Statistics, 64% of U.S. teachers had at least one language-minority student in their class during the 2017–2018 school year, yet fewer than half of those teachers had taken any course on how to teach linguistic-minority students (National Center for Education Statistics, 2022).

In 1984, Richard Ruíz offered a typology that is still helpful today, explaining that schools take one of three approaches to linguistic minority students: "language as a problem," "language as a right," or "language as a resource." Schools that value language as a resource reduce learning disparities between linguistic-minority students and native English speakers (Flores & Rosa, 2015; González et al., 2005; Miramontes et al., 2011). These schools place an emphasis on new teacher mentoring (Catalano & Hamann, 2016), and they interrupt the biases among seasoned educators (Hamann & Reeves, 2013).

Edmund T. Hamann, Janet Eckerson, and Mark Larson write about Lincoln High School (LHS) in Chapter 9. LHS is Lincoln (Nebraska) Public Schools' only majority non-White high school. It also has the highest free and reduced-price lunch–eligible student enrollment of any local high school. LHS boasts a sizable number of newcomer students, representing cultures and languages from all over the world. The school's educators and leaders use an asset-based approach to helping English language learners develop their language skills. Chapter 9 describes the journey of LHS educators, as they developed linguistic inclusion and support services throughout the school. LHS serves as an example because it supports not just Spanish speakers who are learning English, but speakers of Karen,[2] Arabic, Vietnamese, multiple francophone languages from across the globe, and many others. And it does so in such a way that newcomer students are earning competitive scholarships that prepare them for college and careers.

### Criterion 10: Sustain Equitable and Meaningful Parent and Community Engagement

Parent[3] and community engagement can be a key factor in reducing opportunity gaps. Schools can, and should, engage parents in ways that go beyond bake sales, school plays, booster clubs, and grade promotion events. Parent ideas, perspectives, and voices can improve a school's ability to help every student thrive (Auerbach, 2010) and drive equitable school transformations (Ishimaru, 2018). Moreover, meaningful parent and community engagement can make space for helpful counternarratives to emerge—shedding light on issues educators and administrators may not have perceived otherwise.

Chapter 10 tells the story of Rainier Beach High School (RBHS) and its families and community. In this chapter, Ann M. Ishimaru and Dwane Chappelle link shared decision-making with parental involvement, community organizations, and student climate. In doing so, they outline potential ways of cooperatively reimagining the idea of "turnaround" schools—a concept that is situated in deeply rooted historical inequities. RBHS serves a community where most parents are of color. The school's parent leaders help craft the school's budget, enhance master scheduling, and even influence professional development decisions as meaningful partners on the school's leadership team. This is in stark contrast to typically confined parental roles, and many of the lessons described in this chapter confront the vulnerabilities and challenges that emerge en route to deep parent and community involvement.

## THE EXEMPLARY SCHOOLS IN THIS BOOK

Recognized Schools of Opportunity like those discussed throughout this book prove that equitable change that closes opportunity gaps is possible. By illustrating the ways that schools can lower the barriers to learning, the school leaders and researchers who authored these chapters provide a more thoughtful approach to understanding schooling.

The stories and research included in these pages therefore offer ideas for others who aim to close opportunity gaps in their schools. They also offer hope that schools can be part of healing the inequalities in our society. These stories provide concrete examples of how school communities developed and implemented specific reforms, as well as core principles offered to guide the work. Each chapter also points to research that places the stories in the broader context of beneficial school improvement efforts. As you will learn in these pages, equitable changes are implemented a little at a time, rather than all at once. The struggle to be better motivates all of these reforms, and each individual effort contributes to overall school improvement. Equity is not a thing to be achieved, but rather a struggle to engage and sustain.

We offer the Schools of Opportunity rubric (see Appendix B, download-able at www.tcpress.com) as a self-assessment guide for school communities to reflect on where they are succeeding and where they have more work to do. The rubric provides a spectrum of activities, not discrete, concrete steps; as you learn from these chapters, while the goal of equity is the same, the journey each school takes is unique. As we mentioned at the start of this chapter and as you will continue to read through these pages, systemic equitable change is not fast, linear, permanent, or inevitable. This change happens because communities and educators come together to demand it. They then persist, often through major resistance, to keep their equitable ideas moving forward. The journeys that follow were not easy, but they are the journeys we all must embrace as necessary.

## NOTES

1. Dr. Carol Burris was principal of South Side High School, which has repeat-edly been recognized by *U.S. News and World Report* and other national rank-ings as among the nation's best. Those lists have long been dominated by schools that enroll a select population of students—either through school choice or through neighborhood locations. They enrolled students whose outcomes were—and would remain—very strong. Some of these schools were undoubtedly of high quality, but others were not. More importantly, high-quality schools that didn't have elite en-rollment were generally overlooked. Dr. Burris saw in *Closing the Opportunity Gap* (Carter & Welner, 2013) the makings of criteria to recognize schools, including that latter group of schools, that should be held up as exemplars.

2. Karenic languages are historically spoken by some groups living in Myanmar, Thailand, and other parts of Southeast Asia.

3. We use the term "parent" to include anyone who has a primary caregiving role in a student's life.

## REFERENCES

Allensworth, E. M., & Hart, H. (2018). *How do principals influence student achievement?* University of Chicago Consortium on School Research.

Allensworth, E., Ponisciak, S., & Mazzeo, C. (2009). *The schools teachers leave: Teacher mobility in Chicago Public Schools.* Consortium on Chicago School Research—University of Chicago. https://eric.ed.gov/?q=ED505882718-

Auerbach, S. (2010). Beyond coffee with the principal: Toward leadership for authentic school–family partnerships. *Journal of School Leadership, 20*(6), 728–757.

Boyd, D., Grossman, P., Ing, M., Lankford, H., Loeb, S., & Wyckoff, J. (2011). The influence of school administrators on teacher retention decisions. *American Educational Research Journal, 48*(2), 303–333. http://doi.org/10.3102/00028312103 80788

Bryk, A. (2010). Organizing schools for improvement. *Phi Delta Kappan, 91*(7), 23–30. http://doi.org/10.1177/003172171009100705

Catalano, T., & Hamann, E. T. (2016). Multilingual pedagogies and pre-service teachers: The modeling of "language as a resource" orientations in teacher education programs. *Bilingual Research Journal, 39(3–4)*, 263–278.

Coleman, J. S., Campbell, E. Q., Hobson, C. J., McPartland, J., Mood, A. M., Weinfield, F. D., & York, R. L. (1966). *Equality of educational opportunity.* U.S. Government Printing Office.

Craig, S. E. (2016). *Trauma-sensitive schools: Learning communities transforming children's lives, K–5.* Teachers College Press.

Darling-Hammond, L., & McLaughlin, M. (2011). Policies that support professional development in an era of reform. *Phi Delta Kappan, 92*(6), 81–92. http://doi.org/10.1177/003172171109200622

Del Razo, J. L., & Renée, M. (2013). Expanding equity through more and better learning time. *Voices in Urban Education, 36*, 23–34.

Del Razo, J. L., Saunders, M., Renée, M., López, R. M., & Ullucci, K. (2014). *Leveraging time for equity: Indicators to measure more and better learning time.* Annenberg Institute for School Reform, Brown University.

Dobbie, W., & Fryer, R. G. (2009). *Are high-quality schools enough to close the achievement gap? Evidence from a social experiment in Harlem* (NBER working paper). National Bureau of Economic Research.

Flores, N., & Rosa, J. (2015). Undoing appropriateness: Raciolinguistic ideologies and language diversity in education. *Harvard Education Review, 85*(2), pp. 149–171.

González, N., Moll, L., & Amanti, C. (2005). *Funds of knowledge: Theorizing practices in households, communities, and classrooms.* Lawrence Erlbaum.

Gorski, P. (2016) Rethinking the role of "culture" in educational equity: From cultural competence to equity literacy. *Multicultural Perspectives, 18*(4), 221–226. https://doi.org/10.1080/15210960.2016.1228344

Hamann, E. T., & Reeves, J. (2013). Interrupting the professional schism that allows less successful educational practices with ELLs to persist. *Theory Into Practice, 52*(2), 81–88.

Ishimaru, A. M. (2018). Re-imagining turnaround: Families and communities leading educational justice. *Journal of Educational Administration, 56*(5), 546–561. https://doi.org/10.1108/JEA-01-2018-0013

Johnson, S. M. (2019). *Where teachers thrive: Organizing schools for success.* Harvard University Press.

Loukas, A. (2007). What is school climate? *Leadership Compass, 5*(1), 1–3.

Miramontes, O. B., Nadeau, A., & Commins, N. L. (2011) *Restructuring schools for linguistic diversity: Linking decision making to effective programs* (2nd ed.). Teachers College Press.

Mommandi, W., & Welner, K. (2021). *School's choice: How charter schools control access and shape enrollment.* Teachers College Press.

National Center for Education Statistics. (2022). *Characteristics of public school teachers.* National Center for Education Statistics, National Teacher and Principal Survey (NTPS). https://nces.ed.gov/programs/coe/indicator/clr#:~:text=In%20the%202017%E2%80%9318%20school,1.8%20million%20secondary%20school%20teachers.&text=Overall%2C%20the%20number%20of%20public,%E2%80%9932000%20(3.0%20million)

National School Climate Council. (2017). *What is school climate?* https://schoolclimate.org/about/our-approach/what-is-school-climate

O'Day, J. A., & Smith, M. S. (1993). Systemic reform and educational opportunity. In S. H. Fuhrman (Ed.), *Designing coherent education policy: Improving the system* (pp. 250–312). Jossey-Bass.

Oakes, J. (1989). What educational indicators? The case for assessing the school context. *Educational Evaluation and Policy Analysis, 11*(2), 181–199.

Oakes, J. (2005). *Keeping track: How schools structure inequality.* Yale University Press.

Oakes, J. (2018, May). Time in pursuit of education equity: Promoting learning time reforms that cross ideological divides to benefit students most in need. *School Administrator, 75*(5). https://my.aasa.org/AASA/Resources/SAMag/2018/May18/Oakes.aspx

Oakes, J., & Rogers, J. (2006). *Learning power: Organizing for education and justice.* Teachers College Press.

Plumb, J. L., Bush, K. A., & Kersevich, S. E. (2016). Trauma-sensitive schools: An evidence-based approach. *School Social Work Journal, 40*(2), 37–60.

Riser-Kositsky, M. (2021, July 21). Special education: Definition, statistics, trends. *Education Week.* https://www.edweek.org/teaching-learning/special-education-definition-statistics-and-trends/2019/12#:~:text=The%20percent%20of%20students%20with,5.8%20percent%20to%2011%20percent

Ruíz, R. (1984). Orientations in language planning. *NABE: The Journal for the National Association for Bilingual Education, 8*(2), 15–34.

Sadler, D. R. (1989). Formative assessment and the design of instructional systems. *Instructional Science, 18*, 119–144.

Shepard, L. A., Penuel, W. R., & Davidson, K. L. (2017). Design principles for new systems of assessment. *Phi Delta Kappan, 98*(6), 47–52.

Skiba, R. J., Arredondo, M. I., & Williams, N. T. (2014). More than a metaphor: The contribution of exclusionary discipline to a school-to-prison pipeline. *Equity and Excellence in Education, 47*(4), 546–564.

Sleeter, C. (2012). Confronting the marginalization of culturally responsive pedagogy. *Urban Education, 47*(3), 562–584. http://doi.org/10.1177/0042085911431472

Terrasi, S., & De Galarce, P. C. (2017). Trauma and learning in America's classrooms. *Phi Delta Kappan, 98*(6), 35–41.

U.S. Department of Education. (2021a). *IDEA section 618 data products: State level data files.* Office of Special Education Programs, Individuals with Disabilities Education Act (IDEA) database. https://www2.ed.gov/programs/osepidea/618 -data/state-level-data-files/index.html#bcc

U.S. Department of Education. (2021b). Table 204.20. English learner (EL) students enrolled in public elementary and secondary schools, by state: Selected years, fall 2000 through fall 2019. *Digest of Education Statistics.* https://nces.ed.gov /programs/digest/d21/tables/dt21_204.20.asp

U.S. Department of Education, Office for Civil Rights. (2018). 2017–18 state and national estimations. *Civil Rights Data Collection.* https://ocrdata.ed.gov/estimations /2017-2018

Welner, K. (2020, March 10). Answer sheet: At this high-poverty high school, college comes early to students. *Washington Post.* https://www.washingtonpost .com/education/2020/03/10/this-high-poverty-high-school-college-comes-early -students

Welner, K. (2001). *Legal rights, local wrongs: When community control collides with educational equity.* SUNY Press.

Welner, K., & Burris, C. (2014, October 2). Answer sheet: 'Schools of Opportunity'—A new project to recognize schools that give all students a chance to succeed. *Washington Post.* https://www.washingtonpost.com/news/answer-sheet /wp/2014/10/02/schools-of-opportunity-a-new-project-to-recognize-schools -that-give-all-students-a-chance-to-succeed

Welner, K., Burris, C., Wiley, E., & Murphy, J. (2008). Accountability, rigor, and detracking: Achievement effects of embracing a challenging curriculum as a universal good for all students. *Teachers College Record, 110*(3), 571–607.

Welner, K., & Carter, P. L. (2013). Achievement gaps arise from opportunity gaps. In P. L. Carter & K. G. Welner (Eds.), *Closing the opportunity gap: What America must do to give every child an even chance* (pp. 1–10). Oxford University Press.

Welner, K., & LaCour, S. (2021). Education in context: Schools and their connections to societal inequalities. In K. Bowman (Ed.), *The Oxford handbook of U.S. education law. Oxford handbooks online.* https://doi.org/10.1093/oxfordhb /9780190697402.013.3

Wiley, K. E. (2021). A tale of two logics: School discipline and racial disparities in a "mostly White" middle school. *American Journal of Education, 127*(2), 163–192.

Wiley, K. E., Anyon, Y., Yang, J. L., Pauline, M. E., Rosch, A., Valladares, G., Downing, B. J., & Pisciotta, L. (2018). Looking back, moving forward: Technical, normative, and political dimensions of school discipline. *Educational Administration Quarterly, 54*(2), 275–302.

# CHAPTER 1

# A Challenging, Supported, and Engaging Curriculum for All

*Kevin Welner and John Murphy*

Criterion 1: Broaden and Enrich Learning Opportunities, With Particular Attention to Reducing Disparities in Learning Created by Tracking and Ability Grouping

Challenging curriculum and teaching are not a limited resource, or at least they need not be. A top-notch lesson plan in one classroom is not undermined by the same lesson being taught next door. Yet our nation's secondary schools typically provide their best curriculum only to the select few in their highest tracks. While these high-track students are engaged with relevant and meaningful high-expectation projects that connect learning to these students' lives, students enrolled in lower-tracked classes are more likely to be drilled on fundamental skills and asked to complete worksheets and other structured assignments.

Tracking of this sort has been a mainstay of American classrooms for the past century, in part because of power. Tracking helps ensure that today's decision-makers are disproportionately yesterday's higher-tracked students. Youth who are forced to spend years in low-track classrooms are more likely to experience a large number of harmful outcomes—starting with lowered achievement and ending with low college attainment and lower incomes, as well as greater chances of unemployment and incarceration.

Those who dodged that low-track bullet are, predictably, less inclined to perceive problems with tracking. Not only did they not suffer, they might even think themselves to have been advantaged. In fact, they might want their children and grandchildren to have that same advantage.

But when schools track their students into different levels of perceived academic ability or future prospects, they create opportunity gaps. They shun their core obligation of doing their best to teach all their students. The following three results of tracking are particularly harmful:

1. Tracking puts in place a structure of decreased expectations for those students in lower tracks. These expectations are well understood and internalized by teachers and by the students themselves.
2. Tracked systems generally stratify teachers in corresponding ways, with more experienced and accomplished teachers assigned to the higher-track classrooms.
3. Tracking also stratifies instructional approaches, with more engaging pedagogies and enrichment opportunities typically reserved for higher-track classrooms. Low-track classrooms often devolve into warehousing and dull, control-based instruction designed to avoid disruptions.

The disadvantages of lower-track placement accumulate and inexorably drive a continued separation between students placed in higher versus lower tracks. In this way, the placement becomes a self-fulfilling prophesy. Also, since track level is glaringly associated with race and class, tracking contributes directly to the country's persistent achievement gaps. These patterns are true of past, rigid systems of tracking where students were formally assigned to a given level. But they're also true of current, more choice-based systems where students can (usually within some constraints) opt into higher- or lower-level classes. The same practices and results plague all of these systems—the same foreseeable enrollment by race and class, and the same foreseeable stratified learning opportunities.

Yet tracking persists as a regularity in the nation's secondary schools. As we reviewed applications for Schools of Opportunity recognition over the first 5 years of the program, we noticed that tracking was the primary factor that undermined high schools' eligibility. We learned of impressive schools across the United States that had put into practice remarkably engaging, deep, and creative learning opportunities—and then rationed those opportunities. A school is not closing opportunity gaps when only higher-track students have access to the best opportunities.

Moving beyond these structures for rationing and stratifying is, however, difficult for many school leaders and educators to even imagine. After all, psychometricians measure large assessment gaps even at early ages, when children arrive for kindergarten. While some 5-year-old children have relatively well-developed learning habits, knowledge of numbers and letters, and even reading and math skills, others are novices in all these academic areas. Looking at the vast inequalities in our society linked to poverty and racial discrimination, it's easy to understand how these gaps develop. Important advantages and disadvantages, arising from factors as varied as access to high-quality preschool, housing and food insecurity, or exposure to lead, are distributed unequally.

The overall impact of such inequalities increases over the years, because of opportunity gaps that accumulate outside and inside of schools. Accordingly, when students arrive in high school, our inclination is to efficiently sort these students into classes that meet the students where they are. Or, put in the converse: our inclination is to avoid placing students together in the same classes, for which they are prepared to succeed on different levels. Our high schools didn't create the achievement gaps among the 9th-grade students they enroll, and we should understand when they cope with the realities as best they can. No alternative way of coping is apparent.

That's part of the story—and it's the part that we address in this chapter as we describe the beneficial alternative of universal acceleration for all learners buttressed with supports for teachers and students.

Another part of the story, however, is that our high schools are embedded in the broader political and normative context that disadvantages students of color and students from lower-wealth families. When leaders and educators recognize the unfairness of tracking systems and try to provide universal access to a school's best opportunities, they face pushback from powerful parents and school board members, and even from other educators and district/school leaders. These political forces are very real, and they're generally conjoined with pervasive normative beliefs about which children can (and cannot) truly learn at a high level. Although we don't in this chapter directly discuss many of these political and normative hurdles, we encourage readers to explore the nature of, and possible responses to, this part of the story (see Burris & Garrity, 2008; Welner & Burris, 2006).

Below, as we describe the detracking reform at South Side High School in Long Island, New York, we pay particular attention to the steps that the school took as it moved forward with its reform. In doing so, we emphasize what might otherwise seem like a minor point: the school ensured that the challenging curriculum was also relevant, enriching, and supported. Detracked classes will fail if they are not academically demanding, but that's only one part of the reform. In the language of the Schools of Opportunity recognition program: "The curriculum is designed to meet the needs of students while *engaging them in meaningful learning*. The evidence [should show] a substantial amount of innovative, project-based learning in a range of subjects *grounded in the interests, knowledge and experiences of students*."

## THE SOUTH SIDE STORY

South Side High School is a diverse suburban high school located in a community of 28,000 in Nassau County, on Long Island, New York. Current enrollment is 1,067 students. Most of Rockville Centre School District's Black

CRITERION 1: BROADEN AND ENRICH LEARNING OPPORTUNITIES, WITH
PARTICULAR ATTENTION TO REDUCING DISPARITIES IN LEARNING
CREATED BY TRACKING AND ABILITY GROUPING

The curriculum experienced broadly among the [exemplary] school's students includes a range of subjects, activities and experiences that provide a high-quality, challenging education. The evidence in submitted documents shows that the school has little or no formal or informal tracking or ability grouping, with zero tracking in some academic areas. The school has eliminated low-track classes. The school allows any student who wants to take honors, IB and AP courses to do so and provides supports as needed. There is evidence of a high rate of inclusion of low-SES students and students of color in honors, AP and IB classes. Students broadly participate in college counseling programs and in PSATs, SATs, and ACTs.

The curriculum experienced broadly among the school's students includes arts, science, and other enrichment experiences. The curriculum is designed to meet the needs of students while engaging them in meaningful learning. The evidence shows a substantial amount of innovative, project-based learning in a range of subjects grounded in the interests, knowledge, and experiences of students.

and African American students are eligible for free or reduced-price lunch and live in a HUD (Department of Housing and Urban Development) housing project. The majority of Latinx families reside in Section 8, subsidized apartments in the downtown area of the larger village. By contrast, most of the district's White families earn upper-middle-class incomes, and the school is majority White: 77%. Latinx students make up 10.5% of the current student body at South Side, and Black or African American students make up 7.3%. Approximately 18% of South Side students are eligible for free or reduced-price lunch—again, with a stark overlap between this category and the school's students of color.

As discussed below, the school district's detracking reform began because its large achievement gaps were simply intolerable. The demographics made the gaps predictable but not acceptable.

## Outcomes

We want to describe South Side's reform somewhat out of order, focusing first on outcomes and then on how the school achieved these results. These outcomes have been documented in a series of studies that we have conducted along with Dr. Carol Burris, the school's now-retired principal, as well as other researcher-collaborators:

- Atteberry, A., LaCour, S. E., Burris, C. C., Welner, K. G., & Murphy, J. (2019). Opening the gates: Detracking and the International Baccalaureate. *Teachers College Record*, *121*(9), 1–63.
- Burris, C. C., Wiley, E. W., Welner, K. G., & Murphy, J. (2008). Accountability, rigor, and detracking: Achievement effects of embracing a challenging curriculum as a universal good for all students. *Teachers College Record*, *110*(3), 571–608.
- Burris, C. C., Welner, K. G., Wiley, E. W., & Murphy, J. (2007). A world class curriculum for all. *Educational Leadership*, *64*(7), pp. 53–56.
- Burris, C. C., Heubert, J., & Levin, H. (2006). Accelerating mathematics achievement using heterogeneous grouping. *American Educational Research Journal*, *43*(1), 103–134.
- Burris, C. C., & Welner, K. G. (2005). Closing the achievement gap by detracking. *Phi Delta Kappan*, *86*(8), 594–598.

The most recent of these studies looked at the most challenging outcome of detracking classes: success in International Baccalaureate (IB) courses. The IB Diploma Program was created 58 years ago to serve the needs of geographically mobile families whose children planned to apply to and attend a competitive university after finishing high school. Today, the Diploma Program has developed into a world-class pre-university experience for a diverse and global student body, where over half of the member schools are public or regional high schools. The heart of the program has not changed, however. This is a student-centered approach to learning that prepares students for all facets of life after secondary school by focusing on three elements: (a) a diverse, criterion-referenced series of assessments; (b) graded and nongraded student work; and (c) civic-mindedness. While the IB Diploma Program formally begins in grades 11 and 12, the coursework that students experience in grades 9, 10, and earlier is a significant determinant to access and succeed in the program.

As discussed later in this chapter, the school's reformers set greater IB access as a powerful goal. IB participation therefore increased from about 30% to over 80%. The study examined two main questions: how higher-achievers at South Side fared after the gates to IB were opened, and how the newer students (those who likely would not have taken the IB courses) fared when facing the greater challenge. The study's key findings are summarized as follows:

Instead of the world-class IB curriculum being reserved for a relatively small number of elite students, the gates were opened and 82% of the school's students ended up completing an IB English assessment, while 72% completed an

IB math assessment. [It] was district policy in the final cohorts that all students take IB English courses in eleventh and twelfth grade, and though we report that 82% of the final cohort possess IB scores, the district reports that an even greater percentage of students participated in the course—although a subgroup did not complete the assessment [which is not a requirement to participate in the course]. As more students took these challenging courses, they correspondingly challenged two widespread beliefs. First, the school's highest achievers continued to succeed in the more heterogeneous IB classes [as measured by their IB scores]. Second, the average IB scores for the school's lower achievers were the same or higher after detracking began [averaging about 4 on the 1–7 scale], even though many more such students enrolled in those courses. (Atteberry et al., 2019, p. 35–37)

The earlier studies looked at other outcomes (such as success on the required New York Regents exams) and found similar benefits of the reform. For example, Burris and Welner (2005) found that while the pre-reform cohort at South Side had a stark Regents-diploma gap (32% rate for all African American or Hispanic versus 88% of all White or Asian American graduates), the post-reform (detracked) cohort 3 years later had dramatically closed the gap (82% of all African American or Hispanic versus 97% of all White or Asian American graduates).

In short, multiple studies of the South Side reform, examining a variety of outcomes and using a variety of approaches for analyzing the school's data, have documented benefits for the school's students. In fact, the most recent study suggests that the reform was specifically beneficial in math performance for students with the *highest* PSAT scores. Our explanation here is straightforward: the school provides strong supports for teachers, helping them improve their teaching. When classes are engaging and lessons are deep and challenging, all students benefit.

### The Reform Process

The recent successes of the high school date back 3 decades, beginning with a gradual and methodical process involving detracking and "leveling up" curriculum—using high-track expectations and instruction for all students. An analysis of student performance data at the outset of the reform revealed a significant achievement gap between the district's minority population, economically disadvantaged students, and White students whose families earn upper-middle-class incomes. The overarching questions that were posed at the time by the school district's superintendent, Dr. William Johnson, continue to direct the decision-making process today:

1. Do the instructional practices currently implemented match and reinforce the values of the district, especially with regard to equity and excellence?

2. If we are asking more of our students and our teachers, what supports do they need in order to be successful?

3. What sort of an evaluative feedback loop do we need to put in place to make sure that legitimate concerns of students, parents, and teachers are taken seriously?

Students at the district's high school primarily come from one middle feeder school, which is where the district's detracking initiative began. Since the mid-1990s, students at the middle school have been grouped heterogeneously in all classes, with the curriculum revised to ensure that all students have access to those courses that best prepare them for challenging high school coursework. The early detracking effort focused on revising the mathematics curriculum in Grades 6–8 so that every student was prepared to take algebra and the New York Algebra Regents exam in 8th grade.

But detracking was not the district's first response to its achievement gap. Like many places, Rockville Centre first tried to make its tracking system more equitable. At one stage, counselors, administrators, and teachers at the high school made a concerted effort to recruit and place more historically disadvantaged students into higher-track classes. They saw incremental progress, but the results were unimpressive and inconsistent from year to year. Students who were initially willing to enroll in advanced coursework would, more often than not, "level down" or request a schedule change into non-advanced courses when the grades they received did not meet their expectations. In part, these disappointing results could be attributed to two shortcomings. First, at this stage of the process, interventions such as support classes and mandatory extra help periods were either nonexistent or underutilized. Second, the curriculum and assessment models in both the advanced and non-advanced courses were not revised. That is, although the high school encouraged more students to take the higher-track courses, those courses had not yet been revised to include practices that we now know are essential to the success of all students, such as criterion-referenced assessment and differentiated instruction. But beyond these implementation shortcomings, the school's leadership also noted a core equity issue: given two students with similar or identical histories of prior achievement, the best predictor of whether a student chose the advanced or non-advanced coursework was affluence (family wealth). For this reason and others, these leaders realized that student choice was not enough.

Another unsuccessful approach to eliminating the achievement gap involved leveling up the content of the non-advanced courses so that the curriculum and expectations in those lower tracks came close to or met the standards associated with the advanced coursework. Yet the self-imposed expectations of students who saw themselves as "not as smart as the honors kids" created a classroom environment that teachers fought valiantly, but unsuccessfully, to counter. If students are sorted by perceived ability, the lower-track class will invariably look like lower-track classes have always looked. Unsurprisingly, the students in the "leveled-up" lower-track classes still underperformed on state assessments.

Given these discouraging attempts at reform of the high school, district leadership began to take note of the unqualified successes of the algebra reform at the middle school. These district leaders decided to start carrying them through to the high school grades, always keeping in place an evaluative feedback loop in order to ensure that all students were being well served by the changes. By 1999, 9th- and 10th-grade English and social studies classes were detracked, followed by science in 2000 and mathematics in 2001.

At each step along the way, the curriculum and assessment model was revised so that all stakeholders received necessary supports. In particular, teachers received training, wrote curriculum, and met during professional development workshops as new initiatives were implemented. Parents were informed and provided input during PTA meetings, evening presentations, and Board of Education meetings. In grades 9 and 10, the newly detracked classes maintained the requirements set by the New York Regents exams, while South Side High School implemented practices and strategies that promoted differentiation and leveling up curriculum. That is, the high expectations and the targeted standards were non-negotiable; the school's leadership focused instead on improving the approaches for meeting those expectations and standards. In grades 9 and 10, the detracked classes were offered as the standard class, and curriculum was revised with the Regents standards in mind—but with the IB assessment model as the template for differentiation and backward mapping. During these early stages of the reform, IB coursework was an option for students in grades 11 and 12 but was not mandatory.

Another template and anchor for the reform was provided by the IB curriculum and assessment model. For example, all classes began with an open "aim" question based on the topic and content taught. This question was well designed for differentiation in that it would be accessible for all students yet also invite more detailed analysis. These aim questions became standard practice for all lessons at South Side. They provided a focal point and objective for students, and they also helped develop a culture where rich questions subject to divergent and sometimes competing perspectives or points of view become the basis for learning and instruction. The IB assessments that students would experience in grades 11 and 12 provided excellent examples:

- How could [the text being studied] be interpreted differently by two different readers?
- Which social groups are marginalized, excluded, or silenced in the text?

- A moral or a lesson is a common convention in stories. In what ways and for what purposes has the author(s) either adhered to or departed from this convention?
- To what extent did economic factors cause the U.S. Civil War?
- Assess the aims and impact of the Black Panthers from 1966 to the 1970s.

Readings and texts for the detracked classes were carefully chosen to provide students with a rich and challenging experience. Strategies such as the use of guided reading prompts and scaffolding questions were created to assist struggling learners and to guide all students toward a more sophisticated response to the aim question.

Beginning in the early 2000s, South Side created every-other-day support classes in English Language Arts (ELA) and mathematics and deliberately made them open to all students who expressed a need for instructional support. These double-up classes were, in fact, heterogeneous as well—with many non-struggling students opting to take advantage of the learning opportunities. Instead of remediation, the more challenging concepts, skills, and content are pre-taught (usually by the same teacher who teaches the main course) so that students are fully prepared to participate in a larger classroom group. These support classes have been enormously important to the school's detracking efforts, transforming the student who would otherwise be lost and disengaged into an active contributor and learner.

Similarly, when South Side detracked Algebra II/Trigonometry in 2004, an every-other-day course titled Math Advanced Topics was created to introduce topics that exceeded the requirements for the New York Regents exam. This course was designed as a bridge from the Regents-level expectations to the new, higher expectations at South Side. The class provides students with supports on the content and skills required in the school's most advanced 11th- and 12th-grade mathematics courses, IB Mathematics Standard Level and Advanced Placement Calculus, as well as the Algebra II/Trigonometry course.

School staff revised grading and assessment policies in all detracked classes to provide entry points for all students while also promoting high achievement. Teachers created a common formula for calculating quarterly grades, one that rewarded both process and product. For example, in grades 9 and 10 ELA, 50% of quarterly grades were based on process, such as preparedness, class participation, and homework completion, and 50% on product, such as tests and extended writing assignments, projects, and formal oral presentations. In doing so, those behaviors and attributes that were identified as key components to continued academic success became points of emphasis in instruction, professional development, and assessment. When engaging in a better learning process in a challenging, detracked class, even struggling students learned more than they would have in a lower-track class, thus better preparing them for later success—and their improved grades reflected this.

As classes became more heterogeneous, the importance of common assessments became readily apparent. Students deserved to experience a consistent and mutually agreed-upon level of accountability, support, and feedback throughout the year. Further, teachers needed time to collaborate and create assessments that would monitor the achievement of all students and the overall curriculum in a given course. At each phase of the detracking process, teachers in each subject area collaboratively wrote a curriculum that was implemented by all teachers.

As stated earlier, the Regents standards formed the basis of the curriculum, but the IB standards and practices were used for their "backwash effect." Because IB assessments were developed with differentiated instruction and constructivist learning in mind, they were used as anchors for the scope and sequence, to prepare students for the thought processes and skills that would be required in the future. For example, the social studies curricula in grades 9–12 were developed with the "internal assessment" for IB History of the Americas in mind. The internal assessment is a historical investigation of a topic and research question created by the student, in consultation with their teacher. By the time students are introduced to the internal assessment in grades 11 and 12, they have already learned how to create a summary of evidence and how to interpret documents based on their origin, purpose, value, context, and limitations.

A common timeline, scope, and sequence as well as a list of topics and resources were agreed upon to ensure instructional consistency among course sections. While teachers still enjoyed a level of autonomy in terms of day-to-day instruction, a series of common assessments were created and administered at key points in the year to monitor students on an individual basis and across sections. Administered in all courses at the end of the first and third quarters, these quarterly exams complement midterm and final exams.

Multiple access points, open questions that are accessible yet challenging for all students, and criterion-referenced assessments measure students against learning outcomes rather than one another. In each subject area a variety of authentic assessments, both formative and summative, are embedded in coursework to provide students with timely feedback as learning occurs. In the sciences, multiple-step problems include scaffolded entry points and questions designed to help students tackle the more challenging and comprehensive tasks. In English, oral presentations, extended written tasks, and timed exams are used to award a final IB score on a scale of 1–7. In short, students are given multiple opportunities to demonstrate what they do know, rather than to find out what they do not.

It is not a coincidence that the high school detracking efforts coincided with the district moving to an inclusion model in special education. With the exception of approximately 25 students in the school's life skills

Challenging Opportunities for Real-life Experiences (CORE) program, all special education students were fully integrated into general education courses. Based on the individualized education plan (IEP) created for each student by the Committee on Special Education, students were placed in the least restrictive environment to maximize their access to and achievement in the school's most challenging coursework. For students who require the most assistance, two adults, a special education teacher and a teaching assistant, provide supports and instruction in the detracked general education classes in collaborations with the content specialist. These students also meet with the special education teacher during an Academic Enrichment class once a day, where they work on their IEP learning goals as they relate to coursework. Students requiring less support access a resource room class with a special education teacher once a day. A third group of special education students participate in a consultant model, where they are assigned to a special education teacher who monitors their progress and IEP goals. As discussed below, the results as measured by Regents exams and graduation rates have been heartening.

This is a good place for us to stress that detracking requires conscientious assignment of students to classrooms. When South Side's administrators create the school's master schedule, they deliberately and carefully balance enrollment in the general education classes for heterogeneity. Wherever possible, the roster of each class reflects the overall demographics of the high school, including special education and ELL students. Over the summer, after creating course sections and teacher schedules, the school administration balances each course section by hand, based on students' prior achievement. The goal is for each course section in a given subject to include similar numbers of students with histories of high or low achievement. Failure to do this can quickly result in some classes becoming lower-track by default.

The overarching principles that govern each and every decision at South Side are straightforward: diversity is an opportunity every student deserves, class rosters should reflect the diversity of the student body wherever possible, and the success of one student should not and does not come at the expense of another. South Side is a school in a perpetual state of change, one that celebrates diversity and develops an approach and culture that strives for each student to have a sense of belonging. The school provides opportunities for all students to find their own unique talents; make healthy, safe decisions; and become a meaningful part of the school's history.

Along the way, the school formed alliances with other programs and institutions with aligned values. For instance, the growth of the IB Diploma Program coincided with the detracking initiatives, in large part because the IB assessment model, together with the principles and practices espoused by the organization, are designed to open the gates for all students while also maintaining a high standard for advanced students with a history of high achievement. Like South Side, the IB Diploma Program course offerings, instructional practices, and assessments are in a constant state of improvement. The program uses past student performance and the needs confronting current students to inform instruction and programmatic decisions. Similarly, South Side's relationship with the Schools of Opportunity project is a constant source of pride, in large part because it promotes a similar philosophy. One size does not fit all, and no single modification will create success. Yet the overarching design and the approach to learning as previously described serve as a unifying and cohesive force to all modifications and changes to the existing framework.

This is not to say that each stage in South Side's reforms did not include disagreements or controversy. At the initial stage, proposals to detrack English and social studies courses in 10th grade were met with opposition, primarily from parents of higher-performing students. They feared that the new curriculum would water down those experiences found in the school's advanced curriculum and that the heterogeneity of the class would slow the class down. When the curriculum changes were introduced at a Board of Education meeting, a large group of parents attended to voice their concerns. During the extensive question-and-answer period that followed, the administration and the board acknowledged each and every concern, recognizing that the changes created apprehension due to their novelty and the seemingly counterintuitive nature of the approach for families who had felt comfortable and successful within the tracked system. The administration understood that because many community members were products of a highly tracked learning environment, those who experienced educational success found no need to deviate from the status quo. But the community also understood that the proposed reform was grounded in the district's own recent, successful detracking efforts.

The concerns voiced in Rockville Centre were tempered by a discussion of successes at the middle school and 9th grade and also informed by identification of the inequities and issues that surround any stratifying method of course selection. The fact that Assistant Superintendent for Curriculum and Instruction Dr. Delia Garrity was one of the strongest advocates for detracking and was the mother of two high-performing students in the district did not go unnoticed by the community. Eventually, all agreed to move forward with the 10th-grade revisions—with the commitment to monitor progress and ensure a high-quality education for all students. A yearlong curriculum-writing process began immediately. Many teachers were initially apprehensive, but they were also cognizant that in the tracked system they were often fighting an uphill battle in the non-advanced courses. Despite the best and most concerted efforts of the teaching faculty, students in non-advanced coursework self-identified as being less capable than other students, and they lowered their expectations for themselves.

Throughout the detracking process, district and school leaders reminded teachers that their success up to this point made the current initiative possible and that their unique and special talents were among the main reasons why the school's leadership was so confident that this would work. Teachers have the opportunity to attend intensive 3-day IB workshops in their subject areas or area of expertise. Each year, the high school also creates mandatory after-school professional development workshops designed to support and inform the aforementioned assessments and practices. Time is put aside for teachers to read, interpret, and analyze data concerning student results. In addition, teachers participate in workshops based on the Japanese lesson-study model, where they collaboratively create, teach, revise, and reteach a single lesson based on a prearranged theme, topic, or skill set. Once the curriculum is in place and implemented, opposition and concerns largely disappear—including any opposition from the high school's educators.

Evolving over time, the school's consistent efforts have paid off for the South Side community. In 2019, a total of 58% of South Side's graduating class completed the requirements for a full IB Diploma, which requires the completion of six IB subject courses; a Theory of Knowledge course; a 3,000–4,000 word Extended Essay; and a Creation/Action/Service (CAS) portfolio. CAS—the creativity, activity, and service—is a mandatory, nongraded requirement for all IB Diploma candidates. Students create a portfolio of experiences separate from their coursework; at least one activity should be sustained over a year. These activities are channeled through a series of reflective assignments so that students become aware of the benefits to self and others, as well as the challenges, learning outcomes, and consistencies that exist throughout their portfolio. Ninety percent of the graduating class completed one or more IB course(s) and the required assessments. And the school had a 4-year graduation rate of 98%.

## Other Indicators of Success

In New York State, students qualify for a Regents Diploma upon (a) earning a minimum of 22 credits, and (b) passing the following five Regents Exams: English, Global Studies, Algebra, Global History, U.S. History, and one science exam, usually Earth Science or Living Environment. Special education students can, as an alternative, earn a Local Diploma if they score between 55 and 64 on any of the required Regents exams. Students earn a Regents Diploma with Advanced Designation upon passing nine Regents Exams, including a FLACS (Foreign Language Association of Chairpersons and Supervisors) exam in a language other than English that is created and administered regionally. A variety of other provisions have been implemented in recent years to give students other ways to earn a Regents Diploma.

Over the pre-pandemic decade, the 4-year graduation rate for South Side High School has fluctuated between 98% and 100% for all students. For the 2 most recent pre-pandemic years, the school boasts the following results:

1. In 2018, 99% of students graduated with a New York state diploma.
2. In 2019, 100% graduated with a New York state diploma.
3. In 2018, 92% of the class of earned an NYS Regents diploma with Advanced Designation.
4. In 2019, 90% of the class of earned an NYS Regents diploma with Advanced Designation.
5. In both years, fewer than 1% earned only a local diploma.

The Regents with Advanced Designation rate at the school for economically disadvantaged students is 74%; it is 72% for Hispanic or Latinx students, and 78% for Black or African American students. In comparison, the rate for all students in New York State is 33%.

### Recent Changes to the Framework: Flexibility Without Compromising the Goal

Over the past several years, South Side has made two important changes. One area of change, concerning mental health and wellness, is not directly related to the detracking reform but is still important to note here. The second area does concern the detracking reform and is therefore discussed in more detail.

*Mental Health and Wellness.* Academic success should not come at the expense of a balanced life. For this reason, South Side's programmatic approach to learning also focuses on the health and wellness of its students and faculty. This has become increasingly important in recent years, which is why the school's leadership is currently training all staff in mindfulness and meditation techniques. The health curricula in grades 10 and 12 have been revised to place a greater emphasis on social–emotional learning, and a series of social–emotional learning (SEL) lessons are taught by the counseling staff to 9th-grade students. Topics include vaping, drugs and alcohol, stress management, and developing healthy relationships. Recently revised, the school's health and wellness curriculum now has an increased focus on stress management, creating and maintaining healthy relationships, and drug and alcohol abstinence.

*11th-Grade English and Social Studies.* Detracking reforms are almost always subject to pushback. Each such instance should be considered on its own merits. At South Side, the main pushback has been from some parents of students with special needs, and the district listens to those concerns and attempts to address them—but always with the guidance principles in mind.

A recent example involves the IB coursework in 11th grade English and Social Studies. The introduction of Common Core Regents exams in 2010 and the statewide controversy surrounding student performance created heightened levels of anxiety and frustration, especially among students with special needs. The state instituted a series of rules to provide multiple pathways and measures for students to earn a high school diploma in New York, yet the problems that existed in the exams themselves persisted. This coincided with a national epidemic in mental health issues among adolescents that included workload stress, anxiety, and the increasingly competitive and labor-intensive nature of the college application process.

Some South Side parents felt that some of the current course requirements were too arduous for a small group of students with special needs. Despite the history of success as indicated by the district's diploma rates and Regents results, these parents believed that these results came at too high a price. The primary focus of the opposition stemmed from the "IB for all" coursework for English and social studies in grade 11. As in most New York schools, South Side students take the English and U.S. History Regents exams in 11th grade; both are graduation requirements. Since 2011, these classes had been detracked using the IB curriculum and assessment model for the respective subjects. While the final exam in both English and U.S. History was the Regents exam, each course included a series of intensive units that also prepared students for IB assessments that students would take in grade 12. Because the course exceeded the state requirements for graduation, parents felt that the work was too onerous for some students with special needs. A series of town hall meetings were held at the district's middle school and high school. Teachers, building, and central administration met after each meeting, and together they created a solution. Eleventh-grade English and social studies classes would remain heterogeneous. Students would have the option of registering for IB or Regents English and IB or Regents U.S. History, and they would be co-seated so that all sections would include both groups of students.

For those intensive units (where the IB curriculum exceeds the NYS Regents standards), assessments were modified so that students who chose the Regents option would receive the same rich instruction but would complete assessments based on the Regents rather than the IB standard. For example, when students complete an extended written response for the IB Written Task, students who chose the Regents option complete a thematic essay using the same texts, but with a word count, scaffolding questions, and a rubric based on the requirements for the English Regents exam.

It's worth noting that at this same time the IB organization also launched their own investigation into student workload, revising the IB Language and Literature curricular scope and sequence to address workload issues. The writing skills learned and assessed were incorporated into one of the IB exams, thereby lowering student workload while maintaining the same standard for learning. Similarly, a new subject guide was released for IB language and literature, and the number of externally assessed written tasks of 1,000–1,200 words was cut from four to two.

Correspondingly, South Side created a new Pathways program for a small group of special education students (only 12 students were enrolled in the first year, all of them 9th- and 10th-graders). A schedule for each student was created that includes a blend of detracked, heterogeneously grouped classes for those subjects that are an area of relative strength, with supplemental small-group instruction for subjects that require more intensive interventions.

## CONCLUSION

Comprehensive high schools throughout the United States generally contain remarkably engaging classes, where students are challenged, supported, and successful. These classes stand as exemplars of the type of rich learning opportunities that all students need. Yet these exemplars mean little if the opportunities are rationed. If valuable resources and rich opportunities to learn are disproportionately provided to students who arrive at school with greater preparedness and past success, then the school is likely reproducing larger societal inequalities—with the rich getting richer and the poor getting poorer. As the experience of South Side High School illustrates, this rationing is not necessary; it's a tempting path that educators committed to equity must not take. By broadening and enriching learning opportunities for all students, outstanding high schools commit themselves to nourishing the potential of each young person who walks through the door.

## REFERENCES

Atteberry, A., LaCour, S. E., Burris, C. C., Welner, K. G., & Murphy, J. (2019). Opening the gates: Detracking and the international baccalaureate. *Teachers College Record, 121*(9), 1–63.

Burris, C. C., Heubert, J., & Levin, H. (2006). Accelerating mathematics achievement using heterogeneous grouping. *American Educational Research Journal, 43*(1), 103–134.

Burris, C. C., & Welner, K. G. (2005). Closing the achievement gap by detracking. *Phi Delta Kappan, 86*(8), pp. 594–598.

Burris, C. C., Welner, K. G., Wiley, E. W., & Murphy, J. (2007). A world class curriculum for all. *Educational Leadership, 64*(7), pp. 53–56.

Burris, C. C., Wiley, E. W., Welner, K. G., & Murphy, J. (2008). Accountability, rigor, and detracking: Achievement effects of embracing a challenging curriculum as a universal good for all students. *Teachers College Record, 110*(3), 571–608.

# CHAPTER 2

# A Multipronged and Equity-Oriented Approach to Transforming School Climate

## The Story of Revere High School

*Kathryn E. Wiley and Lourenço Garcia*

Criterion 2: Create and Maintain a Healthy School Culture, With Attention to Diversity and to Reassessing Student Discipline Policies

Most people can tell you that schools *feel* a certain way, and not all the same way. The ways schools *feel*—that is, their climate—is partially engendered by elements within the school environment. Let's imagine two different scenarios through the eyes of a student. In the first, you walk up to a bustling campus to find your principal and teachers at the entrance, smiling and high-fiving you as you walk in. They welcome you in your first language and call you by your name. You head toward homeroom to start the day in "opening circle," a time to share joys and concerns with your teacher and peers. This scenario is one of welcome, of inclusion. Now, let's imagine a different scenario. There is no one outside to greet you. Instead, you walk up to the main door and ring a buzzer. Upon entering, you and your peers line up in rows and slowly proceed through the metal detectors. You drop your books, and a security guard shouts at you to "get it together." At this school, you rarely hear your home language. Your name is said in only reprimands and redirects. This scenario is one of objectification and exclusion. The first experience is quite different from the second, in part due to differences in each school's educational environment. A warm welcome, compared to a closed door. The ready recognition arising from having one's name affirmed, compared to words spoken in cold criticism for compliance. Whereas the first school might generate a sense of warmth, well-being, and belonging, the second might create a sense of anxiety, apprehension, and isolation. Although oversimplified, these scenarios are intended to convey an important point:

school environments vary widely, and these school environments matter. These environments, and the feelings they engender, are collectively referred to as "school climate" (Loukas, 2007).

To some, school climate may seem a "soft" topic with negligible connections to student achievement or school quality and safety, but in fact, school climate has important relationships to each. With student mental and emotional health increasingly a concern among school leaders, climate is an important, if not foundational, consideration for a healthy and high-quality school (the National Association of Elementary Principals [NAESP], 2018). In fact, creating a positive school climate may be one of the most important ways that school leaders can impact student learning (Allensworth & Hart, 2018).

Improving a school's climate can be a difficult task. When faced with negative or even hostile school environments, what is a school leader to do? Practices and culture can entrench adverse organizational patterns over time, and competing priorities and conflicting recommendations often leave school leaders feeling overwhelmed. Due to high-stakes accountability systems, instructional interventions tend to be prioritized over "soft" qualities like climate. However, how students *feel* in school has far-reaching implications for student success. According to the National School Climate Council, "a sustainable, positive school climate fosters youth development and learning necessary for productive, contributive, and satisfying life in a democratic society" (2017, p. 4).

In this chapter, we explore climate change at Revere High School (RHS), a School of Opportunity that offers an example of school climate transformation, an important, required criterion in the Schools of Opportunity selection process described below:

---

**CRITERION 2: CREATE AND MAINTAIN A HEALTHY SCHOOL CULTURE, WITH ATTENTION TO DIVERSITY AND REASSESSING STUDENT DISCIPLINE POLICIES**

The [exemplary] school has an extraordinarily safe, welcoming environment that embraces the diversity of race, ethnicity, religion, gender, and sexual orientations among students. There is evidence that the school has reduced instances of bullying, harassment, or discrimination. Clear policies, systems, and practices for reporting, investigating, and addressing such instances are in place and equitably enacted. Such practices attend to student social-emotional well-being and to improving systems to prevent future incidents.

The school has equitably and effectively implemented non-exclusionary approaches to discipline. The school has an active and successful plan to help students learn positive behavior, maintain self-control, and work toward repairing relationships when feasible. Suspended students and their families understand their rights and obligations, and a clear appeal process is

> in place. In the limited instance of exclusionary discipline, students have an environment outside of school (or in in-school suspension) in which to (1) receive educational and social-emotional supports, and (2) complete a reintegration process that welcomes them back to the school.

Revere High School shows how creating and maintaining a positive school climate is possible through whole-school transformation over multiple years led with consistent equity-minded change and social justice leadership. This chapter is coauthored by Dr. Lourenço Garcia, assistant superintendent of Revere Public Schools, who at the time of Schools of Opportunity recognition was RHS's principal and oversaw the school's 5-year transformation, and Dr. Kathryn E. Wiley, an education researcher who studies educational equity and opportunity. We share this story by weaving together Lourenço's memories and experiences alongside the research literature. It is our hope that this chapter inspires readers with a sense of what is possible in school climate transformation.

## THE IMPORTANCE OF SCHOOL CLIMATE

School climate speaks to the "quality and character of school life" and "reflects norms, goals, values, interpersonal relationships, teaching, learning and leadership practices, and organizational structures" (Cohen et al., 2009). There are three dimensions to school climate: physical, social, and academic (Loukas, 2007). Physical dimensions include the appearance of the school building and classrooms, student-teacher ratio, availability of resources, and organization of the school. The social dimension includes quality of relationships between and among students, teachers, and staff; a sense of safety and comfort; students' sense of equitable and fair treatment by staff; and a sense of input into school decisions by students, teachers, and staff. The academic dimensions include instructional quality, teachers' expectations for student achievement, and progress monitoring. According to the National School Climate Council (2017), a positive school climate is one in which "students, families and educators work together to develop, live, and contribute to a shared school vision . . . each person contributes to the operations of the school as well as the care of the physical environment" (p. 4).

Research on school climate has found that positive climate yields a variety of beneficial student outcomes. Reviewing the literature on school climate, Thapa et al. (2013) concluded that positive school climate mitigates students' negative self-esteem, self-criticism, and self-image. It is also linked to lower levels of drug usage and predictive of students' psychological well-being. Their research also indicates that positive climate acts as a protective factor for learning and positive youth development and can reduce some of the negative impacts of socioeconomics on academic success. Although the incomplete research on how positive school climate influences the academic outcomes for students varies, there is general consensus among educators and researchers that it can potentially reduce opportunity gaps among student subgroups, especially those underserved and historically marginalized (Bektas et al., 2015; Berkowitz et al., 2017). Cohen et al. (2009) define a positive school climate as one in which students have what they need for healthy development and learning, and one in which teachers have the supportive conditions to excel at their craft.

## TRANSFORMING THE CLIMATE AT REVERE HIGH SCHOOL

Revere High School is a large racially, culturally, and linguistically diverse urban high school (grades 9–12) located in Revere, Massachusetts—a gateway city located 5 minutes north of Boston. It serves approximately 1,900 students, the majority of whom are low-income. Approximately 61% of Revere's students are Hispanic, 28% White, and 4% Black; 68% of the students' first language is not English. The school's large, three-story white and brown building is trimmed with a blue awnings. An American flag flies outside the main entrance, and a football field and track are visible in the distance. The school is surrounded by single and multistory homes and apartments. Prior to the climate transformation, RHS faced circumstances not unlike other large, comprehensive high schools. Financial resources were limited. Instructional practices were outdated and took a one-size-fits-all approach. Teachers were siloed, having few opportunities to collaborate or learn new instructional methods. Some described the school's approach to teaching as relying on "the banking model" of passive, teacher-centered instruction, offering little in the way of critical thinking.

Revere High School was also beset with deficit mindsets among some staff that contributed to a negative school climate. Some teachers and administrators were reluctant to believe that low-income students, students of color, and students with disabilities could succeed. This was communicated to some students indirectly by the way they were treated as learners in the classroom, where teachers' low expectations and deficit assumptions presupposed student failure. Students did not feel valued as learners nor that teachers and administrators had confidence in them. In addition to mindsets, a variety of policies and practices further created institutional barriers for student success. Language policies in the student handbook were antiquated and posed obstacles for the school's many bilingual language learners. Exclusionary discipline policies and practices further marginalized students. Anything remotely serious was responded to with out-of-school suspension, putting students on track for the school-to-prison pipeline. Relationships between students and teachers were fractured and a source of tension in school. Most staff and students felt alienated, isolated, and disengaged. Student achievement was low; staff dissatisfaction was high. It was clear that RHS's dismal climate needed tending and transformation.

## Sowing Seeds of Change

Because principals shape a variety of policies, practices, and working conditions in schools, their leadership serves as one of the most important ingredients for whole-school learning and change (Leithwood et al., 1998, 2008). A leadership change at Revere High School created a window of opportunity to take the school in a new direction when Lourenço became RHS's new principal in 2010. Lourenço brought with him a new set of ideas to revitalize the school, using his experiences as an educator and dynamic innovator, and as a multilingual, multicultural education leader who had experienced the education system as the child of immigrants. What unfolded next involved a series of changes to create more positive conditions for students and staff. Although Lourenço did not specifically set out to improve school climate, the multipronged approach he took in collaboration with teachers and students created the conditions to support the physical, social, and academic well-being of the entire school community and, in doing so, fundamentally shifted the climate.

*Increase External Partnerships and Funding Sources.* One of the first elements the school leadership tackled was the school's financial situation. Through an aggressive pursuit of external funding, Revere High School acquired a variety of funding sources to offset inequities in the funding system. The high school received $500,000 from the Nellie Mae Education Foundation, a philanthropy committed to reshaping the high school learning experience by working with schools and organizations to implement the principles of student-centered learning and to lay the groundwork for education reform and innovation. The planning grant extended over a 5-year period and had five priority areas: (a) student-centered learning, (b) competency-based learning, (c) digital technology (iPads), (d) flipped learning classrooms, and (e) teacher training, leadership, and capacity-building. Several teachers were selected as building-level coaches, and a student technology team was put together to support any issues that arose using the new technology required for these "flipped" classrooms.

*Extensive, Job-Embedded Professional Development for Teachers.* A subsequent grant for $3 million continued and expanded the work that had begun previously. Grant funds provided extensive training on student-centered learning techniques and built capacity for the school to develop new learning initiatives. One important initiative involved a 2-year deep dive into student data to identify systemic barriers to learning in the school. These efforts resulted in a fundamental reorganization of teaching and learning practices, positioning both teachers and students as having valuable contributions to make in the classroom setting. Through data analysis and teacher professional development, teachers had significant opportunities to collaborate. Collaboration, coupled with significant input into instructional practices, provided teachers with new levels of professionalism and control. To shift the "banking method" approach that had characterized the high school previously, Revere High School teachers participated in a regional and national professional development network. Through these reform partnerships, the staff participated in a series of schoolwide teacher-driven trainings and professional development modules on wide-ranging topics, including differentiated instruction strategies, block schedule teaching strategies, advisory teaching strategies, and teacher leadership. Teacher training was organized so that Revere's own teachers became internal coaches to support job-embedded professional development during school hours. These changes interjected a flood of new resources, technology, and knowledge and skills, which fundamentally reshaped teaching, learning, and relationships throughout the building.

*Improved Programs and Approaches for Multilingual Students.* A third area of change occurred in the way that Revere High School served multilingual students, many of whom were recent immigrants from Latin American countries, including Colombia, El Salvador, Guatemala, Honduras, and Brazil. RHS created an after-school Newcomers Academy and trained staff in second language acquisition and socioemotional learning specific to newcomers. In addition, staff received training to deepen their understanding of the circumstances facing multilingual immigrant students and families and practices to support parent engagement. The Newcomers Academy consisted of students who had experienced interrupted school due to war, civil unrest, migration, or other related factors. Recognizing the challenges faced by these students and to meet their unique needs, RHS developed a series of foundation courses focused on content-based ESL, sheltered sciences, social studies, math, and pre-algebra. Students, depending on their age, literacy, and numeracy skills, remained in the program as necessary and then, based on progress and recommendation, were transitioned into regular ESL classes. A teacher leader in conjunction with the program director coordinated the program.

The changes might have ended with the creation of the after-school academy, but students' experiences in the program led to further improvements. Lourenço recalls how a group of students approached him, in Spanish, and explained, "We want to talk to you about the Newcomers Academy." A meeting between the academy students and Lourenço was held in the school cafeteria. Lourenço recalls the students saying, "While we appreciate the Newcomers Academy and relationships with our teachers, we don't want it to run separate in the afternoon." The students went on to describe how holding the academy in a separate after-school program made them feel like they were not a part of the school community. In addition, the meeting revealed to administrators a previously unacknowledged reality: many of the students worked after school to help their parents financially. In asking students to attend classes after school, administrators had unknowingly created a barrier between students and their families. After the meeting, school administrators took up the concerns, did research, and supported the students' request. They ultimately found a way to hold the academy during school hours as a center that ensured students are supported in grade-level work with the goal of integrating them into general education classrooms. That students voiced their concerns to administrators felt like a significant win for Lourenço, who recalls that it was "a very powerful experience to see the young people take up leadership and ownership of the program, and show what's possible when students trust the principal, and how being a principal that students can relate to, they see in you part of them as a person of color and as a person who speaks their language, and it opens doors."

*Focusing on Academic Engagement and Relationships.* Intentionally creating a relationship-based culture became a central priority among school leaders. To make this shift, though, time itself had to be reorganized within the school's schedule. To identify opportunities for deep relationship-building, Revere High School created a block schedule. The number of daily class periods were reduced from seven to four to extend learning time and increase engagement. This gave teachers four blocks per day—one of which was planning. In addition, an "advisory block" was added three days per week. The purpose of the advisory block was solely for students and teachers to form and strengthen relationships. It provided space to address and talk about issues going on in school—bullying, anxiety, and so forth. Teachers were able to get to know students on a deeper level, to meet students where they were in curriculum, and to adjust methodology to make classes more engaging. School leadership noticed that as freshman, 9th-graders needed help with the transition to high school and skills to navigate the next 4 years. To address these issues, the school created a Freshman Academy. Freshman Academy provided a space for students to hear from and meet guidance counselors, social workers, and assistant principals. They also had opportunities to build relationships and talk about pressing issues as a group.

*Reframing Discipline Policies.* Prioritizing relationships and student well-being included another big shift that the school made in terms of school discipline policy. Lourenço recalls that when he arrived, the school culture was heavily based on compliance, and rule violations frequently resulted in out-of-school suspensions, and sometimes even arrests. These punishments, Lourenço recalls, "often did not fit the crime." Rather, these incidents often stemmed from miscommunications. Overall, though, suspension was not working to improve students' behavior or performance. Furthermore, Lourenço was concerned that suspending and arresting students was putting them on track for the school-to-prison pipeline. The school-to-prison pipeline is more than a metaphor; the use of exclusionary discipline leads to numerous adverse outcomes for students, including poor academic performance, dropping out, and later involvement in the juvenile (in)justice system (Skiba et al., 2014). Exclusionary discipline is used disproportionately with Black and Latino students, often for minor, typical adolescent behavior not warranting harsh discipline response, and adversely impacts students outcomes (Welsh & Little, 2018a,b). It is not surprising, then, that suspending students at Revere High School was not improving students' behavior or academics. To replace exclusionary discipline, new skills and knowledge were needed. RHS adopted a restorative approach and the decision was made to invest in "upskilling" teachers by having them participate in a well-known Restorative Justice training that was available at a nearby university. Rather than suspending students, this change meant that administrators and teachers facilitated students working out their conflicts with one another. Lourenço recalls that "if two students got into a fight, they would have to sit in a circle with other students, facilitated by a teacher, and each student would talk about what happened." He notes, "It allows kids to express themselves and reflect upon actions and behavior, giving them a voice. Plus, this strategy gives other students ideas about how the situation could have been handled differently. Students come away with a sense of voice and empowerment, with an idea of how to handle the situation next time."

Revere High School also put clear policies, systems, and practices in place for reporting, investigating, and addressing incidents of bullying. Such policies and practices attended to student socioemotional well-being and to preventing future incidents. RHS did not eliminate the use of suspension, but school leaders did clarify the suspension policy and provided guidance on family rights and obligations to make the appeal process more transparent. Over time, this shift resulted in fewer suspensions and higher-quality relationships among students and staff. It also reduced instances of bullying, harassment, or discrimination. The percentage of students suspended fell from 7.5% to 1.4%, with declines in suspension rates for Latino students, low-income students, students with disabilities, and White students (Massachusetts Dept. of Education, 2021).

The Revere High School shift from exclusionary discipline to a restorative approach is not unique. Rather, it is a shift that many schools have undertaken in the last decade (Ritter, 2018). What stands out about RHS, however, is that this change was not isolated. Rarely can a single change reduce conflict and the use of exclusion and punishment in schools (Wiley et al., 2018). In fact, implementing new discipline policies without addressing resource inequities, upskilling teachers, or altering instructional practices may not produce the changes in the quality of student and staff relationships and organizational conditions, which in large part drive discipline patterns. RHS significantly restructured relationships between students and staff throughout the building by addressing discipline *as well as* increasing resources, teaching collaboration, technology, and instruction, and by providing supports for language learners and parents. In order for restorative justice to work, a relationship must exist to *restore*. This is what made it so critical that RHS created more opportunities for teacher-student and student-student relationships. These changes created the conditions for a genuine shift in school climate. Students were valued as learners in all aspects, and at all levels. Their emotional needs were addressed and incorporated into curriculum. Their expertise was valued and reflected in lessons. They were given the opportunity to build meaningful relationships with teachers. Their learning was taken seriously. Their voices were valued through opportunities to meaningfully influence change. As a result, students now felt believed in and invested in, which sent the message that they can succeed—and that they are expected to succeed—through the supportive environment of the school community.

### Staying the Course

When schools undergo equity-minded changes to structure, policy, and practice, it is likely that the changes, and those driving them, will face some level of resistance from others in the school community (Oakes et al., 2005; Stuart Wells & Serna, 1996; Welner, 2001). Such changes can result in resistance from parents and school staff (Theoharis, 2007). This was no different at Revere High School. The change in school leadership and the dramatic shifts in school structure disrupted old routines, practices, and paradigms and prioritized marginalized students in ways that had not previously existed in the school building. Initially, staff pushed back against these shifts. Lourenço recalls that "the big ideas had been discussed with and presented to faculty, students and parents, but disagreements, contentions, doubts, and skepticism about the viability and implementation of these changes persisted." This was the case among the most experienced teachers and other school administrators. When Lourenço was new on the job, he remembers being approached by a member of the school redesign team—a team charged with change management—who told him, "Look, here in Revere we do things *our* way. Things are fine the way they are—our school has been this way for a long time and our students, teachers, and staff are happy with what we have." For Lourenço, the response to resistance was clear: "My answer to the administrator was swift: 'Our students and families have been waiting for so long. While I understand your concerns, we have to do what is best for students!'" Of this moment, Lourenço said, "This incident is a powerful reminder to all of us that implementing change can be hard and challenging even to members in our own inner circle and teams." Many teachers also disagreed with the changes and resisted moving forward with the training. In addition, some parents in the school community resisted, specifically White parents whose children were relatively advantaged by the school's pretransformation structure. For instance, when course-taking was expanded to increase representation of students of Color in advanced courses, White parents resisted on the grounds that their children would suffer. White parents also bought into narratives that the school discipline reforms were going to "create a chaotic school." Lourenço recalls it was like "a tsunami of resistance—the White parents knew the dominant language and culture, and they know how to get concessions. They were outspoken, and they wanted the principal to reverse the changes decisions." Conversely, immigrant parents were navigating linguistic and cultural barriers; some were undocumented, afraid to participate, and disenfranchised even as school reforms were trying to change that.

That Lourenço experienced resistance to changes is not unique. Equity-minded reforms, particularly those that challenge the racial, cultural, and linguistic status quo, are often subject to intense backlash. In such circumstances, school leaders play a significant role in sustaining equity-minded changes over the long term in the face of criticism and disapproval. During these challenges, school leaders who demonstrate qualities of social justice leadership can provide a steadying vision for equity-minded change (DeMatthews et al., 2015; Theoharis, 2007, 2008). A social justice leader focuses on challenging societal norms and bringing to the forefront of the school agenda issues of race and marginalized communities (Khalifa et al., 2016; Theoharis, 2007).

To weather this kind of resistance, "the tsunami," required a strategic approach. To build political support and buy-in among the teaching faculty, Lourenço decided to hold a vote as to whether to proceed with the changes at Revere High School. He felt this would provide a chance for faculty to have their input heard and to create an intentional experience to acknowledge the changes in progress. The vote was close, with just a slight majority of teachers in support of the massive transformations at RHS. Despite the close vote, it felt like enough to move forward. Lourenço recalls that "those who were skeptical *did* end up buying in it later on." This is not uncommon. As teachers begin to see for themselves the positive changes in students, resistors can become adopters (Wiley et al., 2018). One particularly effective strategy for building support was having teachers and administrators shadow students for multiple days, following students from class to class and interviewing students about their experience. Lourenço recalls that when the faculty debriefed these experiences together, they noted that it was very eye-opening and that as adults, they had forgotten how hard and stressful it was to be a high school student. The experience caused teachers to reconsider the challenges many students were facing both at school and at home. The teachers felt like they better understood where students were coming from, which gave them the understanding to form more meaningful relationships with students. This also gave administrators and teachers an idea of what needed to be changed in student scheduling to make sure students had the space and time to form meaningful relationships. Many teachers then moved toward supporting the school's new direction.

In addition to these strategies, Lourenço had the benefit of a supportive district superintendent. As Lourenço described, "The foundation and tone for some of those changes really had to be set by the district." The superintendent at the time was a champion for changes at the school and was also committed to disrupting the status quo, seeing this critical juncture as an opportunity to dig deeper into the school's culture, policies, and practices to determine what was working well and what was not working well, and implementing a model that would lead all students to success. The support of the superintendent created a unified front for equity-minded changes. Additionally, the local union president also supported equity-focused reforms in the building, which Lourenço believed reinforced teachers' support of the transformative changes occurring. As a united front committed to prioritizing previously marginalized students and families, a critical mass of supporters helped hold the ship steady in the face of initial resistance from staff and parents. As Lourenço described, the type of whole-school transformation to support students "becomes possible with the superintendent on your side, the union president on your side, these supportive, powerful allies."

## CONCLUSION

Over time, and with steady, equity-focused leadership, the school climate at Revere High School was transformed (Loukas, 2007). Over the transformation timeline, attendance rates increased (from 93% to 95.3%), the percentage of students absent 10 or more days a year was nearly cut in half (from 46% to 27%), and the percentage of students chronically absent declined from 20% of students to 11.4% (Massachusetts Dept. of Education, 2011). Graduation rates for all students increased from 83.5% to 94%, and specifically rose for Latino students from 77% to 93% and for students with disabilities 63% to 77% (Massachusetts Dept. of Education, 2016).

Changing a school's climate is a difficult task. Revere High School's transformation took 5 years. It was not a single strategy that sowed the seeds for whole-school change. Rather, it was a multipronged effort. They found new funding sources to build a budget beyond what was made available by the public system. The staff ventured into outside networks to shift from a teacher-centered, "banking method" to student-centered learning environments. The school restructured the Newcomers Academy and built staffs' skills and understanding about multilingual and immigrant students by listening to students themselves. Shifting from punitive and exclusionary discipline resulted in positive and restorative conflict resolution. Change required centering marginalized students and using evidenced-based decisions to create learning conditions of opportunity. Supportive school leaders, a supportive superintendent, and a union president were willing to hold the line on equity-minded changes in the face of opposition.

Revere High School demonstrates how creating and maintaining a positive school climate is possible but that it does not happen through a single strategy. Schools must be transformed holistically. Creating and maintaining a healthy school climate requires reconfiguring relationships at all levels of a school community: between students, between teachers and students, and between teachers and school leaders. These relational changes are mediated by trust, time, instructional, programmatic changes, and fiscal resources. Revere's story shows the power of using schooling structures in new ways to support both students and staff. Through a 5-year process, RHS became a large, comprehensive school where the well-being and opportunity structures available to historically marginalized students became a fundamental and central priority and, in doing so, created a positive school climate. It required courage to move in a new direction and to resist entrenched patterns of ways of doing things. Even during the hardest situations, a vision of knowing the necessity of the changes and the paths the changes would open for students remained vital. Lourenço, in quoting Nelson Mandela, offers a reminder of the vision central to the whole-school transformation that occurred, saying, "History will judge us by the difference we make in the lives of children."

## REFERENCES

Allensworth, E. M., & Hart, H. (2018). *How do principals influence student achievement?* University of Chicago Consortium on School Research. https://consortium.uchicago.edu/sites/default/files/2018-10/Leadership%20Snapshot-Mar2018-Consortium.pdf

Bektas, F., Çogaltay, N., Karadag, E., & Ay, Y. (2015). School culture and academic achievement of students: A meta-analysis study. *The Anthropologist, 21*(3), 482–488.

Berkowitz, R., Moore, H., Astor, R. A., & Benbenishty, R. (2017). A research synthesis of the associations between socioeconomic background, inequality, school climate, and academic achievement. *Review of Educational Research, 87*(2), 425–469.

Cohen, J., McCabe, E., Michelli, N., & Pickeral, T. (2009). School climate: Research, policy, practice, and teacher education. *Teachers College Record, 111*(1), 180–213.

DeMatthews, D., Carrola, P., & Mungal, A. (2015). Despite best intentions: A critical analysis of social justice leadership and decision making. *Administrative Issues Journal Education Practice and Research, 5*(2). https://dc.swosu.edu/aij/vol5/iss2/3

Khalifa, M. A., Gooden, M. A., & Davis, J. E. (2016). Culturally responsive school leadership: A synthesis of the literature. *Review of Educational Research, 86*(4), 1272–1311. https://doi.org/10.3102/0034654316630383

Leithwood, K., Harris, A., & Hopkins, D. (2008). Seven strong claims about successful school leadership. *School Leadership & Management, 28*(1), 27–42. https://doi.org/10.1080/13632430701800060

Leithwood, K., Leonard, L., & Sharratt, L. (1998). Conditions fostering organizational learning. *Educational Administration Quarterly, 34*(2), 243–276.

Loukas, A. (2007). What is school climate? *Leadership Compass, 5*(1), 1–3. https://www.naesp.org/sites/default/files/resources/2/Leadership_Compass/2007/LC2007v5n1a4.pdf

Massachusetts Dept. of Education. (2011). *Student attendance and retention (2010–11)*. School and District Profiles. https://profiles.doe.mass.edu/profiles/student.aspx?orgcode=02480505&orgtypecode=6&leftNavId=16817&&fycode=2011

Massachusetts Dept. of Education. (2016). *Cohort 2016 graduation rates*. School and District Profiles. https://profiles.doe.mass.edu/grad/grad_report.aspx?orgcode=02480505&orgtypecode=6&&fycode=2016

Massachusetts Dept. of Education. (2021). *2020–21 student discipline data report by all offenses*. School and District Profiles. https://profiles.doe.mass.edu/ssdr/default.aspx?orgcode=02480505&orgtypecode=6&=02480505&

National Association of Elementary Principals (2018). The pre-K-8 school leader in 2018: A 10-year study. https://www.naesp.org/resources/publications/a-10-year-study-of-the-principalship

National School Climate Council. (2017). What is school climate? https://schoolclimate.org/about/our-approach/what-is-school-climate

Oakes, J., Welner, K., Yonezawa, S., & Allen, R. L. (2005). Norms and politics of equity-minded change: Researching the "zone of mediation." In M. Fullan (Ed.), *Fundamental change: International handbook of educational change* (pp. 282–305). Springer.

Ritter, G. W. (2018). Reviewing the progress of school discipline reform. *Peabody Journal of Education, 93*(2), 133–138. https://doi.org/10.1080/0161956X.2018.1435034

Skiba, R. J., Arredondo, M. I., & Williams, N. T. (2014). More than a metaphor: The contribution of exclusionary discipline to a school-to-prison pipeline. *Equity and Excellence in Education, 47*(4), 546–564. https://doi.org/10.1080/10665684.2014.958965

Stuart Wells, A., & Serna, I. (1996). The politics of culture: Understanding local resistance to detracking reforms in racially mixed schools. *Harvard Educational Review, 66*(1), 93–118.

Thapa, A., Cohen, J., Guffey, S., & Higgins-D'Alessandro, A. (2013). A review of school climate research. *Review of Educational Research, 83*(3), 357–385. https://doi.org/10.3102/0034654313483907

Theoharis, G. (2007). Social justice educational leaders and resistance: Toward a theory of social justice leadership. *Educational Administration Quarterly, 43*(2), 221–258. https://doi.org/10.1177/0013161X06293717

Theoharis, G. (2008). Woven in deeply: Identity and leadership of urban social justice principals. *Education and Urban Society, 41*(1), 3–25. https://doi.org/10.1177/0013124508321372

Welner, K. G. (2001). *Legal rights, local wrongs: When community control collides with educational equity.* SUNY Press.

Welsh, R. O., & Little, S. (2018a). Caste and control in schools: A systematic review of the pathways, rates and correlates of exclusion due to school discipline. *Children and Youth Services Review, 94*(September), 315–339. https://doi.org/10.1016/j.childyouth.2018.09.031

Welsh, R. O., & Little, S. (2018b). The school discipline dilemma: A comprehensive review of disparities and alternative approaches. *Review of Educational Research, 88*(5), 752–794. https://doi.org/10.3102/0034654318791582

Wiley, K. E., Anyon, Y., Yang, J. L., Pauline, M. E., Rosch, A., Valladares, G., Downing, B. J., & Pisciotta, L. (2018). Looking back, moving forward: Technical, normative, and political dimensions of school discipline. *Educational Administration Quarterly, 54*(2), 275–302. https://doi.org/10.1177/0013161X17751179

# CHAPTER 3

# Authentic and Equitable Engagement in Learning at Pocomoke High School

*Kellie Rolstad and Jenifer Rayne*

Criterion 3: Provide More and Better Learning Time During the School Year and Summer

Placed in its historical context, Pocomoke High School, a small, 4-year public school of about 350 students, may be viewed as an unlikely place to find exemplary practices centered around equity, racial justice, and education success.

Located in a rural area in Worcester County on Maryland's Eastern Shore, the high school was opened in 1957, three years after the 1954 *Brown v. Board of Education* ruling to desegregate schools nationwide. Despite the desegregation law, Black students were forbidden to attend the newly built Pocomoke High. Jim Crow was also dominant in the wider community at the time. The county's popular beach destination, Ocean City Beach and Boardwalk, had long been off limits to Black visitors, with the exception of a 3-day period after Labor Day when Black people could visit the beach during "Colored Excursion Days." Pocomoke City was the location of Maryland's last recorded lynching in 1933, and Worcester County was the last county in Maryland to desegregate its schools, refusing to close its last Blacks-only school until 1970, sixteen years after the Supreme Court ruled segregation unconstitutional. In 1992, a suit was brought and eventually won against Worcester County for actively violating the voting rights of Black voters; never in its 250-year history had any elected county office been held by a Black person. The Eastern Shore fought on the side of the Confederacy in the Civil War, and Pocomoke City, like other towns and cities on the Eastern Shore, has long struggled with the legacy of slavery and White supremacy and has experienced considerable political turmoil.

## RECOGNIZING THE CHALLENGE

This history of racism and discrimination in and around Pocomoke City is an important context for understanding the antiracist educational climate that has been created by the faculty and staff at Pocomoke High School. Pocomoke is a majority minority school, with 54% of the students from minority backgrounds and 46% White. A majority of the students, 62%, are considered economically disadvantaged (National Center for Education Statistics, 2020).

In many racially diverse towns and cities dealing with the legacy of systemic racism in education, early efforts to desegregate eventually led to resegregation (Kozol et al., 2010; U.S. Government Accountability Office, 2016). For instance, recent news stories in New York City (Richards, 2020), Seattle (Furfaro & Bazzaz, 2019), and Baltimore (Bowie, 2016) reported on the fact that programs designed for gifted and talented children routinely end up serving White children, with a few spots claimed by token children of color; this situation is not new, despite decades of desegregation efforts (Ford, 2013). By contrast, the modern-day Pocomoke High School has worked very hard to create an inclusive setting for the city's high school students, in broad collaboration with multiple community and government agencies. This setting increases opportunities and encourages students to embrace their authentic selves, to use their voices, their differences, and their power to enact change together. Rather than thinking of learning as something that students do for discrete periods of time within tightly controlled settings (during class and while doing homework), Pocomoke has successfully created an environment that recognizes and promotes the notion that more and better learning occurs when every activity, every action, and every interaction holds the promise and possibility of authentic engagement.

Poverty and racism arising outside of the school present Pocomoke's educators and students with very real obstacles. Worcester County has the highest unemployment rate of any county in Maryland (Maryland Manual On-line, 2020), and the county experiences high poverty and the third-highest crime rate in the state (Davis, 2018). High rates of student homelessness have also been the norm in the county, and many students live in substandard housing without running water or electricity. These problems outside the school have a direct effect on students and their ability to succeed, but a lack of communication between the school and community organizations had long meant low levels of collaboration or planning that might begin to address the many needs.

Accordingly, in 2017, Pocomoke High School launched a schoolwide and communitywide plan to dig into the work that was required to provide its students and the larger community with the tools and supports to meet these problems head-on. School leaders asked: How can we facilitate a culture of connection, belonging, and equity? What new ideas, systems, and projects could address these many challenges? How could Pocomoke High

School create an environment of authentic engagement among faculty and students that could ramp up student learning and success with more and better learning time? They decided that they needed a multipronged plan, searched the literature for effective models, and immediately began work on several innovative ideas.

## THE INNOVATION PROCESS

The innovation process at Pocomoke High School begins with the identification of a need, with the process open to all stakeholders. Early on at the school, needs were identified by the principal and vice principal. Gradually, more and more teachers, staff, students, parents, community members, and organizations began recognizing and identifying needs that might be addressed with the school's support. In each case, needs and responses are discussed, and then a team made up of at least one teacher per department and at least two student representatives meet to create goals, a framework, and an action plan, including the rollout of the initiative. A teacher team is responsible for inviting and training school staff to participate in each plan. Every summer, a team meets to measure and improve major initiatives, such as Your60 (described in detail below), an innovative opportunity for students to engage in their own chosen academic and personal activities for one hour each day. The team continues to meet for several years until all improvements are made and the data show that the initiative is positively affecting students.

## MORE AND BETTER LEARNING TIME

Through this process, the Pocomoke High School community has carefully developed structures and elements to create the school's inclusive experience, aimed at providing students with more and better learning time (MBLT) as described by the Schools of Opportunity project.

---

**CRITERION 3: PROVIDE MORE AND BETTER LEARNING TIME**

The [exemplary] school has equitably implemented exemplary programs to extend or enrich learning time, deliberately designed to include all students. Programs go well beyond remediation and credit recovery to focus on broadening and deepening students' knowledge and understanding. These areas may include, but also should reach beyond, core curricular topics. The school likely partners with external organizations to create rich experiences.

The curriculum carefully addresses specific skills and topics through traditional classes. In addition, the innovations developed at the school reach around and beyond class time and classwork to enrich the daily lives and experiences of all students at the school. Students engage in project-based learning as structured elements of the academic curriculum and during Your60 and After School Academies (described below). These opportunities to learn allow them to apply and to personally contextualize disparate elements of the curriculum. Through this project-based approach, the school has created a sense for students that they belong to and are participating in a school culture that is greater than the sum of its parts, greater than just individual students or teachers or classes or programs. Within the school and through the connections that have been forged across community organizations beyond the school, students' learning opportunities are expanded and enriched far beyond what can be drawn directly from any specific topic, skill, or assignment. Students are able to take advantage of all the resources, spaces, and time that the school makes available through its innovations.

What follows is a description of five main MBLT practices that have tremendously impacted Pocomoke High School, its students, and its surrounding community. We then describe seven additional impactful practices that support these core MBLT practices. These innovations and the supporting programs have been developed and continually improved by administrators, faculty, staff, students, and the organizations that have contributed to Pocomoke High School's inclusive culture and positive climate, allowing students to access more and better learning time in the face of tremendous challenges and needs.

## MBLT Practice 1: Your60

A 60-minute period every day, called Your60, is open to students for freely selected rest or activity. The idea expands the traditional 30-minute school lunch block into a full lunch hour with a variety of personalized options. The innovation required some small changes to bell schedules and even slightly extended the school day (by 4 minutes), but Your60 may be the most powerful and important innovation at Pocomoke High School.

Inspired by Jayne Ellspermann, 2015 National Principal of the Year, who created Power Hour at her high school in Florida (Ellspermann, 2014), Your60 was added in 2017. The period has been tremendously successful at meeting the varied needs of the school's diverse student population. During this hour, all students can eat lunch and spend as much of that hour as they like doing whatever they choose, with options including meeting with teachers, socializing, getting tutoring help, participating in club meetings, meeting with community mentors, or attending whatever enrichment sessions they may have requested. These optional enrichment sessions, with foci that change every 2 weeks, cover topics such as test anxiety; the college admissions process; discussion groups on race, prejudice, sexism, and other interest-based groups; dealing with homelessness; and many other topics.

Sometimes a focus may fall into what we think of as remedial, providing much-needed time and support to catch up. For example, one student reported to the judge in her truancy court follow-up that she had succeeded in bringing up her grades because of support offered during Your60, which had enabled her to seek tutoring help during school hours. Other times, a focus may simply be playful. One teacher shows old movies on a vintage film projector, and students make popcorn to share while they watch movies.

Still other activities offer enrichment that connects to the community. For example, a Your60 session involves a weekly visit to the local senior center, which connects elders with interested high school students. One of the elders is deaf, which motivated a student to study sign language. The student then taught a signing workshop to a group of students with developmental delays, which was enthusiastically received. This in turn led to the creation of Leadership Education About Disabilities (LEAD), a student club. This club opted to put together homeroom lessons for all Pocomoke High School students focused on accommodating disabilities; LEAD also conducted a blindness simulation for students and teachers to help sighted people understand some of the obstacles facing blind people.

A special 3-day Comic Con event during Your60 brought art and design representatives from the University of Maryland Eastern Shore and from New York's Pratt Institute to meet with Pocomoke students who were working on graphic novels and/or who had made their own cosplay costumes. A professional photographer brought costumes for students to don as well and took portraits of students in costume.

All adults at the school, including custodians, staff, teachers, administrators, community mentors, and health representatives, are regularly available during Your60 to eat with students, to meet, to tutor, or just to talk. During Your60, students have the opportunity to talk informally with adults, to tell their own stories, and to forge deep connections. Colleges and universities, trade schools, the military, local businesses, and NASA all regularly send representatives to Pocomoke High School to provide information, and often internship opportunities, during Your60. By making information about all of these options available to students without coercing their attention, the school allows students to gain a wide exposure to postsecondary opportunities, piquing student interest, rather than trying to force it. Because of the wide variety and up-to-the-minute choices and options during Your60, bar codes are posted around the school that students can scan with their phones or school-issued iPads to access the constantly updated Your60 schedule.

This change, which was superficially about reallocating time within the school day, facilitated much more substantive changes to how students approach the school and their learning.

## MBLT Practice 2: Community Team Approach

At the school entrance, a team of three adults is stationed every morning specifically to welcome students, greeting each by name to ensure that each day begins with every student feeling connected to adults at the school. In addition to cultivating such school-based, one-on-one student/adult relationships, Pocomoke has established a wider, tightly connected, team approach to student support. This wide-scale, whole-community effort allows for the development of powerful networks among the school, local businesses, government agencies, and community organizations, as recommended by Maier et al. (2017).

The school's community-building efforts bring together families, home workers from social services, the police department, the Health Department, college representatives, trade schools, local businesses, and ROTC. A Health Department representative is located on site at the school. In 2018, the establishment of an in-house Maryland Food Bank added significantly to the school's student and community outreach, reinforcing the importance of every student having access to multiple support networks. Pop-up BBQs are also used for community outreach; Pocomoke staff partner with faith-based organizations and then "pop up" in neighborhoods with food, giveaways, and resources. In fall 2021, Pocomoke High School implemented an initiative called Worcester On Wheels, a grant-funded community project shared between the high school and the middle school. Worcester on Wheels is a customized recreational vehicle that brings meeting spaces into the community at least biweekly for tutoring, parent conferences, literacy initiatives, and even IEP meetings so that families that may lack transportation can participate without having to travel to the school. This allows the high school and the middle school to sponsor events in the community and to make school and community resources more available to families.

Such partnerships with community organizations are one way for schools to create more and better learning experiences for students.

## MBLT Practice 3: Teachers Create Student Learning Enrichment Opportunities

Pocomoke High's teachers work together to create opportunities that enrich students' experiences. The strong culture of teacher and staff empowerment has also led to a significant number of teachers writing grants that bring outside resources to this underresourced school and community. As a school where 70% of the student population receives free or reduced-price meals, Pocomoke High must work extra hard to provide its students with access to additional opportunities. Teachers also engage in field trips and outings that provide additional and enriching learning time for the school's students. For example, two teachers drove six students to New York City to visit the Pratt

Institute, New York University, art museums, and bookstores. One student brought his portfolio to share with the faculty of the Pratt Institute and was later accepted to Pratt as a student, upon graduation from Pocomoke High. The school's literacy coach obtained a grant for "Project Lit," an initiative specifically designed to boost the schools' access to cultural and ethnic representation of the students in their literature selections. Project Lit enables students to access novels, share these texts with the community, and invite community members to positive discussions about difficult and sensitive topics. The project is student-led but overseen by Pocomoke High School's media specialist.

Teachers are committed to helping their students navigate postsecondary education options, supplementing advice and resources provided by the students' parents and other contacts—keeping in mind that many of Pocomoke's parents, like most parents in less wealthy communities, have little experience with postsecondary preparation and support. Teachers also regularly meet to come up with a plan whenever a student is struggling in one or more academic areas. Their goal is to ensure that the student knows of the various supports that are in place, from Your60 tutoring to mental and physical health support. This is particularly important because of the high level of marginalized students served by the school and its programs. The school maintains a strong, positive perspective on all students engaging in their own development, with strong teacher and staff support. While many high schools seek to become large, comprehensive high schools, Pocomoke's accomplishments are facilitated by its relatively small size and close personal relationships.

## MBLT Practice 4: Recruiting Teachers of Color and Strengthening Antiracist Culture

The teaching force at Pocomoke High School was historically all White, reflecting the delayed desegregation of the Eastern Shore of Maryland. In fact, the Eastern Shore still lags behind the rest of Maryland in hiring and retaining teachers of Color. Today, 55% of Pocomoke's student population identifies as African American or biracial, while only four out of 35 teachers are African American. One guidance counselor is African American and has family roots in the area. The school, recognizing the work still needed in recruiting and retaining African American educators, works with Future Educators of America. (For a discussion of research about teacher diversity, see Learning Policy Institute, 2018.) In addition, the school is now collaborating with University of Maryland Eastern Shore (UMES) on a new initiative called MADE MEN: Men Achieving Dreams through Education. MADE MEN focuses on recruitment and development of future male educators of Color. Dr. Richard Warren, professor at UMES, and principal Jenifer Rayne implemented this program as a Teacher Academy of Maryland

(TAM) program at Pocomoke High School in the summer of 2020. In the summer of 2021, a second TAM program called Women Who RISE began in collaboration with Salisbury University. RISE stands for Reach and Inspire Students through Education, and the goal of Women Who RISE is to recruit and support women of Color to become educators. Matt Hoffman, assistant principal and extended day program coordinator, leads efforts in recruitment and retention of these future educators. Currently, seven young men and six young women who are Pocomoke High School students have taken dual enrollment college courses in education.

Overlapping with these efforts are frequent antiracism professional development sessions as well as professional development sessions on bias. Monthly, small randomly selected focus groups of students are asked two questions: "Do you feel personally connected to lessons and to teachers?" and "Do you feel like you are a part of the classroom and school community?" The goal of these focus groups is to collect qualitative data for school improvement initiatives as well as share responses with staff to improve culturally relevant lessons and representation.

## MBLT Practice 5: Wraparound Student Care

Pocomoke High School's extended day program, called After School Academies (ASA), provides more and better learning time through student interest-based enrichment and acceleration opportunities. The ASA runs before and after school, on Saturdays year-round, and during the 5-week summer program. Opportunities include driver's education, community art projects, cooking and baking classes, engineering academy, teaching academies for future educators, and many academic enrichment and acceleration opportunities. Saturday academies offer additional times for students to receive valuable instruction if they feel that they need it. Examples include SAT prep and AP Camp in order to have extra time to prepare for these valuable assessments. ASA is student-interest driven, with activities drawn from student suggestions, and it is highly attended.

A small number of students at Pocomoke High School each year have babies of their own, and these parents meet monthly with an adviser for extra support. Grace Community Center hosts monthly meetings with the young mothers at the school to provide community outreach. Principal Jenifer Rayne is working to create an on-site child care center open to students and staff, where students interested in child care professions can also observe and interact with the babies in a highly supervised environment. School leaders and staff are eager to provide wraparound supports for students, especially when the supports are also learning opportunities for students. As the principal and faculty walk in the hallways, students frequently stop to ask them for hugs or for help with a problem—an important sign that students know the school's educators care deeply about them.

Community-based health care has recently been established on site, including mental health care providers available at the school 4 days per week. Free dental and vision checks are provided in November, as part of the rural health model. Telehealth medical services are being offered in partnership with Atlantic General Hospital to participating students and families. Students with allergies, common colds, or respiratory infections can be diagnosed and treated by a medical provider without having to leave the school building.

The school provides universal free breakfast, and there is a *Second Chance* breakfast kiosk open after first period for those students who missed the breakfast period before school. *Grab a Salad and Go* kiosks are installed at each end of the school, helping students get quick access to healthy food options. These grab-and-go options were initiated to complement Your60, making it quicker and easier for students to eat and still participate fully in Your60 activities; students are not prohibited from eating in workshops or classes. Another student-run, on-site venture is a thrift store that provides clothing to students, free of cost. Teachers and staff are invited to purchase clothing items for a nominal fee. Students working in these on-site ventures can earn life skills credit from Wor-Wic Community College, service learning hours, and valuable business skills.

Another interesting Pocomoke High School project is Poco Percolator, a student-run coffee shop with a kiosk in the school hallway, initiated in 2017 by teachers in the Special Education department. A block away from the school, a commercial coffee shop called Beanery and Bites offers barista internships to Pocomoke High School students.

Several of the students who run the Poco Percolator are non-diploma-seeking students; they are in a certificate track rather than the diploma track due to intellectual disabilities. These are among of subgroup of students with special needs who are supported in attending high school until age 21, and they work on developing their life skills. Educators, staff, and students all take deliberate steps to maintain a welcoming and high-support environment for these members of the school community. One year recently, a group of the school's students ran a successful campaign to elect as Prom King and Prom Queen two students who had intellectual disabilities.

As noted at the outset of this chapter, MBLT includes enrichment of core curricular activities. Below, therefore, we discuss seven additional innovations that Pocomoke High School integrates with its other MBLT approaches.

### Innovation 1: Focus on Student Goals

By itself, setting ambitious goals can be an empty practice, but such goal-setting is a key part of systematic and supported improvement. With the creation of *Project 100*[1] in 2016, all Pocomoke High School students are encouraged to pay close attention to their postgraduation plans and goals from the outset, keeping students mindful from the very beginnings of their high school experience of what they have accomplished and what they have yet to do, since goal-setting and mindfulness are critical for student success (Newman, 2012). The goal of Project 100 is for 100% of seniors to graduate with a commitment or a plan to continue their postsecondary education through college, trade school, apprenticeship, or the military. For those students who do fall behind on their graduation schedule, the school offers an online credit recovery program with teachers who serve as facilitator, motivator and "life coach" in these cases. Project 100 supports families with no college experience to understand postsecondary options for their children. Students often return to visit their Pocomoke High School mentors long after graduation, continuing to seek and receive help and guidance.

As a part of Project 100, *Intent Night* builds student participation and anticipation of their future goals. On Intent Night, under their graduation gown, students wear a T-shirt, or display a prop such as a school pennant, to represent their postgraduation plans, showing whether they plan to attend a college or trade school, go into the military, and so forth. At the end of their graduation walk, they sign the Intent Book. Beginning in 2018, each graduating senior also has been asked to invite one significant adult, their *One*, the adult they feel has supported them most in their development through school, to attend the Intent Night. A student's One is often a parent or other close family member, but it may also be a teacher, a custodian, a cafeteria worker, or other adult from any point in the student's school career. Project 100 and Intent Night are both useful in highlighting student success and showcasing older students as role models for younger students. These highly meaningful events give all students a sense of the range of possibilities they can strive toward and the value of having a solid plan. The initial Project 100 focus on student goals has further developed over the last few years into the building of a whole community of support for each student's postsecondary plan.

### Innovation 2: Connectedness Through Find Your One/Be the One

Individual connections and one-on-one adult/student mentoring are crucial to keeping students fully engaged in their academic growth and goals. In 2018, Pocomoke staff put into action a core value: that all students deserve a relationship with at least one caring adult in the school community they can go to with concerns or to celebrate accomplishments, large and small, and who can help the students navigate their lives in and outside of school. Youth are better able to develop resilience if they have at least one stable and committed relationship with a supportive parent, caregiver, teacher, school staff member, or other adult (Masten, 2018; National Scientific Council on the Developing Child, 2015). Pocomoke's unofficial motto for students is *Find Your One*, which encourages students to reach out to an adult in the school community; "Find Your One" posters can be found throughout the school. The parallel motto for Pocomoke High School adults is "Be the One." In this way, the school culture openly embraces and promotes the importance of connection.

To confirm student/adult connections, a photo of every student in the school is posted in the staff workroom, along with a set of stickers. Faculty and staff are asked to place a sticker "dot" under the photo of students they are confident they have connected with. Any student lacking a sticker by the end of September is then tagged for outreach, so that by the time of the big October "Be the One" event, every student is connected to at least one adult. The check-in board is updated monthly thereafter to ensure that no students slip through the cracks. Teachers also send postcards to every student at the beginning of the year and at holidays, just to say hello and to reach out. Then, as noted above, students honor their Ones at the end of their senior year during Intent Night, which celebrates each graduate's intent to fulfill their postsecondary plans. Principal Rayne facilitates the culminating You're the One event, where each One stands beside their student while the students sign their intent forms. Each year students invite their Ones, who can be any staff member from pre-kindergarten to 12th grade, by proposing to them in a fashion similar to a Promposal (an elaborate way to ask someone to go to prom). The creative and fun ways that students carry out their Intent Night Proposal is a cherished experience for both educators and students.

## Innovation 3: The "Four Tribes, One School" Model

Inspired by Ron Clark Academy's "House System" (https://rcahousesystem.com/), students belong to one of the four houses, or tribes, with each tribe bearing a Latin name representing Courage, Perseverance, Integrity, or Achievement. (For some at the school, this also calls to mind the house system in the Harry Potter stories.) Though not the focus of this chapter, it is important to note that school administration has engaged with students in critical discussion on the use of the word "tribe," what it means in the context and history of Pocomoke, and the multiple meanings the term may hold in Native and non-Native communities.

Bearing in mind that this is a small school, each house has fewer than 100 students, spanning the four grade levels. The students appreciate being able to connect with others with whom they would not normally connect through multi-age mentoring and support. Students can win merit points throughout the day to be used for monthly Tribe Incentives. This model creates yet another dimension of belonging. That is, students feel that they belong (a) to the school community individually (greeted every morning by name as they enter the school and connected through Find Your One), (b) in each class they attend (free to lounge, to move, and to interact with classmates), (c) in the hallways (as they inhabit the whole school and freely interact with peers, faculty, custodians, and staff), and (d) in one of the Four Tribes of their peers, guided by faculty. This sense of belonging is crucial to student success (Lee, 2014).

Many faculty use their Tribe identity as their Facebook profiles, and on rally days, students and teachers wear their Tribe t-shirts. In focus-group discussions conducted with students by Kellie Rolstad, students spoke warmly of their Tribe identities and of the fun of competing against the other houses. The whole school, students, teachers, and staff also participate in pickleball tournaments, in ROTC-sponsored push-up tournaments, and other community-building competitions and events. This initiative, like all others, was planned and facilitated by teams of students and staff. Student and teacher collaboration promotes empathy, understanding, and, most important, provides opportunities for all voices to be heard.

All students are encouraged to take advanced placement (AP) and dual enrollment (DE) classes. Students are supported in advanced classes with AP Pathways, a program aimed at students of promise who may not have achieved top grades, and it especially focuses on the school's African American students, who have historically been underrepresented in those classes. This scheduling pathway is available to all students and is essentially a way for students to take as little or as many DE or AP courses as they choose before graduation. Students who participate in AP Pathways can receive additional support in study skills, take part in time management and small-group scheduling sessions, and participate in a trip abroad as well as making field trips to colleges and universities. Built-in supports through the college application process are available not only through the school counseling office, but through AP classes themselves. The school hosts a special ceremony, the Tribe Induction of Freshmen, welcoming freshmen into their Tribes and honoring student successes. As part of this ceremony, students who are involved with AP Pathways wear lab coats to the Induction of Freshmen ceremony to indicate that they have chosen to take college-level courses.

### Innovation 4: Respect for Students

A deep, authentic respect for students and their freedom of movement and freedom of choice allows students to engage in meaningful ways with their own thoughts and ideas, an important element of successful high school programs (Mertz et al., 2015; Okonofua et al., 2016). At Pocomoke High School, student perspectives and values are fundamental to the running of the school. In 2018, a student voice group called Speak Up was formed as a community celebrating cultural diversity and distinctive differences that seeks to understand the unique perspectives of others through critical conversations that provide acceptance and unity. Membership is open to all students, and they meet every other Friday afternoon. The students discuss ways to cultivate cultural competence and reduce bias, and they have frank conversations with the school's administrators about how to ensure that all students are represented and have their perspectives included. Speak Up topics may be raised by students, or by administrators or teachers, especially when topics arise or events occur at the school for which student views are particularly valuable. The student group may then elect to recruit additional students they think should be included in the discussions.

Another indicator of the school's deep respect for students and their perspectives is the Principal's Advisory Group, made up of students from across the grade levels. This began in 2018, to elevate student voice and improve students' experience. A small group of randomly selected students from each grade is invited to eat pizza with the principal each month to discuss how they think things are going and how the school might improve from the students' perspective. These teams of students, along with teacher leaders, have become the driving force for classroom settings that evolve to meet students' current needs. Creativity, risk-taking, and nontraditional strategies are encouraged to enhance engagement and collaboration.

The deep respect for students that has been cultivated at Pocomoke High School can also easily be seen in the consistent effort to make classrooms comfortable and fun. Throughout the school, classrooms reflect a more collaborative and collegial feeling than traditional classrooms, where students sit separately, facing front, listening passively as the teacher lectures to the whole group. While some schools may allow certain students—for example, those in gifted programs—to have special classrooms that permit greater interaction, all of the classrooms at Pocomoke are set up to encourage extensive student interactions and collaborations. In science classrooms, students lounge on couches, working intently together, all the while discussing scientific concepts and working through problems. The desks in English and math classrooms are grouped in circles, promoting discussion, with student project and activity choices and student research as constant themes. The level of student engagement is extremely high across the board throughout the school, with students engaging in multiple, overlapping projects during and outside of class time. Professional development workshops help faculty incorporate the development of 21st-century learning skills into their lessons and their informal interactions with students; these skills include ". . . critical thinking, problem solving, collaboration, effective communication, motivation, persistence, and learning to learn. 21st century skills also include creativity, innovation, and ethics that are important to later success . . ." (National Research Council, 2012). Project-based learning and 21st century skills have become an integral part of the pedagogy adopted by teachers at Pocomoke High School.

## Innovation 5: Teacher and Staff Empowerment

Teacher visits to other classrooms are now part of the school's weekly routines, and they allow teachers to learn and grow from observing one another's teaching. This initiative was the vision of teacher leaders in 2017. Teachers take time every Tuesday to visit one another's classrooms for 5–10 minutes during instruction, and they can provide feedback and recommend that others come to observe particular instructional strategies that another teacher is using particularly well. (See Hendry et al. [2013] for research supporting such practices.) Outside each classroom is a "Pineapple Pop-In" poster board where students and teachers can jot down specific praise for something they see a teacher do, all of which is included in instructional assessment. This has led to a strong culture of teacher collaboration, where teachers feel comfortable and welcome in one another's classrooms, and which students benefit from seeing as well.

In addition to empowering teachers, however, the school succeeds in showcasing the contributions of the staff, including the custodial staff. All adults at the school are clearly respected by all, and all adults take on the responsibility of meeting, talking with, and mentoring students. This deep respect for all is highlighted whenever students ask a custodian or cafeteria worker to stand with them on Intent Night as their One. Faculty and staff are all empowered by this culture of deep respect for the contributions of every member of the school community.

## Innovation 6: Assessment and Universal Design for Learning

Formative Assessment for Maryland Educators (FAME) is a Maryland State Department of Education program that encourages schools to implement a yearlong collaborative professional development process that guides educators in improving assessment. The school embraces FAME as well as Universal Design for Learning (UDL). The school draws a distinction between UDL, which approaches instructional planning to ensure challenge and engagement for all students, and versus differentiated instruction, which calls upon teachers to adjust existing lessons to ensure the same challenge and engagement. The school also believes that UDL allows for more flexibility and builds in individual student voices and feedback in how students access content, represent their learning, and are assessed. All staff received professional development in FAME during the 2018 school year.

## Innovation 7: Community Celebration

Finally, as part of the Pocomoke High School administrators' efforts to communicate effectively with a variety of organizations to bring them together for collaborations, they instituted an important community festival that has become the highlight of the year, attended by the entire community. The festival is called the Pocomoke Back to School Block Party, and it includes not only the student, teacher, and parent populations of Pocomoke High School and the middle school and elementary schools, but also the Police Department, the Fire Department, the Health Department, and all the area churches. The Block Party is held at the middle school, the community's most central location, and features a DJ, a dunk tank, and other fun, interactive events. The Block Party highlights and celebrates the team efforts so clearly emphasized as the foundation of Pocomoke High School's community for student supports and success.

## DISCUSSION

Located in what might commonly be dismissed as a high-poverty and high-crime area, Pocomoke High School has created a caring community of students, parents, educators, support agencies, and local businesses that all work together to focus on supporting students in multiple ways. Its added initiatives work to ensure that all students feel they are connected to the school community, feel a sense of belonging, and are a part of a shared vision. Students, teachers, staff, and administrators can regularly be observed interacting and working together to support students and one another, offering encouragement in the halls, in the office, and in the classrooms. Despite high rates of student homelessness, and with many students living in homes without running water or electricity, the students and staff at Pocomoke High School have banded together as an inclusive, welcoming community where students engage in more and better learning time than is typically provided through core curriculum alone.

This school and its families face common challenges of racism and discrimination in the wider community. Historically, this area has been deeply racist, with White supremacist efforts to suppress Black votes and to maintain segregation in housing, finance, law, and education. Foundational challenges at the school have also included a lack of communication among the various stakeholders, as well as between the school and a host of community organizations that could potentially have been beneficial to students' well-being. These groups are now effectively woven into the fabric of the school and the experiences of its students, as well as into the entire community.

More than anything else, what is striking about Pocomoke High School is how well its educators know and understand their local context, their students and families, and their responsibilities and their abilities to help these students to succeed and to dream big. By knowing and understanding all this, and by paying close attention to the wider world of education research and practice, they have succeeded in creating and adapting the structures and elements to build a caring, inclusive community within a marginalized area. Pocomoke High School is a powerful and positive place for students to learn and grow. One veteran teacher, who chose to move to Pocomoke High School to teach after having taught for years at wealthier schools, told Kellie Rolstad, "This school is doing more to build character and relationships with kids than any other school I have seen." The teacher went on to say that the school's priority is on students doing research, rather than on testing, and that the school "is constantly trying to think outside the box." Students in focus groups asserted emphatically that they and other students are respected and listened to at this school. One student said, with great enthusiasm, "If you have an idea that might help the school, everyone wants to hear it." That idea might concern classroom curriculum, or it might be about starting a podcast. The students clearly feel empowered and excited to have their voices heard and their ideas taken seriously. Censorship of student topics and student voice by the school is avoided so that students feel trusted to be responsible and sensitive to their community.

While many schools seek to separate students by perceived abilities, Pocomoke High School instead seeks to engage all students in collaborations that excite and motivate further learning, recognizing that all students have strengths that can be tapped in collaborative, mutually beneficial learning activities and projects. Tracking is not practiced at this school, supported by research that has shown that tracking is detrimental to student success, and that it often aligns with racist and classist ideologies and outcomes (Kalogrides & Loeb, 2013; Oakes, 2008). Administrators and teachers often discuss the distinction between equality and equity; in the history of this place where the "separate but equal" doctrine was only officially rejected in 1970, it remains critical to ensure that the schoolwide goal is equity. The prevalent racialized poverty harming students outside of school guarantees that merely equal in-school opportunities fall short of ensuring overall equitable access to opportunities. The faculty regularly attend professional development workshops dedicated to strategies to boost student engagement and a sense of belonging, especially among the students who face the greatest challenges (based on factors such as poverty, having to work after school, gang activity in their neighborhoods, low levels of formal education among family members, and racism in the community).

While more traditional schools tend to prioritize obedience and quiet order, particularly for minoritized and other marginalized students, Pocomoke's students are pleasantly rambunctious and outspoken, appearing happily engaged at the same time, which suggests that quiet, obedient students are not more highly valued or supported than more boisterous students. Students freely describe their earlier life and school struggles, and how Pocomoke High School's approach turned them around. More senior students describe how they had started as freshmen with fairly low prospects and low interest in academic success but had become passionate about their education because of the many innovations at the high school and their feelings of being respected and supported by teachers and administrators.

Students from across a spectrum of ages and diversity assert that race, class, gender, and sexual orientation pose no particular challenges when they are safely at their school and that all students feel welcomed and supported. The students openly discuss the content of their classes, statements from teachers, and the plethora of special clubs and Your60 offerings—some proposed by students themselves—that have increased students' confidence that all are encouraged and supported in reaching for their dreams. Their beliefs in the equity in their school is especially significant because of the history of this part of Maryland, which lies in the path of the Underground Railroad and Harriet Tubman's successful journeys leading enslaved people to freedom in the North. Racism remains a grueling reality of life on the Eastern Shore, but the Pocomoke High School community is working hard to create an antiracist, engaging, and welcoming community.

## NOTE

1. Former principal Annette Wallace created Project 100. Wallace was named the Maryland High School Principal of the Year in 2016. In 2018, she left to become the chief operating officer of the Worcester school system. Jenifer Rayne was selected to serve as the new principal of Pocomoke High School. Rayne has continued to develop Project 100 and has contributed several additional innovations.

## REFERENCES

Bowie, L. (2016, February 13). Teaching of gifted children changes course in Baltimore County. *Baltimore Sun.* https://www.baltimoresun.com/bs-md-gifted -schools-20160129-story.html

Davis, J. (2018, September 6). Legislative study: Worcester taxes low, crime rates high. *Bayside Gazette.* https://baysideoc.com/legislative-study-worcester-taxes-low -crime-rates-high

Ellspermann, J. (2014). Power hour! *Principal Leadership, 14*(6), pp. 26–28.

Ford, D. Y. (2013). *Recruiting and retaining culturally different students in gifted education.* Prufrock Press.

Furfaro, H., & Bazzaz, D. (2019, October 22). What's next for Seattle schools' gifted programs? *Seattle Times.* https://www.seattletimes.com/education-lab/faq -whats-next-for-seattle-schools-gifted-programs/

Hendry, G. D., Bell, A., & Thomson, K. (2013). Learning by observing a peer's teaching situation. *International Journal for Academic Development, 19*(4), 318–329.

Kalogrides, D., & Loeb, S. (2013). Different teachers, different peers: The magnitude of student sorting within schools. *Educational Researcher, 42*(6), 304–316.

Kozol, J., Tatum, B. D., Eaton, S., & Gandara, P. (2010). Resegregation: What's the answer? *Educational Leadership, 68*(3), 28–31.

Learning Policy Institute. (2018). *Teachers of color: In high demand and short supply.* https://learningpolicyinstitute.org/press-release/teachers-color-high-demand -and-short-supply

Lee, J-S. (2014). The relationship between student engagement and academic performance: Is it a myth or reality? *Journal of Educational Research, 107*(3), 177–185.

Maier, A., Daniel, J., & Oakes, J. (2017). *Community schools as an effective school improvement strategy: A review of the evidence.* Learning Policy Institute. https://learningpolicyinstitute.org/product/community-schools-effective-school -improvement-brief

Maryland Manual On-line. (2020). *A guide to Maryland and its government.* https:// msa.maryland.gov/msa/mdmanual/01glance/economy/html/unemployrates .html

Masten, A. S. (2018). Resilience theory and research on children and families: Past, present, and promise. *Journal of Family Theory and Review, 10*(1), 12–31.

Mertz, C., Eckloff, T., Johannsen, J., & Van Quaquebeke, N. (2015). Respected students equal better students: Investigating the links between respect and performance in schools. *Journal of Educational and Developmental Psychology, 5*(1), 74–87.

National Center for Education Statistics. (2020). *CCD, Common core of data.* https://nces.ed.gov/ccd/schoolsearch/school_detail.asp?Search=1&DistrictID =2400720&ID=240072001330

National Research Council. (2012). *Education for life and work: Developing transferable knowledge and skills in the 21st century.* The National Academies Press.

National Scientific Council on the Developing Child. (2015). *Supportive relationships and active skill-building strengthen the foundations of resilience* (Working Paper No. 13). www.developingchild.harvard.edu

Newman, R. (2012). Goal setting to achieve results. *Leadership, 41*(3). 12–16, 38.

Oakes, J. (2008). Keeping track: Structuring equality and inequality in an era of accountability. *Teachers College Record, 110,* 700–712.

Okonofua, J. A., Paunesku, D., & Walton, G. M. (2016). Brief intervention to encourage empathic discipline cuts suspension rates in half among adolescents. *Proceedings of the National Academy of the Sciences (PNAS), 113*(19), 5221–5226. https://doi.org/10.1073/pnas.1523698113

Richards, E. (2020, January 13). "New York is in an uproar over plans to ax gifted education. This school is doing it anyway." *USA Today.* https://www.usatoday .com/story/news/education/2020/01/13/nyc-doe-racist-segregation-brooklyn -specialized-high-school-exam-gifted/2763549001/

U.S. Government Accountability Office. (2016). *K-12 education: Better use of information could help agencies identify disparities and address racial discrimination.* https://www.gao.gov/products/GAO-16-345

# CHAPTER 4

# Authentic Assessment Embedded in Project-Based Learning

*Jeffrey Palladino and Lorrie A. Shepard*

Criterion 4: Use a Variety of Assessments Designed to Respond to Student Needs

This chapter is about "assessments designed to respond to student needs." In an educational environment dominated by test-based accountability, developing healthy and supportive assessment practices may be more difficult than enacting any other of the Schools of Opportunity principles. This is especially true for schools in high-poverty neighborhoods, where pressure to raise test scores can distort learning goals, limit opportunities, and pre-judge students as less-than-capable learners. The story of Fannie Lou Hamer Freedom High School (FLHFHS) is a rare exception to this rule.

Fannie Lou Hamer Freedom High School is located in the West Farms section of the Bronx, New York, in the heart of the poorest congressional district in the United States. Ninety-one percent of its students are identified in the Highest Economic Need category, 8% higher than the rest of the Bronx and 20% higher than the rest of New York City. Thirty-two percent of Fannie Lou Hamer students are classified as students with disabilities, and 13% are classified as English language learners. Sixty-three percent of 9th-graders coming to Fannie Lou Hamer scored in the lowest quadrant on the district's 8th-grade math exam, and 37% scored in the lowest quadrant on the 8th-grade English Language Arts exam. After joining the FLHFHS community, however, the comparisons become strikingly positive. Ninety percent of Fannie Lou Hamer students say that their school "offers a wide enough variety of programs, classes, and activities to keep them interested in school," compared to a 77% endorsement of their schools by students citywide. Importantly, 74% of Fannie Lou Hamer students graduate in 4 years, based on 2019 data, competitive with the citywide 4-year graduation rate of 77%—and much better than comparison schools with similar demographics. In New York City, 9th-graders choose their high schools by rank-ordering their preferences. FLHFHS's students, however, are over-whelmingly drawn from the nearby Bronx neighborhood.

Fannie Lou Hamer Freedom High School does not focus on testing. Instead, it focuses on teaching students to use their minds well and on pre-paring them to live productive, socially useful, and personally satisfying lives. Dedicated teachers are recruited who share the belief that students learn best by investigating authentic issues in ways that require collabora-tion, personal responsibility, care for others, and a tolerance for uncertainty. These crucial "habits of mind and work" are nurtured in classrooms where students are engaged in projects they design and carry out themselves and by work that students undertake outside of traditional classrooms through real-world learning. To these ends, the school coherently integrates their instructional approaches with a variety of assessments designed to support student learning.

This inquiry-oriented, deep-learning curriculum is closely integrated with a performance-based, portfolio assessment system that supports stu-dent learning on an ongoing basis. After improving individual work products based on faculty feedback, students collect their written papers and projects in portfolios demonstrating mastery, which they then defend in oral presen-tations. The pivotal reason why FLHFHS can use a learning-focused ap-proach to student assessment is the school's long-standing membership in the New York Performance Standards Consortium. Pursuant to a waiver granted by the state's Board of Regents and its Education Department, stu-dents in Consortium schools are exempt from all but the English Language Arts Regents exam and instead demonstrate graduation requirements through performance-based assessments. Further, and as described in more detail later in this chapter, students in the Consortium schools complete

---

**CRITERION 4: USE A VARIETY OF ASSESSMENTS DESIGNED TO RESPOND TO STUDENT NEEDS**

The (exemplary) school has established sound practices for using test-ing and other assessments to inform instruction in a healthy, student-centered way. Teachers are actively engaged in the analysis of students' assessment results to understand students' needs, revise curriculum, and improve instruction. Assessment is varied, and teachers rely on multiple forms of assessment to analyze student learning. The school provides time and resources to support this analysis. Students receive prompt, informa-tive feedback. The school has implemented a teacher evaluation system that promotes collegiality and minimizes the impact of accountability test scores.

graduation-level written tasks, known as PBATs (performance-based assessment tasks), including an analytic essay on literature, a history research paper, an extended or original science experiment, and problem-solving at higher levels of mathematics in order to meet New York State graduation requirements.

To tell more of the story about performance-based assessment at FLHFHS, this chapter is organized in three main sections: History and Legacy, Curriculum and Assessment, and Supports and Collaborations. Explaining the school's beginnings is critical to understanding the vision and commitments necessary for ensuring that students in underfunded and underserved neighborhoods have access to challenging and meaningful curriculum. Although Fannie Lou Hamer has the benefit of progressive, alternative school efforts begun over 40 years ago, those ideas and the power of those early organizing efforts are still relevant today. In the Curriculum and Assessment section, we describe the present-day, project-based curriculum with emphasis on both the instructional and learning purposes served by PBATs and culminating assignments. In addition, we explain how this system works requires an understanding of the philosophy and commitments of the school beyond the mere structures and processes in place. In making this case, we refer to several additional Schools of Opportunity principles—especially "broadening and enriching learning opportunities" and "maintaining a healthy school culture"—emphasizing how these commitments all work together. In the third section, we identify supports and collaborations outside the school, thus going further in answering the question, what makes Fannie Lou Hamer Freedom High School possible?

## HISTORY AND LEGACY

### Who Was Fannie Lou Hamer?

Fannie Lou Hamer was a courageous civil rights leader who fought for African American voting rights in Mississippi in the early 1960s. She was brutally beaten after being arrested when she and other civil rights activists sat at a Whites-only lunch counter, sustaining permanent damage to her eyes and kidneys. Undeterred, she cofounded the Mississippi Freedom Democratic Party (MFDP) and gained national attention in 1964 when she spoke to the Democratic National Convention Credentials Committee demanding that state delegations be integrated. Fannie Lou Hamer had a resonant voice, which she used in uplifting hymns and fiery speeches. She had a knack for incisive quotations still remembered today. Most famously she declared, "I'm sick and tired of being sick and tired." The relevance of her struggles for students today is exemplified by the banner that repeats on the Fannie

Lou Hamer Freedom High School website: "Nobody's free until everybody's free."

In 2017, the year marking Fannie Lou Hamer's 100th birthday, FLHFHS students made her life and the history of the school the focus of their project-based learning efforts. In a letter requested by one of the students, the first director, Peter Steinberg, explained that he named the school after his hero, Fannie Lou Hamer, because daily social, political, and economic oppression faced by the school's students and families was "strikingly similar to that which Mississippi blacks faced in the 1960s." Steinberg added, "If [students] could understand her strength in the fight for a better society, they could understand their potential power to reshape their society."

Steinberg chose the second part of the school's name, "Freedom," in honor of the 1964 Freedom Summer in Mississippi, when Black young people came together for the first time to learn about Black history, the reality of oppression, and the value of basic academic skills. The philosophy of these schools "was that people should become agents in their own liberation," according to Steinberg. "'Freedom school teachers were trained to ask students questions and challenge them to find their own solutions.' That philosophy was strikingly similar to the principles of the Coalition of Essential Schools, the basis for our new schools."

## Central Park East and the Coalition of Essential Schools

The vision of two schools—Central Park East Elementary School and later Central Park East Secondary School (CPESS)—and what they accomplished for East Harlem students is foundational to the history of Fannie Lou Hamer because a number of the founding teachers and leaders of FLHFHS came from CPESS. As described by founding teacher and Fannie Lou Hamer's long-time principal, Nancy Mann, they brought with them the progressive vision of democratic schooling and lessons learned from Central Park East's leader, Deborah Meier:

> [Deb taught us] that each child had a right to be intellectually challenged and was capable of engaging in all the controversies of history, literature, science and the mysteries of math. And Deb taught us that schools cannot be places of intellectual challenge for students if they are not intellectually challenging for teachers. And that nothing is more challenging—or more important—than teachers coming together in a school to use their collective knowledge, wisdom, ingenuity and relentlessness to solve the problems of education in THIS school, in THIS classroom. Debbie understood the democratic meaning of schools and helped us explore democratic governance in schools. (Mann, 2005, p. 3)

For those interested in how such schools are built from the beginning, we have the benefit of Deborah Meier's own account (1987) plus two detailed case studies of Central Park East Secondary School: one by Darling-Hammond et al. (1995) and the other by Duckor and Perlstein (2014). Central Park East Elementary School was made possible in the mid-1970s by the space created for a network of New York City *alternative* schools. At a time when "open" and progressive education was being rejected in favor of standardization policies, Meier and her colleagues were allowed to start on a very small scale to build a school culture based on respect for students, care, trusting relationships with families, and a curriculum designed to ensure full citizenship. The requests to attend Central Park East were so great that by 1984 the program had expanded to three elementary schools, and the decision was made to create CPE Secondary School.

The obstacles to creating a progressive secondary school were myriad, including beliefs about alternative schools being only for "difficult" kids, district course requirements, and Regents exams (Meier, 1987). As part of an alternative school special project, CPESS enjoyed a waiver from New York's Regents Diploma requirements, and Ted Sizer's Coalition of Essential Schools was an important resource in developing and sustaining CPESS because of its national visibility and shared ideals. As reported by Darling-Hammond et al. (1995, p. 25), CPESS modified four of the 10 Coalition of Essential Principles as follows and used them to guide its integrated approach to authentic teaching, learning, and assessment.

1. *Less is more.* It is more important to understand some things well than to know many things superficially. Schools must focus on the essential skills, areas of knowledge, and habits of mind that are central to students becoming well-educated members of society.
2. *Student as worker.* Learning is not an observer sport. Students must be active participants and active citizens, discovering answers and solutions, and learning by doing rather than simply repeating what texts or teachers say.
3. *Goal-setting and assessment.* High standards are set for all students. Students should be evaluated on the basis of their performance, not hours spent or credits earned. Performance assessment should be as direct and authentic as possible. Graduation should be based on demonstrated mastery over clearly stated competencies related to the school's goals.
4. *Personalization.* Schools should be personalized to the greatest extent possible. Learning units should be organized so that students and adults remain together in small communities over several years so that they can get to know each other well.

Focusing on intellectual challenge, authenticity, and relationships forced CPESS creators to conceive a very different kind of assessment system. They developed an alternative portfolio-based graduation system very much like the assessment system still succeeding at FLHFHS today. As noted by Duckor and Perlstein (2014, p. 3), "Learning by doing became synonymous with assessing by doing." The commitment to developing students' habits of mind meant that assignments and projects needed to engage students—on an ongoing basis—in five habits: examining evidence critically, looking at multiple viewpoints, making connections, seeking alternatives, and looking for meaning. Duckor and Perlstein (2014) titled their article "Assessing Habits of Mind: Teaching to the Test at Central Park East Secondary School," and they used the idea of "teaching to the test" somewhat ironically to call attention—in contrast to goals implied by multiple-choice tests—to the new, authentic ways that these ultimate goals for learning drove expectations for how students would develop their body of evidence as well as the skills needed to explain and defend their portfolio entries. What was expected for seniors to graduate from CPESS was backward-translated into project work and critical inquiry for all of the grades. For example, the 7th- and 8th-grade U.S. history course was organized around the study of power rather than a chronological recounting of events. This preparatory work, in turn, meant that feedback on early efforts could be used formatively to revise and improve students' understandings as well as the quality of their final products over time.

## First Steps at Fannie Lou Hamer Freedom High School

In the section after this one, we describe the present-day workings of the performance-based, portfolio assessment system at Fannie Lou Hamer, which carries forward the spirit and basic structures of what began at CPESS. It would be a mistake, however, to think that a system based on shared expectations and trusting relationships could be transplanted whole to a new school. Even with seasoned and dedicated faculty, the first years at FLHFHS were quite challenging. As described years later by Nancy Mann (2005, p. 6), "None of us had understood what persistent school failure had meant to the 60 young people who were the first entering class at FLH." Creating a portfolio system that had real meaning, instead of credits and exams, was only one small part of community-building efforts emphasizing work and person-to-person relationships, including mediation of conflicts in and out of school, and developing relationships with families.

Reflecting on hard-won success after 10 years at FLHFHS, midway through her 20 years as teacher and principal, Nancy Mann (2005) had this to say about portfolios:

> Portfolios are not panaceas. They are not a "pure" form. They embody the contradictions and dilemmas we see as educators, but they communicate to the teachers and the students one of the key foundations of our community. Work. Work that has meaning and work that is individual and work that you can see.

Collected into a portfolio and discussed with your teachers and family, work is tangible. You can see progress, you can see what someone liked, you can begin to formulate next steps. (p. 14)

## CURRICULUM AND ASSESSMENT

### Habits of Mind

The Habits of Mind framework is very visible at Fannie Lou Hamer, not only because of how specific assignments might be structured but also because of a broader commitment to treat students as intellectuals. Focusing on these critical thinking skills helps get students out of the mindset of "doing school" by just reading and then answering questions about the text. When students develop the ability to have opinions and thoughts about work, they develop ownership.

Figure 4.1, which is from an assignment in Humanities, illustrates the explicit use of Habits of Mind in the curriculum. These ways of thinking are part of everyday discourse, part of the ways that teachers and students talk about academic work and even service projects. Asking about evidence while inviting students to draw connections or consider possible alternatives is consistent with a curriculum focused on "going deep"—and in keeping with the long-standing Coalition of Essential Schools principle that "less is more."

### Project-Based Learning

This idea of going deep is evident in the organization of the curriculum and the commitment to project-based learning. Instead of covering the history of the world over a 2-year period, teachers take one topic and dive deeply into it for 6 weeks. This allows students to develop a clear, real understanding.

---

#### HABITS OF MIND

- **VIEWPOINT**: Identifying and understanding various perspectives on an issue.
- **EVIDENCE**: Being able to support a particular point of view and critically examine different forms of evidence.
- **CONNECTIONS**: Seeing larger patterns and connections between ideas, the individual, and the larger society.
- **CONJECTURE**: Being able to envision alternatives and ask, "what if?"
- **RELEVANCE**: Understanding the importance of an issue and asking, "What difference does it make?"

**Figure 4.1. Humanities PBAT 2020**

**Task:** Choose a question from the list below. Use at least 3 of the units from this year to write a response to your question.
1. Should violence ever be used to fight injustice?
2. Can freedom and safety live side by side? Which one is more important to protect?
3. Do laws and governments always protect us?
4. Can counter-narratives be used as a form of resistance?
5. What inequalities or oppressive systems have existed (in history) or currently exist (today)? What can we do to resist these unequal, unjust, and oppressive systems?

**Guidelines:**
- 2.5–4 pages
- Use Unit 6: Slides for Weeks 1–3. You can copy and paste your viewpoint, evidence, and connections directly from those slides.
- Use at least 3 of the units from this year to write a response to your question.
- Employ ALL Habits of Mind:
  » Viewpoint
  » Evidence
  » Connections
  » Conjecture
  » Relevance

**Units/Themes From This Year: A Block Exhibitions, B Block Exhibitions**

- Immigration
  » *Enrique's Journey* by Sonia Nazario
  » *Which Way Home* Documentary
  » Push/Pull Factors
  » Family Separation
  » Immigrant Rights
  » Counter-Narratives
    ○ *When They See Us*
- *Medea*
  » *Medea* by Euripides
  » Gender Roles
  » Revenge vs. Justice
  » Inequality
- Intent vs. Consequences
  » Death Penalty case study
  » *13th* Documentary

- Philosophy/Human Nature
  » Locke, Hobbes, Rousseau
    ○ State of nature, social contracts
  » Wollstonecraft, Mills, Pateman
  » Freedom vs. Safety
  » Kantianism/ Utilitarianism
  » Inequality
- Dystopian Fiction
  » Your Dystopian Book
  » Power, Government Control
  » Technology
  » Revenge, Justice, Injustice
  » Freedom vs. Safety

They immerse themselves in the content and wrestle with it. This enables them to find places where they can come up with their own connections to the work. When they connect in this fashion, they can talk about it in a way that has real meaning. For example, when responding to the Greek tragedy *Medea*, some students took up the topic of gender roles, others related the story to immigration issues, and still others tackled the issue of societal norms. It's a powerful learning strategy to let students wrestle with things based on how it connects to their lives.

Several of the internal structures at FLHFHS are important supports for project-based learning. In keeping with Coalition of Essential Schools principles, time and space are organized so teachers and students work in smaller groups for longer time periods. Block scheduling with longer class periods makes it possible to have time to sit down and undertake project work with students. Unlike traditional high school ratios of 150 students per day, Fannie Lou Hamer teachers are responsible for only 60 students and stay with the same group of students for 2 years. Content teachers are also advisers for a smaller group of students, which lets teachers build strong relationships with students and their families and helps them to know students' interests, their strengths, and their weaknesses. Students also loop in cross-generational classes. Because 9th- and 10th-graders take classes together, 10th-graders are able to shepherd 9th-graders' transition into the culture of FLHFHS. Ninth-graders come from traditional schools. As a result, they are surprised, for example, when they find themselves heading off to the Bronx River to take water samples for class. But 10th-graders assure them, "Oh, no, I didn't think I would do this either, but you will."

Studying the biology and chemistry of the Bronx River is perhaps the longest-standing real-world learning context for FLHFHS students. Teacher Maarten de Kadt (2006) wrote about the first class visit to the river, when they used a bucket to collect water samples to test. Later on, through community grant funding, students had access to more sensitive probes that could be sent deeper to detect the saltwater concentration below the clear water at the mouth of the estuary. An important aspect of de Kadt's (2006) account was the connection of the students' investigations to various local organizations:

> Sharing our test results with community groups also monitoring the Bronx River increased the kids' level of pride and self-confidence, as their work—authentic research valued by organizations outside of our school—was being made public in a way that was rare for a class. (p. 105)

In subsequent years, FLHFHS students wrote essays and participated with community advocacy groups to get the NYC Department of Parks to convert an abandoned concrete plant on the river into a park. Later, students participated in a Parks Department project to grow the plants that would be used to reclaim the riverbank and prevent erosion.

Because a strength of project-based learning comes through its meaningful connections to the world outside of school, the curriculum at FLHFHS necessarily entails many relationships with community organizations. These relationships are symbiotic. Community organizations in the Bronx exist to educate the community on impactful issues and policies, while students learn the importance of their actions in their community and develop ownership of their schoolwork and their own neighborhoods. In 2015, for example, a GE Skills Grant made it possible for 40 9th- and 10th-graders to participate for a full year in Rocking the Boat's on-water educational programs. Students worked on building nesting boxes as part of a tree swallow repopulation project and participated in a Wildlife Conservation Society project to monitor American eels. Fannie Lou Hamer students have also partnered with Sustainable South Bronx to research the impact of environmental racism in the Bronx on their community's air and water quality. By having access to AirCasting data documenting patterns of pollution, FLHFHS students come to understand the connections between air quality, industry, and community health.

Students have also developed their communication, organizational, and advocacy skills by leading community workshops under the sponsorship of the Bronx River Watershed Alliance and Youth Ministries for Peace and Justice. As mentioned previously, in 2017, students made Fannie Lou Hamer's life and the history of their school the focus of their research projects. As a school, they decided to undertake different challenges in preparation for a celebration of her 100th birthday. One group decided to ask New York City to rename the street outside of the school Fannie Lou Hamer Road. They did research, wrote letters, got petitions signed, went in front of the Parks Department and other local agencies, and eventually got the street named in honor of Fannie Lou Hamer. This kind of activism as the focus of project work is consistent with the axiom often attributed to Deborah Meier as her original vision: *You cannot prepare kids for democracy unless they experience living in a democracy.*

## Portfolios and Exhibitions

Alternative ways of assessing students' skills and content knowledge have always been a part of the school's mission at FLHFHS. Performance-based assessment tasks (PBATs) provide direct evidence of student learning as part of the inquiry-oriented, project-based curriculum. While these final products collected in a student's portfolio are evidence of each student's best work and mastery of required content, the portfolio *process* additionally provides for ongoing feedback and reflection to support learning and development. Thus, portfolios serve both formative and summative assessment purposes.

Formative assessment "refers to assessment carried out during the instructional process for the purpose of adapting instruction to improve learning" (Penuel & Shepard, 2016, p. 788). Summative assessments provide documentation of what students know and can do, generally at the conclusion of a specified period of learning. Ideally these two purposes for assessment are coherent with each other and are substantively aligned so that they work together to further and represent intended learning goals.

In the early days at FLHFHS, the founding teachers introduced the idea of a Language Portfolio for 9th- and 10th-grade students because they felt that students needed support in the first years of high school, to be better prepared to participate later in the portfolios leading to graduation. They decided to focus especially on language and literacy skills because so many entering 9th-grade students were significantly below grade level on state tests (Mann, 2005). Today there are seven required components of the school's "Division I Language Portfolio" (at FLHFHS, "Division I" roughly translates into 9th and 10th grades), including documentation of reading, of public speaking, and of real-world learning. It also includes a component on humanities, one on second language, and even one on math or science. Finally, there's a cover letter, serving as a personal reflection.

Work for this portfolio is based on exhibition projects completed in each course, reflecting the learning goals and essential questions for that class. Students work with teachers to revise their work and to submit projects in final form to their Digital Portfolio. The Division I portfolio, for 9th and 10th grades, is still called the Language Portfolio because reading and writing skills are so necessary to receive final, "red-tag" approval from the teacher to certify that a piece of work has been revised multiple times and reflects the needed improvements.

The portfolio and exhibition structure at Fannie Lou Hamer help to orchestrate a shared intellectual or academic culture among students and teachers. Nancy Mann (2005) referred to this as a "portfolio culture." Because students are expected to present their work publicly and document their progress, it helps "teachers and students have a dialogue over the question of what good work (is) and how you could revise—improve your work" (p. 13). This rationale is exactly like Royce Sadler's (1989) iconic article on formative assessment, where he put forward the idea that helping students to internalize the features of quality work is an essential element of effective feedback. Instead of a series of graded assignments where the teacher is always the arbiter of quality work, the ongoing dialogue and revision process helps students to develop the vocabulary and insights about features of quality work. Ultimately, this helps students "develop the capacity to monitor the quality of their own work during actual production" (Sadler, 1989, p. 119) and develop their own strategies for improvement.

Rubrics designed by teachers as part of the New York Performance Standards Consortium provide criteria and an organizing framework that support this process of formative feedback—deeply embedded in ongoing instruction—leading to demonstrations of mastery. As noted previously by Duckor and Perlstein (2014), this is a kind of teaching to the "test" that does not narrow the curriculum or distort valued learning outcomes, because the test is not narrow. It includes both the culminating project report and an oral defense of what was learned from that project. An important feature of Consortium rubrics is that they are structured around Habits of Mind and disciplinary practices rather than by discrete content strands. Thus, they are built specifically to help students develop appropriate modes of inquiry and critical thinking skills within each subject area. For example, the dimensions of the Mathematics Rubric are Problem Solving, Reasoning and Proof, Communication, Connections, and Representation. As illustrated by the Literary Analysis Rubric included in Figure 4.2, some of the dimensions are more general, such as Organization, Style and Voice, and Conventions, thus helping to develop writing and communication skills to be used across contexts. Other dimensions clearly require that students develop a deep understanding of the particular literary works and context they have selected for their project. As part of Analysis and Interpretation, for example, they must show their understanding of the text and the author's craft and must draw connections between "another work of literature or historical/cultural context, or film version of the text."

Keeping in mind that Consortium rubrics underpin all classes each semester, it becomes clear how these ways of thinking and "thinking about thinking" are an ingrained part of expectations for students. The portfolio process is structured explicitly to support student agency and metacognitive awareness. As noted, the Language Portfolio for 9th- and 10th-graders includes a Cover Letter and Personal Reflection. For every exhibition, students are asked, "What was it like to learn this material?" "What was hard, what was easy?" "How did this end up looking the way it does?" Later, for the Graduation Portfolio, student reflections are expected to consider both intellectual and very personal aspects of their own learning. For example, in science, students are asked to reflect on the connections between science and society and at the same time to look inward and answer the question, "Has your study of science changed the way you look at the world? Why or why not?"

Completed portfolios then serve a summative purpose, when students must present and defend their work orally. In the spring of each student's 10th-grade year, the student's adviser works with the discipline teacher to organize a panel of teachers to serve as evaluators. The evaluating teachers are explicitly selected to be different from the student's regular teachers. These teachers evaluate each student's written portfolio and oral defense to determine whether the student has met the requirements for advancement to Division II, which roughly translates into grades 11 and 12. Evaluators consider each student's "understanding and use of the Habits of Mind,

**Figure 4.2. New York Performance Standards Consortium Assessment: Literary Analysis**

| Performance Indicators | Outstanding | Good | Competent | Needs Revision |
|---|---|---|---|---|
| Thesis | Has a clear, compelling argument that is debatable and coherent | Has a clear, coherent argument | Has an implied argument, though may lack focus at times | Has a central idea, but vague, unfocused, and undeveloped |
| Organization | Develops argument logically and persuasively<br><br>Uses relevant, convincing evidence and quotations that thoroughly support argument<br><br>Makes explicit and elegant transitions from one idea to next | Develops argument coherently<br><br>Uses relevant evidence and quotations that support central argument<br><br>Makes seamless transitions, flows easily from one idea to the next | Has mostly cohesive argument structure<br><br>Uses mostly relevant evidence and quotations to support central idea<br><br>Uses transitions but may lack smooth flow from one idea to the next | Unfocused organization<br><br>Little, irrelevant, or no evidence used<br><br>Little or no use of transitions |
| Analysis | Provides deep insight and creates meaningful interpretation of texts<br><br>Elaborates on central argument and meaning of supporting evidence; answers question, So what?<br><br>Considers author's language, craft, and/or choice of genre<br><br>Analysis drives discussion of literary elements when relevant | Creates meaningful interpretation of texts<br><br>Explores central argument and meaning of supporting evidence; answers question, So what?<br><br>Considers literary elements when relevant | Provides basic interpretation of texts<br><br>Develops central idea and explains choice of evidence and quotations | Summarizes or uses faulty analysis<br><br>Little or no interpretation of texts<br><br>Little or no use of evidence or quotations |
| Style and voice | Evidence of ambition, passion for subject, or deep curiosity | Evidence of a mind at work, grappling with ideas | Communicates ideas clearly<br><br>Shows some | Relies on conversational language |

(continued)

Figure 4.2. New York Performance Standards Consortium Assessment: Literary Analysis (*continued*)

| Performance Indicators | Outstanding | Good | Competent | Needs Revision |
|---|---|---|---|---|
| | Writer willing to take risks Displays intellectual engagement Creative, clear, and appropriate use of language and word choice | Clear and appropriate use of language and word choice | awareness of appropriate language and word choice | Little or no evidence of formal or appropriate use of language and word choice |
| Connections | Makes insightful connection between text and something outside the text: Another work of literature or Historical or cultural context or Biographical context or Film version of text, or Substantial criticism | Makes appropriate connection between text and something outside the text: Another work of literature or Historical or cultural context or Biographical context or Film version of text, or Substantial criticism | Establishes a connection between text and something outside the text: Another work of literature or Historical or cultural context or Biographical context or Film version of text, or Substantial criticism | Inappropriate or no connection made between the text and something outside the text |
| Conventions (for writing assignment only) | Mechanical and grammatical errors are rare or nonexistent; follows accepted conventions of quotations and citations; uses transitions effectively | Few mechanical or grammatical errors; follows accepted conventions of quotations and citations; makes some use of transitions | Some mechanical or grammatical errors but communication is not impaired; demonstrates knowledge of accepted conventions of quotations | Communication is impaired by errors; little or no use of conventions or quotation and citations; shows little awareness of appropriate use of transitions |
| Presentation (for oral component only) | Communicates ideas clearly in appropriate, sophisticated, and original way to audience; able to respond to questions and expand on ideas; presents complex, accurate, substantive ideas and information clearly | Communicates clearly in appropriate and original way to audience; able to respond to questions and expand somewhat on ideas; presents accurate, substantive ideas and information clearly | Communicates clearly in appropriate way to audience; able to respond accurately to questions; presents some substantive ideas and information accurately | Neither clear nor appropriate presentation to audience; cannot respond well to questions; does not present accurate or substantive ideas or information |

understanding of the content area, and his/her capacity to use appropriate tools, above all the tools of effective research and communication, showing the student's ability to present information and ideas in variety of forms." Over time, this structure of having teachers from different advisories sit on student panels has contributed to the interconnectedness of the school community—building a shared culture of intellectual curiosity. Teachers who aren't your teacher are involved in your academic journey. Students come to understand three sayings at the school: *We are all in this together, No one is invisible,* and *No one is a passenger.*

For Division II, the portfolio process continues with the completion of PBATs as part of each class. In addition, for their Graduation Portfolio, students must complete mastery and reflection work in seven different content areas. These include Regents content areas of Science, Mathematics, Social Studies, and Literature. In addition, there are three FLHFHS-required topics: Social Issues plus two of three elective choices—Autobiography, Internship, or STEAM (Science, Technology, Engineering, Arts, and Math). These mastery projects do not attempt to cover all the material studied but instead should reflect an in-depth understanding of a particular issue within the context of the overall discipline and must reflect the student's internalization of Habits of Mind and Work. Although projects typically begin as part of classwork with support of the teacher, they also require a significant amount of independent work, with an eye toward college expectations and New York Performance Standards Consortium rubric criteria. All seven mastery exhibitions are evaluated at the end of each student's senior year to determine graduation. Specifically, to meet New York Regents requirements, students must defend or "panel" their work in the four core subject areas. These presentations are evaluated by other teachers in the school (someone who is not the student's regular teacher) and by external evaluators who might be teachers from other Consortium schools or adults from students' internship settings. Students' written work is evaluated based on Consortium rubrics for each discipline, and their oral defense is evaluated according to the Consortium's Oral Presentation Rubric. During junior and senior years, a good deal of thought and energy are focused on the portfolio process. In addition to relevant class time, students have time in Advisory to prepare and rehearse their portfolio defenses.

## Outcomes Data

Development and defense of portfolios at Fannie Lou Hamer is a rigorous process. To meet these requirements, New York City school performance data[1] document sustained support of students across their years at FLHFHS. Seventy-seven percent of 9th-graders and 77% of 10th-graders earn enough credits to be on track for graduation, compared to 71% and 61% respectively of 9th- and 10th-graders on track in comparison schools.[2] In 2019,

**Table 4.1. Percentage of Students Graduating "College Ready"**

| 8th-grade test score | Graduated college ready |
|---|---|
| Level 3 or 4 | 91% (Comparison Group: 78%) |
| Level 2 | 59% (Comparison Group: 46%) |
| Level 1 | 28% (Comparison Group: 15%) |

Fannie Lou's 4-year graduation rate was 74%. Another 4% of students take additional time and graduate within 6 years. Importantly, 46% of students graduate college-ready, according to CUNY's standards to avoid remedial classes. This compares to 31% who graduate college-ready in comparison high schools. Indeed, 47% of FLHFHS seniors enroll in a college or other postsecondary program within 6 months of graduating. Support provided at FLHFHS to lift students up to grade-level standards is illustrated by the data in Table 4.1 showing the level students were at when they entered the school (based on 8th-grade test scores, with Level 4 being the highest score) but nonetheless graduated college-ready.

The data that best reflect the shared intellectual commitments at Fannie Lou Hamer are from the School Survey administered by the New York City Department of Education in 2019. Seventy-eight percent of Fannie Lou Hamer students responded. Their answers convey their experiences regarding two aggregate dimensions: Rigorous Instruction and Supportive Environment. Eighty-five percent of FLHFHS students responded positively to questions about Rigorous Instruction compared to 79% of students in Bronx high schools overall and 79% citywide. Rigorous Instruction includes questions such as whether classes make them think critically (82% yes), work in small groups (72% yes), learn a lot from feedback on their work (75% yes), and knowing what their teachers want them to learn (84% yes). Seventy-nine percent of students responded positively to questions about Supportive Environment compared to 71% of students in Bronx high schools overall and 72% citywide. This dimension included questions about whether most students work when they are supposed to (72% yes), adults talk with them about what they plan to do after high school (83% yes), and most students try hard to get good grades (79% yes).

## SUPPORTS AND COLLABORATIONS

### Internal Coherence and Supports

Students, families, and teachers at Fannie Lou Hamer Freedom High School are fortunate to have a rich tradition of project-based learning, performance-based assessments, and graduation portfolios that they work to sustain, rather than needing to develop them from scratch. Yet it is interesting to note that the ethos at the originating school, Central Park East, changed dramatically in the years after Deborah Meier left (Suiter, 2009). This suggests that explicit attention must be regularly paid to these shared commitments. Sustaining the vision is not automatic. FLHFHS's portfolio culture is likely effective precisely because the elements of curriculum, instruction, and assessment are coherently integrated and mutually reinforcing. In addition, these commitments are highly visible. Teachers and students have a shared vocabulary for talking about expectations and learning goals. This vision and set of commitments are also clearly acknowledged by new staff as they are recruited to the school and agree to take up this work.

For educators in other schools that are considering what resources are needed to begin a performance-based, portfolio assessment program like Fannie Lou Hamer's, it is important to recognize that the system is built on relationships as much as intellectual and academic commitments. To make this mutually supportive system possible, the school began back in 1994 with only 60 students and still today is a relatively small high school with fewer than 500 students. The total enrollment per grade level is then divided into smaller "houses" to enable the smallest number of students to connect with the smallest number of teachers. The school's schedule, as noted earlier, allows each teacher to work with only 60 students. In addition, teachers loop with their students for 2-year cycles both in content classes and as advisers. These structures make it possible for families to know their children's teachers and advisers well. Block scheduling, creating class times of 1 hour, 15 minutes to 2 hours, and dyad pairings of math/science and humanities teachers also support project-based learning, allowing teachers substantial amounts of time to interact with students and go deep into content.

A collaborative spirit among teachers is also critical to the success of a performance-assessment portfolio system. Teachers work closely with one another to plan instruction as well as support schoolwide goals by serving on cross-house portfolio evaluation panels and on external panels for the New York Performance Standards Consortium, described in the next section. There is built-in time for teachers to work together and establish clear expectations among the staff that "this is what we do here." In addition to recruiting new staff based on shared commitments, teacher leaders have a strong role in onboarding new staff, showing them all of the elements of how the system works. In 2019, ninety-five percent of FLHFHS teachers responded to the New York City School Survey, and 95% of those teachers answered positively to questions on the Collaborative Teachers scale. This overall dimension included sections addressing Cultural Awareness and Inclusive Classroom Instruction, Innovation and Collective Responsibility, Peer Collaboration, Quality of Professional Development, and School Commitment. Specific questions indicate, for example, that 94% of teachers say they receive support to incorporate students' cultural and linguistic backgrounds in their practice; 89% say that teachers maintain discipline in the entire school, not just their classroom; 94% say they design instructional programs, lessons, and units together; 91% say they had opportunities to work productively with teachers from other schools on professional development; and 97% look forward to working each day at their school. These very strong responses are in contrast to only 81% of teachers in Bronx schools and 80% of teachers citywide who responded positively to questions about Collaborative Teachers.

### New York Performance Standards Consortium

Fannie Lou Hamer enjoys support from many external partners, but its most critical and essential support comes from the New York Performance Standards Consortium. From its earliest days, FLHFHS was a participant in the collaboration among schools, officially established as the Consortium in 1998. Together the founding leaders and schools developed the vision of a portfolio-based graduation system, all while working against the headwinds of an increasingly intensive test-driven accountability context. Explaining this history, the website for the New York Performance Standards Consortium (2018) notes that it focused explicitly on authentic assessment and "a pedagogy in which curriculum and instruction drive the assessment, not the reverse. It is unique because it values inquiry teaching and learning, promotes student voice, fosters depth over coverage, and promotes school cultures built on professional communities" (p. 1). Today the Consortium provides the organizational structure that enables teacher professional development and teacher collaboration and that continues the development of PBATs and assessment rubrics. During the COVID-19 pandemic, the Consortium's Center for Inquiry was the virtual place where teachers came together to participate in summer workshops focused on remote learning resources and to develop meaningful curriculum units specific to the pandemic.

Significantly, the Consortium is also a collective that generated and maintains the political will whereby students in Consortium schools are exempt from all but the English Language Arts Regents Examination. Teachers who have taught in both contexts say that in Regents-driven high schools it is not possible to go deep in the same way that the practice has thrived in performance-based schools like FLHFHS.

Consortium staff lead the effort to petition the New York State Department of Education, every 3–5 years, to continue exemptions and extend participation to additional schools. Originally, in the late 1990s, waivers from the Regents exam requirements were granted on the basis of the ideals represented by project-based learning and authentic assessment. In more recent years, the argument has been amplified by compelling evidence that Consortium high schools in New York City outperform other high schools despite serving larger proportions of high-needs students.

One explanation, especially regarding college readiness, college-going, and college persistence, is that Consortium schools engage students in critical thinking, project reports, and oral presentations that much more directly resemble college learning expectations. The Consortium's staff also conduct moderation studies (a kind of consistency check) to establish the reliable implementation of PBAT scoring rubrics, undertake evaluation studies, and support external researchers as well as Consortium teachers who wish to investigate particular aspects of the Consortium's teaching, learning, and assessment model (Barlow & Cook, 2016; Tashlik, 2010).

## Other External Supports

Relationships and emotional supports for students and their families begin with Advisory at the school but also depend profoundly on FLHFHS being a Children's Aid Community School. Such collaborations are not always easy, in part because community-based organizations and schools often have different missions, but they can be enormously rewarding. In any case, a tremendous amount of collaboration is necessary for the community school model to be effective. The critical partnership between FLHFHS and Children's Aid (CA) took over 15 years to develop. CA provides academic support with one-on-one tutoring and after-school enrichment programs. CA staff also partner with FLHFHS counselors to provide college and career advising and even college trips. Beyond educational resources, CA attends to the social and emotional needs of students and their families. Social work staff provide individual and family counseling, support youth leadership development by facilitating youth-led community events like an event they called the "Peace Block Party," and meet with students in small groups to discuss personal topics and build social–emotional competencies. CA programs have a welcoming and community-building aspect, including events such as a Women's History Month celebration and fitness classes along with financial aid/FAFSA workshops. CA also provides critical services for families in crisis, including legal and financial assistance. When the school was locked down because of the COVID emergency, FLHFHS staff worked with CA to hand out more than 250 computers and Wi-Fi hotspots. True to community schools' comprehensive services approach, CA also provides medical care through its clinics and from other partner organizations, dental and vision screenings, and sexual education.

Together with CA, FLHFHS teachers and leaders have developed extensive relationships with external organizations that offer workshop and internship programs where students can gain access to career-relevant, real-world experiences. For example, New York City offers a Summer Youth Employment Program (SYEP) that pays students a stipend of $700–$1,000 and connects them with professionals in a potential field of interest. Each spring advisers work with all of their students to help them apply. Students who participate in Summer Youth are then eligible for the New

York City–funded Work, Learn, and Grow program, during the school year, that offers readiness training as well as part-time work experience.

Because the FLHFHS Internship and STEAM portfolio projects both require that students document connections between their project and real-world work experiences, virtually all FLHFHS students participate in internships or outside-of-school experiences related to their career interests. Occasionally these opportunities are based on a connection that a student made individually, but more often they depend on service learning relationships that individual teachers have established (as was the case with Bronx River project connections described earlier), or they depend on relationships between the school and external organizations. For example, educators in the New York University EXCEL program partner with students who want to work on social justice issues. One student extended her Food Justice research project into a pitch that helped her gain funding to create a Food Pantry at Fannie Lou Hamer when she realized that many of her classmates are impacted by food insecurity.[3] Another partnership with the MSG Networks and the Madison Square Garden Company gives students opportunities to connect with professionals working in various roles in the television industry.[4] These real-world projects are what give meaning to students' academic work, but they are a constant work-in-progress, requiring significant logistical coordination and relationship-building. The national Big Picture Learning network, yet another external support, assists FLHFHS in the quality and connections of real-world learning. This relationship enables students and staff at FLHFHS to network and collaborate with students throughout the world on the importance of student-centered learning and assessment.

## CONCLUSION

This chapter is focused on assessment and the 4th Schools of Opportunity criterion: Use multiple measures to assess student learning. Yet singling out that criterion is a bit incongruous because, like other schools in the New York Performance Standards Consortium, Fannie Lou Hamer is intentionally curriculum and instruction focused, not test- or assessment driven. But that might be the point. Performance-based assessment tasks (PBATs) and portfolio oral defenses are quite different from standardized tests, and FLHFHS's focus on student intellectualism and on quality project-based learning is what enables the school's success. Unlike standardized testing contexts, at FLHFHS assessment may not be the driver, but it is the glue that connects formative feedback—focused on students' inquiry skills and habits of mind—to official documentation via portfolio entries and reflections.

At Fannie Lou, curriculum, instruction, and assessment are coherently integrated and mutually supportive. FLHFHS addresses all 10 of the Schools of Opportunity principles, but this is possible only because they are not separate or discrete undertakings. The portfolio culture described in this chapter makes it possible for the school to "create and maintain a healthy school culture" (criterion 2 of the Schools of Opportunity selection criteria). All students benefit from "broadened and enriched learning opportunities" (criterion 1) created through project-based learning and supports for internships and other out-of-school, real-world experiences. Student choice and teacher-designed curricula enable a "challenging and supportive culturally relevant curriculum" (criterion 8), "provide rich, supportive opportunities for students with special needs" (criterion 6), and "build on the strengths of language-minority students" (criterion 9).

Fannie Lou Hamer has a proud history of recognizing students' intellectual capabilities and working to further develop critical thinking skills as part of deep content learning and project work. Teachers and students have a shared understanding of the school's commitments and help to induct new staff and new students into "how things work here." School structures—block scheduling, academic houses, Advisory, dyad teaching teams, and looping—are all designed to build relationships and to allow teachers to engage with students individually and with their families. "Teachers are supported as professionals" (criterion 5) by the highly collaborative within-school practices and by the professional development opportunities created through participation in the Consortium. Because of the extensive economic needs of students and the neighborhood, FLHFHS is a Children's Aid Community School. FLHFHS teachers and CA staff together "sustain equitable and meaningful parent and community engagement" (criterion 10) and "provide more and better learning time" (criterion 3) through internships, individual tutoring, and summer programs. CA specifically "provides students with additional needed services and supports" (criterion 7), addressing both physical and mental health.

Fannie Lou Hamer serves a community where children and their families have long suffered the harms of racism and racialized poverty. But within that context, its success with a 74% high school graduation rate and college attendance by nearly half its graduates is made possible by a coherent and ambitious vision and by incredibly dedicated staff. Project-based learning and graduation portfolios are demanding work. But FLHFHS's success is also highly dependent on its two chief external sources of support: the New York Performance Standards Consortium and the New York City Children's Aid Community Schools. Building similar structures throughout the nation will help to make these beneficial practices more widespread.

## NOTES

1. https://tools.nycenet.edu/snapshot/2019/12X682/HS/#INFO
2. The New York City Department of Education identifies comparison schools based on Grade 8 ELA and math scores, the school's percentage of students with IEPs,

the school's Economic Need Index, the school's percentage of ELLs, and the school's percentage of overage/undercredited students.

3. https://steinhardt.nyu.edu/metrocenter/excel

4. https://www.gardenofdreamsfoundation.org/msg-classroom-fall-2018/

## REFERENCES

Barlow, A., & Cook, A. (2016). Putting the focus on student engagement: The benefits of performance-based assessment. *American Educator, 40*(1), 4–11, 43.

Darling-Hammond, L., Ancess, J., & Falk, B. (1995). *Authentic assessment in action: Studies of schools and students at work.* Teachers College Press.

de Kadt, M. (2006). The Bronx River: A classroom for environmental, political and historical studies. *Capitalism Nature Socialism, 17*(2), 99–110.

Duckor, B., & Perlstein, D. (2014). Assessing habits of mind: Teaching to the test at Central Park East Secondary School. *Teachers College Record, 116*(2), 1–33.

Mann, N. (2005). *It takes 10 years to build a school.* Lecture presented at The Child Development Institute, Sarah Lawrence College.

Meier, D. (1987). Central Park East: An alternative story. *The Phi Delta Kappan, 68*(10), 753–757.

New York Performance Standards Consortium. (2018). *History: Teaching over testing.* http://www.performanceassessment.org/history

Penuel, W. R., & Shepard, L. A. (2016). Assessment and teaching. In D. H. Gitomer & C. A. Bell (Eds.), *Handbook of research on teaching* (5th ed.) (pp. 787–850). American Educational Research Association.

Sadler, D. R. (1989). Formative assessment and the design of instructional systems. *Instructional Science, 18,* 119–144.

Suiter, D. (2009). Sustaining change: The struggle to maintain identity at Central Park East Secondary School. *Horace, 25*(2&3).

Tashlik, P. (2010). Changing the national conversation on assessment. *Phi Delta Kappan, 91*(6), 55–59.

# CHAPTER 5

# Preserving, Deepening, and Growing a Professional Teaching Culture
## Lessons From Casco Bay High School

*Linda Molner Kelley and Derek Pierce (with Matt Bernstein, Susan McCray, and Rebecca Lynch Nichols)*

Criterion 5: Support Teachers as Professionals

Schools of Opportunity close opportunity gaps by establishing exemplary, evidence-based practices in numerous critical areas, including student-focused approaches to broad, meaningful learning experiences and assessments; an inclusive, healthy school culture; and instruction that meets the needs of all students in an academically challenging and supportive environment. Foundational to these efforts are the working conditions and supports afforded to teachers in Schools of Opportunity who are entrusted to create and safeguard opportunities and to dismantle inequities that are within their control.

Engagement in equitable practices for today's students calls for skilled teachers who know their students and local communities well and who assimilate relevant historical and complex cultural perspectives in their teaching, student interactions, and all aspects of school life (Gorski, 2016; Sleeter, 2012). Accordingly, teachers need access to meaningful, job-embedded professional development opportunities that are culturally responsive if they are to succeed with students and remain committed to their own work and the profession at large (Darling-Hammond & McLaughlin, 2011).

A school's working conditions—including a nourishing professional culture, inclusive and supportive leadership, and strong collegial relationships—matter greatly to teachers and ultimately contribute to improved student learning outcomes (Allensworth et al., 2009; Boyd et al., 2011; Bryk, 2010; Johnson et al., 2012). These large-scale studies on teaching conditions in New York City, Chicago, Massachusetts, and North Carolina schools report that poor school climate and organizational culture, rather than student demographics or zip codes, are the strongest predictors of teacher dissatisfaction and turnover. This research aligns with the experiences of many Schools of Opportunity that successfully serve high numbers of students living in poverty.

These approaches, focused on working conditions, strong professional development, and cultivation of positive social environments for teachers, stand in stark contrast to recent "school-turnaround" efforts. Those turnaround approaches address teachers as isolated workers; they often rely on teacher performance evaluations tied to their students' test scores; and they include a great deal of staff turnover and churn—even replacing professional teaching staff with new teachers who come to the profession through alternative pathways.

The good news is that creating positive conditions to support, develop, and retain teachers who work effectively and equitably with today's students can be within every school's reach. In Schools of Opportunity, these are reflected in collective student and teaching cultures that are learner focused and fully inclusive, and that give everyone a voice and a place to belong.

## TEACHER SUPPORT IN A SCHOOL OF OPPORTUNITY

In this chapter we introduce you to Casco Bay High School, located in Portland, Maine, where teachers thrive in an interdependent professional environment thoughtfully constructed to encourage them to do their best work with their students and one another. Set within the context of the school's ongoing commitment to equity initiatives, the following Casco Bay story includes the voices of its principal, a coauthor of this chapter, and three of the school's teachers.

We focus on Casco Bay's established supports for staff to see how Schools of Opportunity and other great schools tackle equity and social justice issues while they create the best working conditions and inspiring professional development opportunities for teachers. We also learn how such schools deliberately design positive cultures for both teachers and students so that those intertwined cultures mirror each other and thrive through interdependence and a shared vision. Notably, we see through Casco Bay's recent history how this involved dismantling equities. We present Casco Bay as a living example of what it looks like to support teachers as professionals. The story presented in this chapter includes exemplary and inspiring professional development and related approaches that might be replicated in other schools. But it also includes a variety of other practices that many of us might not normally associate with teacher development; in fact, the chapter illustrates how difficult it is—and should be—to separate teacher development from holistic approaches to improve student learning.

---

**CRITERION 5: SUPPORT TEACHERS AS PROFESSIONALS**

The [exemplary] school successfully employs a variety of collegial and sustained professional development activities that build upon school-level expertise, build teacher leadership, and provide ample opportunities for teacher collaboration. The school has high-quality induction processes in place. Professional learning emphasizes the development of a cadre of well-trained teachers who have a deep understanding of diversity and how to address diverse learning needs without promoting inequitable learning experiences. The school develops healthy and beneficial attitudes and beliefs among administrators, teachers, school personnel, and students regarding teaching, learning, and student ability.

---

Portland families may choose among three public high schools. As an Expeditionary Learning (EL Education) high school option, Casco Bay embraces active, inquiry-based learning and a challenging, interdisciplinary curriculum that centers instruction on real community needs and the passions and interests of its diverse student population. Casco Bay opened in 2005 with a freshman class of 80 students committed to the idea that all students—and each student—could achieve greatness with the right support and challenge. In its opening years, the school established many of the structures and policies that have been foundational to its commitments to equity and access. Untracked, standards-based courses are open to all. And learning "expeditions" focus academic instruction on the big social justice issues of the day, from race relations and income inequality to climate change.

As Casco Bay grew over time from 80 to just under 400 students in 2020, it maintained its focus on equity and access. Any interested student may apply, and the school's weighted lottery process ensures that the student body reflects the diversity of the district in terms of English Language Learners (ELLs), special education students, and economically disadvantaged students. Approximately 40% of Casco Bay students are students of color, 18% have Individualized Education Plans (IEPs), and nearly 50% receive free and reduced-price lunch. About 20% of Casco Bay's students are ELLs, with first languages consisting of Arabic, Somali, French, Spanish, and Portuguese.

The school has little teacher turnover, and over 70% of the majority-White staff (26 of 35) have 10 or more years of experience. The school actively supports the district's initiative to recruit and retain more educators of color to reflect the change in community and school demographics. In 2020, three out of five school hires were staff of color; two of those recruits were Casco Bay graduates.

## EQUITY-FOCUSED TEACHER AND STUDENT LEARNING
## AT CASCO BAY HIGH SCHOOL

The school leadership at Casco Bay anchors many of its conversations about professional development and working conditions with the question, *How do we create and sustain a vibrant professional culture that is positive, productive, and continuously improving its ability to support a full range of students and dismantle inequities?* In this chapter, we present seven concrete guidelines that Casco Bay's leadership uses to place teacher support in this central role while also maintaining dynamic, adaptable organizational structures. In brief, these guidelines are as follows:

1. Adhere to a common vision of excellence and equity that encourages students and teachers to aim for greatness.
2. Pay attention to the pace, process and psychology of making change.
3. Build clear and continuous processes for feedback, reflection and learning for both individuals and the collective.
4. Create structures that cultivate teacher interdependence and professional capacity.
5. Empower and expect teachers to be leaders.
6. Sustain excellence by attending to staff wellness.
7. Cultivate an adult culture that mirrors what you want to see in your students.

### Guideline 1: Adhere to a Common Vision of Excellence and Equity That Encourages Students and Teachers to Aim for Greatness

Grounded in the "3 Rs" of rigor, relevance, and relationships, Casco Bay defines student achievement along EL's three related dimensions: mastery of academic skills and content, high-quality work, and character. Students and staff understand and embrace these dimensions, and all are encouraged to aspire to greatness. In practice, this plays out in major and minor ways, such as student learning presentations that require countless drafts and rehearsals until they are ready for an outside audience (often of experts). Every senior must apply and be accepted to at least one college, and the school provides strong supports to ensure this is achieved—by 98% of graduates to date.

Since students' success is tied to their teachers' success, Casco Bay provides its teachers with the time and collegial support to expand their perceptions of what is possible by dreaming big and planning big for their curriculum and students. To meet rigorous expectations for themselves and their students, teachers work collectively to design interdisciplinary, project-based exhibitions and assessments of complex ideas that place students at the center of their learning, often through exploration of societal injustices, and often in conjunction with community partners.

As an example, Casco Bay juniors in 2018 completed a cross-disciplinary, 5-month expedition that began with an examination of the economic and cultural realities of Maine mill towns and the increasing polarization in the state. Students researched divisive issues from gun control to immigration reform and presented and defended policy briefs to local experts at a Public Policy Symposium. Next, they embarked on a weeklong "Junior Journey" to Millinocket, Maine. Once there, teams of students lent a hand to local service projects and conducted oral histories of Katahdin region indigenous locals. Back at school, the junior class converted these oral histories into a full-length documentary film that premiered in Portland and aired on Maine Public Television.

Flexible learning options, opportunities, and assessments of student work all take place in an untracked curriculum. All classes are "advanced" in the sense that they are academically challenging and taught with high expectations, but the teaching is also differentiated. This requires teachers to provide scaffolded instruction with multiple access points and opportunities to exceed standards for every student, including those receiving special education or English language supports. All students participate in expeditions and public sharing, and there are multiple opportunities for supportive feedback along the way.

Rebecca (Becca) Lynch Nichols, a contributor to this chapter and Spanish teacher with 22 years of experience in three schools, addresses the challenges of teaching at Casco Bay, given the school's complex curriculum and high expectations of students and teachers:

> The learning curve at an EL school was steep, especially with language teaching, but it was challenging in a good way. Here the bar is high. People feel pressure to be excellent, and there is a self-expectation to be excellent. My biggest challenge is myself: Am I being excellent enough?

To expand what is possible for Becca and other Casco Bay teachers, principal Derek Pierce (coauthor of this chapter, but for clarity referred to in the third person—often just as "Derek"—throughout) embraces democratic decision-making processes open to all, allocates time for collegial interactions, and divides roles and leadership opportunities among the entire staff. The school leadership is also intentional about its use of professional development activities, which research suggests can improve learning outcomes if they are content-specific, highly collaborative, and driven by the teachers themselves (Berry, 2008; Bryk, 2010; Darling-Hammond et al., 2017; Johnson, 2019). In following this research-based approach, Casco Bay deliberately places teachers' interests and students' learning at the center of an array of empowering and appealing professional supports.

Casco Bay's inclusive methods foster a level of community engagement that Sleeter (2012) has identified as a critical aspect of culturally responsive pedagogy. Framing many learning activities as "quests" or "expeditions" within an interdependent culture generates interest and opportunities to excel for both teachers and students. Interdisciplinary projects with social justice themes have included exploration of issues such as *What forces people to flee their homes for another country?* and *What can be done to create a moral and just migration system?* Seniors self-design their own culminating expeditions. Representing the intersection between a personal passion and a need in the world, recent projects have included Queer Activism and Muslim Art.

Student opportunities include daily crew (advisory) gatherings, often student-led, that function as a "family at school" to support students and build community. As part of their equity goals, staff members devised a structure within crew gatherings to talk about challenging issues through "courageous conversations." Trained student facilitators now lead crew sessions focused on topics such as race, income inequality, gender identity, homophobia, and mental health. These and other efforts to incorporate character into the learning environment recognize the importance of promoting a schoolwide culture of respect and compassion and of including social and emotional learning alongside academic learning.

The school's teachers benefit from a similar culture of empowerment, inquiry, and ongoing support, again as a result of deliberate design by the school leadership. This is reflected in a learner-centered work environment that catalyzes a deep-seated culture of relational trust. At Casco Bay, it is safe to take healthy risks and make mistakes, and collegial decision-making is the norm. These are recognized essential features of transformative professional growth (Darling-Hammond & McLaughlin, 2011).

Susan McCray, another chapter contributor and a 30-year veteran English and humanities teacher who has worked at Casco Bay since its inception, describes to us her experiences within the school's dynamic and collegial organizational structures and culture. "People think culture just means we should teach everyone to treat each other with respect and that we should be happy," she says. "But I think positive school culture is really about the structures that provide opportunities to talk with each other—it's an organic process that doesn't *feel* structured or overly stilted."

Susan's colleague Matt Bernstein, a 9th-grade humanities and social studies teacher and fellow contributor to this chapter, observes that the underlying expectations for having a culture of support and trust have existed since the school's founding. "We talk about culture and how structures lead to the culture, but I think a part of it is that an expectation is always there. We are a team, we are a family, and that's not really something we need to debate anymore." Matt describes adults in the school working alongside him who "have his back" and support him as a colleague along with their own students, as well as "a sense of camaraderie that is readily apparent because of the ways people interact on a daily basis."

Susan's and Matt's comments represent the widespread views of the entire Casco Bay staff. An externally administered survey that Casco Bay and all Portland school district teachers complete annually indicates strong agreement among the school's teachers about its positive working conditions. Teachers believe that Casco Bay is a good place to teach and learn and is committed to helping teachers improve instructional practices. In fact, 100% of Casco Bay's teachers identified strong leadership at the school that (1) articulates a clear vision that drives priorities and decision-making, (2) prioritizes equity and inclusion and encourages teachers to learn and grow in these areas, (3) follows through on commitments, (4) models behavior for staff, and (5) regularly includes input from teachers. Teachers also report that their peer culture is strong, that all staff contribute to students' success, and that their work makes a real difference for students.

Identifying and committing to new priorities and growth areas, both as a staff and as individuals, allow Casco Bay teachers to contribute to a shared community vision. The most important recent such effort began in 2017, when the school's community embarked on an "equity literacy" initiative inspired by Gorski's (2016) principles. Gorski (2016) pushes back on superficial "cultural proficiency" approaches that can limit schools' efforts to mere *appreciation of* cultural diversity and that risk perpetuating stereotypes about marginalized communities. He argues for a more ambitious equity literacy framework for schools that addresses forms of injustice such as racism that many students and families face in today's schools (p. 222).

The staff at Casco Bay realized that however deep their commitments to social and racial justice might be, students' perceived realities sometimes differ from the teachers', with occasional resentments spilling over in unexpected, messy ways. Acknowledging that their comprehensive efforts must start with teachers' and students' respective perspectives, the school took on equity literacy as a long-term initiative that became embedded in the school's vision and professional development efforts. The equity literacy initiatives that Casco Bay has undertaken engage teachers in deep justice-oriented work that targets critical underlying issues. These include examining positions of privilege and teachers' assumptions about students that can, however unintentionally, feed bias, racism and other inequities that occur in schools. Gorski's (2016) framework anchors Casco Bay's educators' work in four areas: (1) recognizing even subtle forms of inequity existing in the school environment, (2) responding immediately to identified inequities, (3) addressing inequities for the long term (e.g., working on incipient institutional problems that hinder access and opportunity), and (4) sustaining the equity efforts, even when they become messy or difficult (p. 225). This equity literacy work brings Casco Bay teachers into a conversation that itself contributes to a shared community vision.

### Guideline 2: Pay Attention to the Pace, Process, and Psychology of Making Change

A major tension at Casco Bay was finding the right balance between maintaining the necessary sense of urgency without provoking the defensiveness, hopelessness, or righteousness that can derail the work. All agreed that there were substantive, complex inequities and biases that do daily damage to many kids, especially students of color, and that needed to be acknowledged and dismantled. But all understood that deep change required sustained effort—it required time.

Pursuant to the schoolwide goal of improving their equity literacy, Casco Bay teachers spent the first (2017–2018) school year exploring their own implicit biases, privilege, and particular experiences with equity and injustice, using approaches similar to what Sleeter (2012) has described as "critical multiculturalism" frameworks. With leadership and guidance from a teacher-led equity task force, staff members analyzed their own identities and perspectives in addition to discussing broader racial issues and unequal power relationships. These included social class, sexual identity, religion, and other backgrounds, identities, and potential triggers that could create conflict for staff and students. (A Faculty Leadership Team works closely with the Equity Task Force, regularly seeking input from staff, reviewing student data, and overseeing professional development efforts with an eye toward narrowing the gap between the school's aspirations and daily practices.)

Teachers noticed that after the 2016 presidential election, more students expressed concerns about inequity and racism they perceived and sometimes experienced personally in their own communities. As tensions escalated among some students of color and faculty and others in the school community, the teachers, who were used to being viewed as "the good guys" able to handle almost any student behavior challenge without personalizing or internalizing a student's critical comments, did not feel equipped to deal with the increasing anger and frustration they were observing.

During the school's 2017 Summer Institute, an annual 3-day staff gathering designed for big-picture planning and team-building, staff addressed these issues. To explore the difficulties of having conversations that implicated their own beliefs and actions, the staff role-played how and why they might react differently to hearing "You're a racist" from a student than, for example, "You're the worst teacher ever." They brainstormed productive ways they might listen and respond to such accusations and to deescalate conflict and tensions in positive ways, finding ways to learn and move forward. This activity and others stimulated the staff's self-exploration as they developed school and faculty equity-focused learning targets and strategies to guide their professional development efforts.

At the outset, after exploring their own biases, these efforts included increasing individual and collective equity literacy and differentiating instruction. Over time, learning targets evolved as staff found better ways to measure opportunity gaps, to develop pedagogies and skills as antiracist educators, and, during the COVID-19 crisis, to improve remote and hybrid instruction for harder-to-reach students. The teachers' journey toward dismantling inequities exemplifies successful professional development, outlined by Darling-Hammond and her colleagues (2017), that ties highly collaborative efforts to school priorities, embeds professional support activities during the school day, and involves teachers in their own active learning over a sustained period of time.

Throughout the equity literacy efforts, a leadership team consisting of teachers and administrators has paid careful attention to the tone, sequence, and pacing of the work. Recognizing that not all teachers are in the same place at the same time, they have created multiple pathways for teachers to identify and dismantle inequities, differentiating options both individually and collectively. Casco Bay's shared concepts of what it means to "preserve, deepen, and grow" serve as keys to the school's sustainable change processes. Maintaining a balance among the three concepts—preserving, deepening, and growing—means that teachers have numerous opportunities to validate what they are accomplishing, improve their practices with colleagues' help, and expand their own learning through new, mutually determined initiatives.

To help teachers remain open to understanding their relative privilege and better empathize with others who have had different experiences, the school has embraced the idea of naming and celebrating the particular lens through which each person views equity and identity issues. Noting that the work to dismantle inequities is as never-ending as it is vital, Derek finds that staff resilience for the work is bolstered by regularly dedicating some time to looking at how far they have come (as a school, as a staff), as well as anywhere else they need to go.

To this end, the school's staff, administrators, and students self-assessed their equity progress using the scoring rubrics developed for the 10 Schools of Opportunity criteria. Undertaking this challenge at one of the school's Equity Summits (consisting of several days of staff planning and professional development), the community collectively and individually identified numerous school strengths as well as new improvement targets.

The school's educators shared their Equity Summit findings in their application for recognition as a School of Opportunity. In part, this meant highlighting their exemplary practices that provide opportunities and dismantle equities for their students and teachers—practices well worth preserving. These include an untracked curriculum focused on issues of social justice and diversity, myriad opportunities for people of diverse backgrounds to contribute to the school, support structures and differentiated assignments for all students, and implementation of restorative justice principles in response to student misbehavior. But it also meant recognizing that there was more work to be done to grow together as a community and to identify and eradicate inequities and injustices in their school and the broader world. This included continued work on their individual practices and curriculum as well as school policies and structures. Throughout the process, teachers and leaders supported one another as they read and discussed relevant books and articles, engaged in activities and continued role-playing, and reflected on their own practices. This work, and even the acknowledgment of the need for that work, is an example of the school's commitment to "preserve, deepen, and grow."

As noted briefly above, the school's staff development was not pursued in isolation; it was interlinked with other reforms and was connected to the voices of the school's students. To inform their equity work, teachers co-designed professional development sessions with student leaders and then participated in a student-planned "fishbowl" activity that by all accounts forever changed the whole school community in profound ways.

The goal of the fishbowl activity was to help faculty understand students' lives, especially those of immigrant students and students of color. A cross-section of 20 Casco Bay students answered questions posed by a senior student leader. Faculty encircled the students and listened as students spoke candidly on questions that ranged from "What do you love about Casco Bay?" to "Where and when have you experienced injustice or inequities at the school?" Faculty received lots of kudos, but they also heard some hard truths that were delivered by students with maturity and civility. These ranged from student frustration at having their names or pronouns botched to requests for more uplifting and nuanced tales and representations of oppressed or marginalized people in the curriculum. Afterward, small groups of staff and students reflected on deeper questions about what each may or may not yet fully understand about each other.

Susan and Matt both made note of the value of pacing and thoughtful change processes that include students as partners in successful equity work. "It's that whole progression and evolution that has allowed us to get where we are," Susan says. "And we have a culture that says, no community is perfect, but the best community is willing to dig into those hard places and have hard conversations with each other and with our students. It's been really important to have students involved."

Matt agrees. "The equity work is challenging," he says, "but it needs to be hard to be meaningful." Describing reflections with his professional learning community (PLC) team after another fishbowl activity intended to address occasional hallway issues and conflicts, Matt adds, "I wanted to think about my practice and how it can be more equitable. I think the key for me is that we are intentionally and specifically focused on equity. That's what we have to keep our laser focus on, and so accessing student voice to me has been crucial, in addition to PD and reading and deep scholarship we can all learn from. But listening to student voices and being self-reflective with the explicit goal of equity has been the key factor for me."

### Guideline 3: Build Clear and Continuous Processes for Feedback, Reflection, and Learning for Both Individuals and the Collective

Frequent opportunities to reflect, such as the fishbowl activity, allow for real change and are ingrained elements of the school's culture. They give teachers space and time to process their beliefs and learn from one another in a safe environment, a critical feature of meaningful teacher growth (Sun et al., 2013). As Becca tells us, "We had an equity observation tool we created, and I had an opportunity to be observed by a colleague—which I really, really appreciated. It's super validating to have ideas and then have other staff members reflect with you on what you're doing," she says. She adds, "I can talk to a colleague, go to a veteran teacher and say, 'Can we brainstorm about this? I'm struggling.' Pretty much everybody has moments when they don't feel great. It's part of what makes us good teachers."

Becca also values her 3-year involvement as a grade-level PLC coach at the school and its opportunities for peer collaboration and reflection. After meeting with the full group of schoolwide coaches each month, Becca works with the other 11th-grade teachers in her PLC to choose and enact their own equity goals. "I am improving my awareness of how to connect better with students in a more equitable way," she says, "and I'm more aware of my own bias in my instruction and how students might view staff in all kinds of situations."

As part of their humanities team structure, Matt and Susan engage with their English and social studies partners during weekly planning time to be, as Matt describes it, "collaboratively reflective." Humanities teams and grade-level teams each have common planning time with special educators and culturally and linguistically diverse (CLD) teachers. The teams share ideas, plan, and reflect, sometimes taking advantage of the school's scheduling flexibility for co-teaching to occur. Matt and Susan emphasize the value of this teamwork and collaboration in helping improve their instruction of special education or English language students. "After looking at data and getting feedback from my students, I'll touch base if I feel like I'm not doing a good job of meeting their needs or if I could use some help accommodating or modifying some of the upcoming curriculum," Matt observes. "That's another really helpful touchpoint." Similarly, Susan noted that with the help of the special education and CLD colleagues she has consulted after struggling with differentiation and accommodating different students' needs, she has made significant structural changes to her teaching.

Twice a year, Casco Bay teachers share an example of their best practices related to the schoolwide professional development goal for that year. As part of that sharing, they put the example on a wall so that others can view colleagues' work. The teachers then participate in a "Promising Practices Walk," with teachers reflecting on what they are seeing and a "note catcher" colleague compiling the ideas. In a similar "Equity Learning Walk," teachers visited colleagues' classrooms to share and reflect on their work in response to equitable classroom criteria that PLC coaches developed for them.

Susan values these opportunities to improve her own equitable practices, noting, "Mostly it's to share, and we're gleaning ideas from it, and I think, 'I'm going to steal this notion, and there's an example of embedded differentiation I'm going to use.'"

The school's Expeditionary Learning model is anchored in relevant issues related to social and environmental injustices. To stay current and provide support to one another, teachers also share their entire expedition plans twice a year. Each grade-level or humanities team presents an expedition idea, with other staff members providing feedback using an established sharing protocol. "We know there's trust," Susan says, "and we know that we won't get shot down. We give feedback and it's great. We get good ideas and the process builds culture." Matt adds, "Providing support like this shows what the school values—the school prioritizes supporting teachers."

The school seeks feedback on the curriculum as well. Once teachers began to work on advancing broader, more inclusive instruction, the school instituted a curriculum review process through its "Futures Task Force," charged with moving the school closer to actualizing its long-term vision. Composed of two staff members and eight students, the Futures Task Force has provided a strong voice for student ideas and, accordingly, proposed revisions to the scope and sequence of the curriculum to better reflect the diverse backgrounds and interests of Casco Bay students.

As a result of the Futures Task Force recommendations, grade-level and humanities teams developed new expeditions and assessments of related student learning, one of which included expanding representation of indigenous populations. Matt's own 9th-grade team took this on with a deep dive into the history of Wabanaki nations who live in Maine, New Hampshire, and the Canadian Maritime provinces. After studying indigenous history before the impact of European arrival, the teachers and students brought their study into the present and looked at ongoing oppressive, racist practices that harm indigenous populations.

"Students picked topics they felt passionate about and created a 30-minute lesson plan that they taught to 3rd-, 4th-, and 5th-graders," Matt explained. "Their goal was to promote truth-telling and amplify indigenous voices in our district and in our community." In what Matt considers to be exceptional work, the 9th-graders educated the elementary students based on what they had learned from the interdisciplinary expedition and visiting guest experts that had included Wabanaki art, indigenous ecological practices, Wabanaki historical fiction, and Wabanaki history in Maine.

### Guideline 4: Create Structures That Cultivate Teacher Interdependence and Professional Capacity

At Casco Bay, interdependence is the norm. In what the school leaders and researchers (Donohoo et al., 2018) refer to as "collective efficacy," each teacher believes that "my success is your success" and that it is teachers' work together that overcomes challenges and makes a real difference for student learning. Through a collective culture of teacher and student interdependence, actions are understood to have a ripple effect and impact everyone in the community. This creates a system that incentivizes teachers, stretching their instructional practices and ambitious work for kids. Faculty are sustained in their work because the community understands that no one is ever alone—there are always people rooting for you. As Rosenholtz, cited in Berry (2013), noted, "learning-rich" schools such as Casco Bay embody "collective commitments to student learning in collaborative settings . . . where it is assumed that improvement of teaching is a collective rather than individual enterprise" (p. 190).

Naming the interdependency cultivated at the school as "collaboration on steroids," Susan observes:

> It's more than people working together. I think we have real connections with each other because at every level we work together. A team structure is in place at the grade levels, and we have a leadership team, and a crew structure and crew team leaders and special teams with content teachers and Culturally and Linguistically Diverse teachers and special educators. All of these "meetings" are part of our structure, but because this all happened in a way that's very organic and natural, I can now turn to a colleague and say, "Oh my god, I just had a crummy lesson. I need some help." I can go to my neighbor or Derek and talk it out.

Matt voices similar sentiments:

> Two words that come to my mind are "team" and "family." It really feels like all the staff are on the same team. The thing that has struck me as I've now seen a few classes graduate is this sense that the students are *all* of our students at all times. My heart soars when students present their public presentations. It feels like rather than being in silos, we're all in it together, we're all one team, all the time.

In contrast to other schools where she taught, Becca observes that she, too, feels like a member of a family. "Everyone is all in. You have a sense that you are supported and that we *all* have students' best interests in mind as opposed to places where there is a paranoia that the administration is not supporting you. Here you assume that everyone has the best intentions." Becca also emphasizes the importance of Casco Bay's leadership in creating a positive, collegial culture for teachers:

> If you have a problem, you're encouraged to go right to the root of the problem and talk to each other. I think it comes from Derek. He has complete faith in all of his staff. And he empowers us by making us all feel like professionals. He sees the strengths in all of us, he knows it takes a village, and that makes us feel connected to the community.

Holding to a conception of teacher learning as ongoing and fluid, the school offers teachers flexible organizational structures, choices, and supports that enable all teachers, regardless of experience level, to be part of a positive working and learning community. The Casco Bay leadership stimulates an environment that, as Darling-Hammond and McLaughlin (2011) recommend, fosters robust teacher learning communities through fluctuating professional development activities—all with various "life cycles" depending on the school's goals and teachers' interests (p. 86). As Susan points out,

> Derek is brilliant about creating those structures and protocols and making them flexible and fluid, as well. If we need to pop up a new one, we pop up a new one, if we need to form a new committee for something to happen, it happens. So structures are there, they come and they go, and they reinforce and naturally create this incredibly intimate culture.

Time is provided for teachers during the school day for daily teamwork and opportunities to engage and support one another in their planning, equity work, and other activities. The school allocates 90 minutes of additional ongoing collaborative and proactive planning every other day within and across departments (for example, grade-level teams, 9th- through 12th-grade humanities teams, and 9th- and 10th-grade mathematics teams). English language learning and special education teachers are part of these teams. The teams analyze student work and progress; plan curriculum, exhibitions, and assessments; and communicate with families. An early release of students every Wednesday provides time for additional planning sessions and professional development activities for entire grade-level teams.

All teachers are members of PLCs. Organized by grade levels, each PLC focuses on responding to its own identified student and teacher needs. Examples include differentiation of instruction, antiracist instructional practices, and classroom culture. Matt describes the role the PLCs played during the spring of 2020, as teachers faced the challenges of teaching remotely during the initial semester of the COVID-19 epidemic. PLC coaches were preparing the final PLC meetings for the year, and their initial plan was to lead workshops about remote learning tools and tips. But after the footage of George Floyd's murder became public, Matt observed that it sparked not only a national reckoning but also important feedback from Casco Bay students:

> Thanks in large part to the courage of students surfacing hard truths, it became clearer than ever that we needed to redouble our efforts to closely evaluate our own institution and practices and prioritize and center antiracist work. We were able to change the plans for the PLC session to a series of readings, including James Baldwin's "A Talk to Teachers" speech in 1963, Clint Smith's 2017 *New Yorker* article about the relevance of the Baldwin piece to today, followed by a discussion of how those readings resonate with us and what they inspired us to work on over the summer and beyond.

This session then became the launch point for the staff's summer book-group reading, initiated and led by teachers, of Bettina Love's book *We Want To Do More Than Survive: Abolitionist Teaching and the Pursuit of Educational Freedom* (2019). Twenty-six faculty and staff (out of 40) signed up for the book study, later using Love's book as an anchor text for PLC work the following year, as the school continued to strive to become a more antiracist and abolitionist institution. Additional professional resources, curated by and for staff and others, are available to staff through the school's Anti-Racism Resources for Casco Bay Educators site on Google Docs.

The Portland school district has recognized that Casco Bay's professional development can serve as a model for other schools. A district-wide professional development course titled "Race and Democracy" is now offered and taught by a Casco Bay teacher and is based on a student "intensive" course offered at the school.

These broader activities and structures are in addition to the school's (and district's) approach to traditional teacher-development practices. New teachers participate in a district-sponsored induction program as well as a combination of frequent school-developed on-site meetings and one-on-one support led by Casco Bay teacher mentors. Intended to provide both nitty-gritty logistical information (e.g., how the grading system and calendar work) and philosophical, theoretical, and instructional support, mentors observe and coach novices by providing nonevaluative feedback and opportunities to reflect. Remembering his first year at Casco Bay, Matt says, "That support was really influential for me because I could get a lot of great feedback in a way that felt nonevaluative. I wasn't scared because I didn't feel like I was going to get fired if it didn't go well, and it was a great learning opportunity."

Matt also notes that the formal teacher evaluation system at Casco Bay is a "safe space" for a novice teacher to learn and grow. He describes his postobservation discussions with Derek as "organic" and promoting self-reflection:

> At no point in time did I feel like I was being judged and that it was about whether I was going to make it as an educator or not. It was as if this was just really a system of how you're doing, how you feel about it, what you can work on to improve. It was very safe space as opposed to evaluative. That whole system made me feel really supported. I will say because of that I felt empowered as a young teacher to take some healthy risks. That was huge for me.

### Guideline 5: Empower and Expect Teachers to Be Leaders

Abundant leadership opportunities for teachers at Casco Bay endure in a nimble working environment that shifts and adapts depending on the school's goals and teachers' interests. At the beginning of each school year, teachers volunteer for any of the school's teams and committees, many of which are described in this chapter. The teachers can serve in positions that rotate by design so that everyone has a chance to participate. Most teachers in leadership positions receive stipends. Teachers and students also serve on hiring committees and help to select—and eventually support and welcome—new staff into the school community. In addition, Casco Bay teachers are encouraged to choose other professional development pathways suited to their individual needs. For example, three teachers at the school have earned National Board for Professional Teaching Standards (NBPTS) certification. Casco Bay teachers routinely share their work with fellow educators, either at the EL National Conference or with the 100-plus educators who visit the school annually to learn from their exemplary practices.

By empowering all teachers to take on a range of revolving leadership roles, the school ensures that teachers have opportunities to grow and to drive their own professional development activities. According to Susan, there are always new opportunities to learn at school. "There's so much *room* at our school," she says. "There's always more equity work to do, there's the next issue of the day, and I want to be on cutting edge of whatever is happening in our society and at school. I get to do that at Casco Bay High School."

Matt describes a conversation he had with a colleague who suggested learning more about restorative practices. The conversation later turned into a new Restorative Justice Task Force—a growth endeavor that has benefited Matt and the school. After approaching Derek and the director of Student

Life to express their interest in working on restorative justice practices for the Casco Bay community, Matt and his colleagues received appreciation and encouragement to initiate the work. "It was a typical 'water cooler' conversation," Matt says, "and the majority of those conversations in most workplaces go nowhere. But for us, we were able to put something we feel passionate about together, and it turned into something meaningful." Now overlapping with equity work in the building, the restorative justice efforts have expanded to include staffwide training and new peer mediators for resolving conflicts using restorative justice principles. "There are creative spaces to do new work," Matt adds. "Water cooler conversations get to go places, which is fun."

Becca, in addition to her work on the equity PLC and other school leadership, has many opportunities as a Spanish teacher to serve on district-level committees and to develop her content skills and attend conferences with other EL and world language teachers. As she designed an expedition titled "Heroism in the Face of Political Adversity," Becca teamed with a teacher in Boston at an EL dual-language school. Students from both schools collaborated on activities and assignments related to South American heroes in countries with political unrest. Casco Bay students traveled to Boston to engage in shared experiences with their Boston peers and to unveil a joint publication.

Teachers at Casco Bay value working conditions and learning opportunities that inspire them toward excellence as they grapple with challenging curricula and new ways of thinking about equitable teaching. Susan describes her own sense of empowerment at the school:

> My mom was a principal and kept asking me, "When are you going to become a principal?" And I'm thinking, "I don't have to." I love teaching, and at Casco Bay High School I have full empowerment to be involved in every aspect of the school. So the elements that I would love about being in that leadership role I already have at Casco Bay as a teacher. I am a vision person, and I can be at the table helping to define vision and make decisions.

### Guideline 6: Sustain Excellence by Attending to Staff Wellness

Casco Bay High School has allocated funding for a series of faculty wellness initiatives. These include appointing a faculty "Wellness Czar" to establish healthy opportunities and rituals for teachers, including staff meals at a local restaurant, on-site 10-minute massages, gifts, and lots of formal and informal (and often humorous) faculty team-building, from modeling goofy games crew advisers can use, to weekly faculty memes.

Individual goal setting and coaching from school leaders also takes teachers' physical and mental health into account. For example, as they identify personal growth targets, some teachers—due to personal circumstances such as sick parents or the arrival of a baby—may not be able to take on a "grow" year involving lots of new activities or leadership commitments. In these situations, teachers are encouraged to choose to "deepen" a practice (e.g., differentiating their instruction) that they already have initiated but want to improve. When faculty were faced with the stress and challenges of delivering online and hybrid learning during the COVID-19 crisis, wellness supports for curricular planning, screen-time parameters, and additional connections among faculty became part of an annual teacher learning target.

Every school year ends with a faculty appreciation circle. Each teacher draws the name of a colleague and then fashions a brief tribute and small gift, such as a summer read. The goal is to end the year by recognizing the greatness in each staff member, just as Casco Bay teachers do with students all year long.

### Guideline 7: Cultivate an Adult Culture That Mirrors What You Want to See in Your Students

As the range of successful practices for teachers at work in Casco Bay reveals, schoolwide commitments to "Preserve, Deepen, and Grow" apply to individuals and to the collective, as the entire Casco Bay community rallies to repair inequities and have a say in school practices. Teachers and students tackle hard issues together. As Susan reflects,

> What's happening at the staff level, we're trying to create at the student level. . . . [W]e have to be sure students and faculty are sitting together at almost every table. And all of the ways we talk to each other are the ways we talk to students. And then it's the way students talk to us, and to each other.

Visitors can hear this in the precise and supportive feedback peers give to one another about draft work. Doris Santoro, an education professor at Bowdoin College and a Fellow at the National Education Policy Center, knows the school well. An expert in sources of teacher dissatisfaction and ways to mitigate turnover, she holds Casco Bay up as an exemplary model for her education students. Santoro frequently places and coaches Bowdoin's preservice teachers at the school and, along with a local principal, conducted a site visit as part of the Schools of Opportunity application review process. She notes, "Student and teacher behavior is constantly mirroring each other in their words, actions, and intentions, especially regarding a growth mindset in how to make their school continually better. At Bowdoin, we take a professional culture of ongoing learning and inquiry as a significant consideration when placing our student teachers. Casco Bay is always at the top of our list for this reason."

## CONCLUSION

Treating teachers as professionals pays off for schools and for students; it also pays off for the teachers as employees and as persons. As in all good stories, Casco Bay's lessons endure for those who live them, and the school's teachers express gratitude for the opportunities they have to grow both professionally and personally. According to Matt, he is a better person for working at Casco Bay High School. "On a human level, I'm more thoughtful, more caring, and more committed to doing really hard, necessary work than if I had been had I done something else or been somewhere else," he reflects. "I feel like I'm always growing. I'm a teacher but I'm also a learner. I have so many inspiring people around me every day, from 14-year-olds to 70-year-olds, and I'm learning from all of them. It's a gift."

Becca echoes these sentiments. "I feel very fortunate and I want to come to work every day," Becca says. "It's a really positive place to be in this crazy world we live in."

Susan appreciates the ways that support for relevant, meaningful teacher work at Casco Bay propels teachers toward becoming part of something much bigger:

> Schools are microcosms. Within the larger society, it's easy to feel powerless. But a school building is driven and defined by hope and possibility and transformation and growth, because that's the definition of school, right? We're working to help people grow and transform, so at the end of my day I get to feel like I did something. I am fully empowered all the time, watching our students evolve and watching us evolve as a school. I am playing a role in figuring out the important issues like dismantling inequities. I'm driven by hope and possibility. I feel every day that I'm part of the work that has to happen for our society and our world. And for that I'm just grateful.

Finally, Derek observes, "Perhaps most important, my sense is that the students and adults who experience our community—the inclusivity, the omnidirectional caring, the intentionality, the play, the embracing of difference, the commitment to opportunity for all—spend much of their lives outside of our community being committed and trying to re-create it in their particular context."

## REFERENCES

Allensworth, E., Ponisciak, S., & Mazzeo, C. (2009). *The schools teachers leave: Teacher mobility in Chicago Public Schools.* Consortium on Chicago School Research—University of Chicago. https://eric.ed.gov/?q=ED505882

Berry, B. (2008). Staffing high-needs schools: Insights from the nation's best teachers. *Phi Delta Kappan, 89*(10), 766–781. http://doi.org/10.1177/003172170808901017

Berry, B. (2013). Good schools and teachers for all students: Dispelling myths, facing evidence, and pursuing the right strategies. In P. L. Carter & K. G. Welner (Eds.), *Closing the opportunity gap: What America must do to give every child an even chance* (pp. 181–192). Oxford University Press.

Boyd, D., Grossman, P., Ing, M., Lankford, H., Loeb, S., & Wyckoff, J. (2011). The influence of school administrators on teacher retention decisions. *American Educational Research Journal, 48* (2), 303–333. http://doi.org/10.3102/0002831210380788

Bryk, A., (2010). Organizing schools for improvement. *Phi Delta Kappan, 91*(7), 23–30. http://doi.org/10.1177/003172171009100705

Darling-Hammond, L., Hyler, M. E., & Gardner, M. (2017). *Effective teacher professional development.* Learning Policy Institute. https://learningpolicyinstitute.org/sites/default/files/product-files/Effective_Teacher_Professional_Development_REPORT.pdf

Darling-Hammond, L., & McLaughlin, M. (2011). Policies that support professional development in an era of reform. *Phi Delta Kappan, 92*(6), 81–92. http://doi.org/10.1177/003172171109200622

Donohoo, J., Hattie, J., & Eells, R. (2018). The power of collective efficacy. *Educational Leadership, 75*(6), 40–44. http://www.ascd.org/publications/educational-leadership/mar18/vol75/num06/The-Power-of-Collective-Efficacy.aspx

Gorski, P. (2016) Rethinking the role of "culture" in educational equity: From cultural competence to equity literacy. *Multicultural Perspectives, 18*(4), 221–226, http://doi.org/10.1080/15210960.2016.1228344

Johnson, S. M. (2019). *Where teachers thrive: Organizing schools for success.* Harvard University Press.

Johnson, S. M., Kraft, M., & Papay, J. (2012). How context matters in high-need schools: The effects of teachers' working conditions on their professional satisfaction and their students' achievement. *Teachers College Record, 114*(10), 1–39. https://doi.org/10.1177%2F016146811211401004

Love, B. (2019). *We want to do more than survive: Abolitionist teaching and the pursuit of educational freedom.* Beacon Press.

Sleeter, C. (2012). Confronting the marginalization of culturally responsive pedagogy, *Urban Education, 47*(3), 562–584. http://doi.org/10.1177/0042085911431472

Smith, C. (2017, September 23). James Baldwin's lesson for teachers in a time of turmoil. *The New Yorker.* https://www.newyorker.com/books/page-turner/james-baldwins-lesson-for-teachers-in-a-time-of-turmoil

Sun, M., Penuel, W. R., Frank, K. A., Gallagher, A., & Youngs, P. (2013). Shaping professional development to promote the diffusion of instructional expertise among teachers. *Educational Evaluation and Policy Analysis, 35*(3), 344–369.

# CHAPTER 6

# Clark Street Community School

## A Place for All Students to Live, Learn, and Create

*Jill Gurtner and Julie Mead*

Criterion 6: Meet the Needs of Students With Disabilities in an Environment That Ensures Challenge and Support

I (Jill) remember the day the idea came together. I was out for a run in the quiet of the north woods of Wisconsin. As a school administrator and mother of young children, I knew that time alone was rare, and I often found myself inspired by creative ideas when the opportunities for quiet presented themselves. This particular run and creative brainstorm would prove to be life-altering.

Our school district, a suburban school district near Madison, Wisconsin, serving a predominantly White, socioeconomically middle- to upper-class population, was deep into discussions about moving to an Integrated Comprehensive System (ICS) model (Capper & Frattura, 2008) to improve our programming for all students. An ICS model is grounded in strong instructional design and implementation for inclusion and equitable outcomes. With the requirements of the No Child Left Behind Act, we had begun to disaggregate our data, and not surprisingly to those of us who had worked closely with struggling students, our disaggregated data painted a significantly different picture than our overall data. For years, we had touted student achievement that ranked us among the best school districts in Wisconsin. Disaggregating our data demonstrated clearly that for our students of color, our students living in poverty, and our students with disabilities, the experience in our school district was not at all equivalent to that of their more affluent, nondisabled, White peers. Because these minoritized and marginalized groups represented a small portion of the student population, their outcomes had been masked by the very high achievement of the majority population. As an insider in this system, it was clear to me that we fit Doug Reeves's (2006) definition of a "lucky" school district quite nicely. For a number of reasons, our district attracted predominantly well-educated, well-resourced families whose students performed very well on standardized assessments irrespective of our schools, not necessarily because of them. When forced to look at the data for our students who needed us the most, it was clear that we were not serving them well. The move to an ICS model was part of the plan to improve our responsiveness to students we had been neglecting, including those with special needs.

This chapter introduces a charter school,[1] Clark Street Community School, which arose out of the experiences and lessons of that school district. In this chapter we describe the change processes that Clark Street School, a high school serving about 120 students in grades 9–12, undertook to address disparities in learning as Clark Street's educators reimagined and implemented interesting, personalized, and challenging learning opportunities for their students. While the team designing the school anticipated a population of students that matched the local and national average of 12–15% students with disabilities, several factors led to them serving, and succeeding, with a student population that was closer to 40–50% students with disabilities. Clark Street's story shows us that innovative, rich curriculum centered on student and community interests benefits all students and particularly offers an excellent way to serve special needs students. Clark Street has been recognized as a School of Opportunity for its innovative approaches to learning and notable effectiveness with special needs students, as described in the following criterion.

In an ICS model, a goal is for each school, or program within the school, to have student demographics that match the overall student demographics in the district and to eliminate any schools or programs that are instead designed to serve just a select portion of the population (Capper &

---

**CRITERION 6: MEET THE NEEDS OF STUDENTS WITH DISABILITIES IN AN ENVIRONMENT THAT ENSURES CHALLENGE AND SUPPORT**

The [exemplary] school is distinguished for providing rich, supported learning opportunities for students with special needs. The school has fully resourced programs designed to identify and support students with special needs in the least restrictive learning environment. Only the most severely disabled students are placed in self-contained classes. Inclusion is the norm, and inclusion classes are not low-track classes filled with high-needs learners. The school supports all modifications and provides layers of support for students with special needs. Special education students are actively engaged in the social life of the school.

Frattura, 2008). At the time of the district's adoption of the ICS model, I was the principal of a small alternative high school within the district that had been designed to serve students at risk of not graduating from high school. While this model of identifying students as "at-risk" and creating a separate school for them was in strong opposition to the ICS model, the school had nonetheless experienced a lot of success for many students. The district's desire to move toward an ICS model had me thinking about how we could build on those successes to create a school that served *all* students well, by design.

These past successes at the alternative high school had revealed a few truths. First, these students were quite talented. They simply had not performed in school at a level that was consistent with their ability. Second, students produced their best efforts when the work they were asked to do had a very clear relevance to their lives and to the lives of others they cared about. As discussed later in this chapter, we have applied these lessons to special needs students at Clark Street as well, in contrast to the many special education programs that have historically limited opportunities for richer, authentic learning experiences.

At the school that preceded Clark Street, we had often engaged in visioning conversations that started with some version of "Can you imagine what school could be like if all of our experiences with kids were like the ones we had when we were out in the community doing real work?" The discussions about ICS had now opened the door for us to talk about creating a school that would serve all students, not just those who had been labeled at risk, in a manner that really connected them to things that mattered to them personally. On my run that morning, I made the decision to take this conversation back to the alternative high school staff. If the district was heading in this direction, then it would make the most sense for the pilot-school effort to be led by those of us who had seen the transformational power of connecting even struggling or academically challenged students to relevant learning experiences.

## ORGANIZING THE DREAM

This is how Clark Street Community School (Clark Street) began to take shape. As a staff, we started talking and dreaming. I pitched the idea to district leaders. We held community conversations about the schools that parents and community members dreamed of for all students. Through all of these discussions, the theme remained the same: We had a great idea, and it was hard to believe there were not more schools approaching their work this way. Even the passage of Act 10 in 2011, a Wisconsin law that ultimately removed many protections for teachers and reduced their compensation packages, did not deter the staff from creating our dream school together.

We received a grant to study innovative schools around the country, and we spent a year planning our school prior to opening.

Ultimately, the vision for Clark Street settled around a theme of engagement, grounded in the work of Phil Schlechty (2011). Schlechty observed the participation of students in school and critiqued many of the measures of engagement in use. He found that most of these tools did not measure (and indeed schools did not foster) student engagement at all, but instead simply promoted varying levels of compliance. Schlechty (2011) argued that while compliance certainly had a role in any system, learning in a manner that allows students to retain and transfer the resultant knowledge truly only happened when learners were engaged. He explained that when learners are engaged, they will persist even when the work becomes challenging, since they find personal meaning in doing the work. As such, they are driven by their personal desire to "get it right" rather than simply complete the work for some externally driven reason. We wanted Clark Street Community School to foster engagement rather than compliance. We note in particular that engagement is an effective teaching and learning strategy for all students with special needs (Kennedy & Haydon, 2021; Sethi & Scales, 2020), including many students with special needs (Long et al., 2007). In service of this mission, we drew upon and then modified our original three "pillars" of project-based learning, place-based learning, and democratic education.

Today, Clark Street serves approximately 120 students in grades 9–12. Enrollment is open to any student in the district regardless of disability status, and we serve students with a wide variety of disabilities. A lottery is held if we have more student interest than capacity. While our racial demographics of about 30% students of color match the district demographics, we consistently attract a higher population of students who identify as members of the LGBTQ+ population and students who qualify for financial assistance when compared to the district as a whole.

## Pillar 1: Personalized and Project-Based Learning

We ultimately replaced our former emphasis on project-based learning with personalized learning; we realized that projects were just one way of engaging ideas, and we did not want our pillars to limit students from finding the best way for them to connect with their learning. Importantly, our use of the term "personalized" was not about adaptive computer programs, as the term is used by advocates of digital learning (Martinez, 2001). We rejected this digital conceptualization of personalization, which offers students very little agency over what they learn, the manner in which they learn it, or the method used to demonstrate their understanding. Instead, we committed to starting with an emphasis on giving students as much voice and choice over as many aspects of their educational journey as possible. As students join our school, we ask them to begin thinking about who they are, what they are most passionate about, where they want to be in 5 or 10 years, and what areas they may want to focus on for improvement. Students return to these questions regularly throughout their high school experience and use them to drive decisions about what they learn, how they learn it, and how they demonstrate what they now understand. This is true of all Clark Street students, certainly including our students with disabilities such as Lewis, whose experience we include below. Helping students with disabilities to develop a deep understanding of self and their learning allows them to significantly participate in creating their Individualized Education Plans (Sanderson & Goldman, 2020) and is a critical part of the work of case managers and all educators (Kleinert et al., 2010; Lindstrom et al., 2007).

Lewis, a somewhat shy, quiet African American male who had attended a lot of schools and endured a lot of change in his life, arrived as a 9th-grader. In his transition IEP meeting, the team had highlighted his significant struggles with reading and writing. His passion for social justice and excellence as an orator had only minimally been acknowledged. His parents were full of questions about our unique school design. Lewis, who had aspirations of attending a competitive university and someday running for public office, had heard a presentation on Clark Street and was sure it was the right school for him. His parents were skeptical about whether this relatively new school with no letter grades and a lot of flexibility could provide their talented young son with the structure and support he would need in order to meet his goals. We are all so fortunate they trusted us and trusted him enough to give Clark Street a try.

Lewis is, without question, a rediscovered version of himself because of the opportunities he has had to develop his skills as an independent learner and personalize his learning experience. In his senior year he was able to co-teach a seminar on activism to his peers and received rave reviews. Through the feedback and revision process, he has learned how to effectively communicate his ideas in writing and in oral presentation. The passion he has developed about the power of Clark Street's educational design combined with the craft he has perfected in public presentations put him in position to deliver a kickoff message to a gathering of the entire school district staff at the start of the school year. As he stepped onstage and delivered a flawless, powerful message to an auditorium full of educators to help them see their power to positively impact lives, I cried. I was overcome by the thought of the opportunities he may have missed if he had not advocated for himself as a rising 9th-grader who somehow knew that a personalized, competency-based school with a strong commitment to community was exactly what he needed to thrive as a learner.

## Pillar 2: Place-Based Learning

Place-based learning emphasizes a focus on the communities, both local and global, that students are a part of right now and that frame their real-world learning contexts (Smith, 2002). A place-based learning approach helped us take down the figurative walls that separate schools from the communities in which they are situated and allow students to see that learning takes place all around them, all of the time. It's not something that happens exclusively or even most frequently in schools. This approach also creates opportunities for students to play very real roles as problem solvers, creative thinkers, and laborers working to address problems and maximize opportunities that exist in their communities. For students with disabilities, this approach also helps us better prepare students for transition to postsecondary life (Best et al., 2017; Kauffman & Landrum, 2007; Test et al., 2015).

## Pillar 3: Democratic Education

Our final pillar, democratic education, drives a focus on creating the opportunities for students to engage in the process of designing and maintaining a school environment in which both individual and collective needs are honored (Dewey, 1916). Through opportunities to participate in meaningful decisions within the school and to work together to resolve conflicts when they arise, students feel more connected to the school and develop the skills they must have to learn to express their needs and desires while honoring the needs, desires, and perspectives of others.

We opened our doors to Clark Street in the fall of 2012, driven by a belief that although our idea would be a challenge, we were on the right track. Success, we felt, would certainly follow. We had thrown out many of the conventions that had constrained us as educators and replaced them with ideas that, though not new, were rare in actual practice in high schools. Gone were grades, Carnegie units, courses that focused on discrete content areas, students separated based on their ages, teacher-directed classrooms, administrator-directed schools, punitive and exclusionary discipline, teachers working in isolation, and education contained within the walls of a school. In their place were an interconnected collection of practices deliberately chosen to advance our three pillars:

- Assessments based on self-, peer-, and adult-review and a process of expected revision and improvement for nearly every piece of work
- A set of standards for which students needed to demonstrate proficiency
- The creation of a portfolio demonstrating both growth and best work

- Interdisciplinary learning experiences that often took students into the community or invited the community into the school
- Mixed-age classes
- High levels of student voice and choice in all aspects of school management and individual educational planning
- Restorative practices
- A commitment to keeping students in school and in classes

Yet the path awaiting us was packed with obstacles. Ten years into this crazy experiment, we have learned a great deal. We have experienced incredible transformations of students whose former selves are truly unrecognizable in light of the confident, empowered learners they have become. We have also experienced deep challenges to our vision and our belief in ourselves as competent educators. The journey has been nothing less than extraordinary—at times deeply painful and at others insanely rewarding and reinforcing.

## FROM THEORETICAL APPROACH TO PRACTICAL DESIGN

We based our school design on a firm belief that every individual belongs in our school community and that everyone brings talents, gifts, and personal genius that will enrich our learning community. While this chapter is written to highlight how the practices at Clark Street support the success of students with disabilities, it is critical to keep in mind that the commitment to designing instructional and systemic practices in a manner in which *all* students will find success is one of the most important contributors to success with students with disabilities. As research has supported for years, we have found that solid instructional design, which begins with fostering strong relationships and a deep understanding of the talents and needs of all students, clearly does lead to success for learners with disabilities (Murray & Naranjo, 2008; Murray & Pianta, 2007). While Clark Street is open to all learners in our district, we have seen a consistent pattern of higher levels of interest from students with disabilities (with our student body ranging from 30–50% served with IEPs or 504 plans, as compared to approximately 10–12% for the rest of our school district). Our most common disability areas are autism, emotional/behavioral disturbance, specific learning disability, and other health impairments—particularly related to attention, anxiety, and depression. This reality has challenged us to hone our practices related to universal instructional design, and it has demonstrated how effective this can be, even in a setting where the percentage of students with special needs is disproportionately high.

All of our seminars (which schools typically call classes) are fully inclusive and designed in a manner that allows every learner to belong and thrive in the learning environment. One of our long-term goals for all learners is that they be able to identify and ask for what they need from a learning environment. It is our constant goal and focus to create a school environment that can support all of these needs. We have accomplished this ambition by focusing heavily on universal design of instruction that is highly differentiated and that offers a great deal of opportunities for personalization of learning. As we create learning partnerships with students to help them become more independent, we are able to support them in identifying what they need from the environment, how they best learn, and how they can most effectively demonstrate their learning and understanding. We support our students with IEPs in actively engaging as members of their IEP teams, and we prepare them to ultimately lead their IEP meetings.

Along with these commitments, we work to consistently create and reinforce a culture of belonging in which everyone develops a deep appreciation for the power of a diverse learning community. We teach students how to support their fellow learners and how to work effectively and advocate for their needs within a community. Our special education staff work to support all other staff in designing learning environments in an inclusive manner and assisting in making modifications to curriculum, while supporting all learners in developing the skills they need to be successful in our setting. As a result, students and staff form deep, genuine connections with one another both academically and socially.

In order to create this type of learning environment, the Clark Street school design is driven by five key tenets, which frame the remainder of this chapter. As we walk through these tenets, please note that they were not designed specifically for students with special needs. Rather, they were designed to benefit all students but deliberately inclusive of those with special needs.

### Tenet 1: Full Integration

The foremost tenet at Clark Street is the full integration of all students in all contexts coupled with the commitment to differentiation and thoughtful planning of universal instruction in order to ensure that all students can find success in the classroom where the instruction is delivered. In this model, our staff certified in special education serve as experts supporting the system design, the educators, and the students to ensure that our universal design is as inclusive and accessible as possible. As they co-serve with our other staff, they are always working to improve the experience not only in the classroom, but in the system as a whole. The development and constant iteration and improvement of standard operating procedures, as we find strategies and approaches that are most effective, has helped us move from pockets of success to systems that support success for all. With this commitment to universal design and support, our practice of designing our learning experiences around highly relevant and engaging content can have the maximum impact on engagement. When all students are supported in a manner that allows them to engage fully and bring their unique talents and perspectives to the experience, it truly creates an environment in which everyone can be fully honored as the unique learner they are.

## Tenet 2: Interdisciplinary Learning

A second, and related, tenet is the commitment to offering students high-interest, interdisciplinary learning experiences with ample opportunities to produce and share new knowledge with an authentic audience in a personalized manner. Students select seminars that allow for deep and individualized exploration. One successful example is "Colonize or Rehab," where students wrestle with the big question of "Should we rehabilitate this planet or work to figure out how to colonize another planet?" Students ultimately pick a personal project of interest to research and share their learning in a concise, tangible manner with the community at our Exhibition Night or our Clark Street Market. The latter practice, Clark Street Market, showcases products designed by students and inspired by our school garden. They create a full marketing plan, determine a production plan and price point, and then sell their wares to the community. These practices provide students with opportunities to see their power as learners, producers, and contributors. Through such experiences, they come to deeply understand their own sense of agency and their interdependence with the community around them. For students with disabilities, who have often been marginalized in school and made to feel as if they could not meaningfully contribute, these experiences, which by design ask each student to personalize their learning experience around a collective goal or concept, ensure that the unique talents, perspectives, and dispositions of each learner contribute to the whole in deep and meaningful ways.

## Tenet 3: Community Partnerships

A third critical aspect of our design is a commitment to learning partnerships. Much of our early design work was inspired by the work of Shep Zeldin and others around youth adult partnerships (Zeldin et al., 2012). While much of their research had been done in community settings such as 4-H, community centers, and youth representation in local government, the applicability of the concepts and structures in their model was clearly aligned with our vision for our school.

Inspired by Zeldin's findings of positive outcomes, we created structures that ensure that youth and adults have the opportunity to learn from one another on a regular basis. Roles within groups honor that all individuals have unique talents to offer. They also recognize that each group member's learning advances the effectiveness of the group at doing our work in a way that gives every person an opportunity to employ their strengths on a regular basis. Students know that they are expected to be very active participants in their educational journey and to ask for what they need. Staff, whether certified teachers or teaching assistants, know that our goal is to create a consistent, predictable system that allows us to support and respond to the needs, requests, and passions of each learner.

A critical piece of this work has been shifting staff understanding from one in which they were independent contractors working to hone their personal craft to members of an interdependent but empowered team that includes other staff, students, and families. Reinforced by Hattie's research (Donohoo et al., 2018; Hattie & Zierer, 2018) on the impact that collective teacher/adult efficacy has on student outcomes, we have thoughtfully and collaboratively designed communication systems and standard operating procedures to ensure predictability, while allowing for maximum flexibility and responsiveness to staff and student needs and passions based on shared beliefs rather than on inflexible rules and policies.

### Tenet 4: Formative Assessment

An additional critical tenet in our design is our emphasis on formative assessment. These practices help students become more independent in their learning while recognizing the power of interdependence in learning (Israel et al., 2018; Kiely, 2018). We centered the school's assessment practices on a common set of rubrics in reading, writing, numeracy, communication, and research. These rubrics provide all learners with clear, transparent guidelines related to what is needed to do high-quality work. Students enter the work and the formative processes wherever they are and are credited for working through a supported process of improvement. Feedback is personalized and gives students specific suggestions for improvement.

Unlike the typical use of grades, the feedback they receive is not based on an arbitrary benchmark that ranks them against others their age. Instead, the feedback tracks their progress with specific, identifiable skills they work to master. Each piece of work students create goes through a series of feedback and revision cycles where students review their own work against a standard, receive feedback from peers, and receive targeted suggestions from teachers. Through this process, students begin to internalize a few key concepts:

- Our work can always get better.
- Honest, constructive feedback is a gift.

- Our work gets better when we share it with others and seek to understand deeply how they received what we have created. As the creator/author, we retain the right to determine in what ways we will adjust our work based on that feedback.
- We can learn and grow through deep engagement in a single project where we commit significant time and energy to the final product and through a series of faster, less formal iterations that allow us to take multiple perspectives.
- A strong design for learning makes each of us unique and more fully ourselves and helps each of us continue to hone our unique way of sharing our learning with others.

## Tenet 5: Restorative Culture

The final critical tenet is a strong commitment to creating a climate and culture that is inclusive of all and "safe enough" to allow all to learn and grow within a diverse community. We adopted a philosophy based in restorative practices as a part of the creation of the school and quickly added a clear commitment to not using any exclusionary discipline unless there was a clear and imminent threat to safety. At the root of the creation of this restorative culture are two beliefs: that when we are in community together, there will inherently be conflict, and that deeply engaging in learning is at its core an emotional, tension-filled act. In order to effectively manage and even harness the energy of these two realities, we must actively teach, reinforce, and support the social-emotional skills and the interpersonal communication skills that are needed to be your best in a learning community.

Our approach employs the regular use of circles and a circle protocol in both academic and social contexts along with structured supports and strategies to help all members of our community repair harm when it occurs and return to the community strengthened. In doing so, we honor that each struggle, whether personal or communal, is an opportunity for growth and that part of our obligation as an educational institution is to support all learners in the development of these critical skills. For many of our students with disabilities, their struggles to regulate their emotions or to communicate effectively have had significantly negative impacts on their ability to stay in a learning environment, much less to engage deeply in learning. We work to honor that we all, no matter our disability status, struggle at times when interacting with others and become disregulated when pushed out of our comfort zones as learners. By designing a system to support all of us in improving our skills in these areas, we create space for students with significant struggles to participate fully in our community. The story of Kala, one of our 9th-grade students, illustrates how this helps students.

Grace, struggling with anxiety steeped in a competitive mentality, benefited from our focus on personalized learning and assessment as a process. Grace is a highly intelligent, passionate young lady who also suffers from debilitating anxiety. After a year and a half in a traditional high school setting, she had become so paralyzed by her need to perform "perfectly" that she simply could not function. As she and her parents became increasingly concerned about her mental health, they began to desperately seek support and solutions. Because she had always been a highly successful student and because the environment in the traditional school was so deeply steeped in a competitive mentality, her mother's attempt to advocate for her was treated as if the parents were part of the problem. In addition, Grace's very real and dramatically increasing mental health struggles were misinterpreted by school staff as manipulative. When she was finally diagnosed with a disability based on her mental health needs, she was suicidal and struggling in very significant ways.

When she first arrived at Clark Street, we set a clear goal of simply attending, participating as much as possible while she was in school, and then practicing leaving the stressors of school behind once she walked out the door. Because it was so clear that she was highly intelligent, our first goal was to help her stabilize and begin to reconnect with her sense of self, a task much more important than the feedback she received on assignments. We took advantage of the school's flexible demands and limited summative assessment, setting aside time where there were no expectations for any work to be completed outside of class. We then progressed from simple attendance to encouraging her to work at home when her mental health allowed, but to stop as soon as the patterns of burden and stress began to appear. Our mantra of "ask for what you need" was a regular one with Grace and critical in her path to becoming an independent learner. All this was made possible by the design of our school, where no grades are given and learning is always a process of building on students' strengths, identifying opportunities for growth, and giving students agency over where they will focus their improvement efforts.

Over time, as she regained her trust in herself and in the adults around her, Grace began to blossom. Her meek presence was gradually replaced with a confident demeanor, a quirky sense of humor, and an infectious laugh. She also became a fierce warrior for the development of better mental health supports in our system. As is so often the case, she was able to find her voice and confidence as a learner through our process of feedback and revision. Experiencing the power of sharing her work as a means of creating work *she* was proud of rather than producing for a grade empowered her to truly shine. As she now explores her options for postsecondary education and a career, she is fueled by a confidence and a sense of herself as a contributor and leader. She has consistently jumped into leadership opportunities and has become increasingly comfortable being vulnerable in order to grow and to become her best version of herself. The young woman who appeared to be afraid of her own shadow and struggled to advocate for herself in even the smallest of ways is now a passionate advocate for all marginalized populations and has a very clear sense of her agency and her ability to make a difference.

## CHALLENGES

### Internalized Low Academic Expectations

We could have never imagined the extreme negative impact of our students' earlier school experiences—the 9 years prior to arriving at Clark Street. Many of these students had spent those years looking for ways to survive school, and they had deeply internalized a message that only some individuals could be successful learners. And they were convinced they were among those who could not. Many of them had no experience with the productive struggle that was required for learning and had little tolerance for persisting in the type of challenging situations we all need to learn. They believed to their core that there was no chance of success, so the necessary struggle held no promise for them.

I have a vivid memory of one brilliant young man with a learning disability who patiently explained to me in one of our early years at Clark Street, "You know this isn't how it works. I am never going to do any work. I know if I sit here long enough, someone else is going to do the work for me. That's how it has always worked." He had the awareness and verbal capacity to give voice to what we were seeing exhibited all over the building: students simply refusing to engage in the production of any work because they had spent the previous 8 or 9 years learning avoidance as a method of survival and because they had no sense that the game of school was one they had any chance of winning.

This painful realization forced us to reassess our model, which was heavily based on a belief that if we created high-interest opportunities, gave students a great deal of choice and autonomy, and continued to invite them in, students would naturally begin to choose to engage. In hindsight, the naiveté of this belief represents well how deeply we had bought into a myth of traditional schools offering opportunities for students and students simply choosing to pick up these opportunities at varying rates. What we recognized instead was clear evidence of a system that was, by design, training large groups of students to accept that they were not learners and did not have meaningful gifts to contribute to their community or their world. These students were forced to attend schools each day where their unique talents and

Fireball. That is the only word I have to describe this amazing young woman. As a 9th-grader, Kala was already an amazing social justice warrior, but her academic struggles and her tumultuous previous experiences as an African American in a predominantly White community both in and out of school had fueled an anger in her that she was often unable to manage effectively. Her responses to problems were often disruptive and even violent—the sort of actions that would yield suspensions in most schools today. But we engaged, instead.

I remember sitting with Kala on far too many occasions processing a situation where she had again lost her cool. In these times, she consistently had an ability to assess what had triggered her and how she could have handled it differently in order to get the result she was looking for without any violence. And yet, the pattern persisted. I remember learning about how when young people are feeling powerless in situations where they are trying to maintain some level of control, the options of flight or freeze are not really even on the table because they cannot face the loss of power that not responding would represent. This was Kala. Time and time again, she would seem to switch automatically to fight mode and then shortly thereafter be able to logically process the whole event and offer up far more productive potential options.

Adding to this tendency to respond with aggression were some very real academic struggles and a deep-seated belief that she could not be successful as a student. For Kala, we found our entry in the fact that she was able to form strong relationships with adults very quickly. She seemed to find comfort in the fact that adults tended to be more predictable in their behavior, and most of us were genuinely able to see beyond the anger to the amazing human who was waiting to show herself. Over time, we collectively honored that her anger was justifiable given what she had experienced and that it had, in fact, served in some protective capacity for her. And yet, it was also destroying her from within and limiting her potential in very tangible ways. The more she let us in, the more we were able to set up escape strategies and create productive outlets for her passion for social justice and the rights of victims. Eventually, as our system supported her and she was able to experience enough small successes, she started seeing the possibility of being successful as a learner as well. She began seeking help and allowing adults to push her academically in ways that had not been possible previously. As her skills grew, so did her confidence. Ever so slowly, her need to approach the world with fists clenched began to ease.

Her experience with us culminated with a trip to New York City as a part of one of our seminars. For her, this opportunity to see communities full of life infused with the energy and passion of people of color who were thriving was incredibly powerful. She returned to us full of a far more positive energy, power, and optimism and ready to persist to complete her high school requirements and take on whatever came her way next.

gifts went unrecognized, and they came to define themselves based only on their limitations. The lucky ones were those who had found spaces outside of school where they could deeply engage and find success. Yet, when we attempted to connect to these experiences of engagement, we frequently encountered astonished disbelief. Our students did not believe us when we tried to convince them that school should be engaging and that the best learning takes place when learners are engaged in meaningful struggle. We therefore had to restructure to ensure students found success, and we had to intensify our efforts to help students develop an identity of self as a successful learner. Shawn's story illustrates these points.

The Christensen Institute (n.d.) has developed a "Jobs to Be Done Theory" that helps organizations design for success by clearly identifying the "jobs" that customers are hiring a product to do. They have identified two of the jobs students "hire" school for: (1) to make learning progress, and (2) to connect socially with others.[2] School was not meeting the expectation for ensuring that students felt as if they were making progress, so they were not "hiring" school for this job. Our system redesign had to ensure that we were fulfilling this job if we wanted to help students become successful learners. Our approach needed to ensure that students were having success and then help them see what they had done to create this success so that they could replicate it on a consistent basis. In order to do this "job" for all students, we needed to be clear in our systems so that all staff could provide support in a consistent manner.

### Redesigning Systems for Inclusive Instruction

This challenge of redesigning our system in order to ensure that all students would become independent learners who could find success was exacerbated by sheer numbers. While our vision for the school was based on an ICS model and school classes with average proportions of students with disabilities (Capper & Frattura, 2008), the efforts at the district level to make the shift to integrating children in this way had fallen apart. The leader who spearheaded the goal had left, and the infrastructure to implement such a significant change had never been built. Ultimately, this lack of structural supports resulted in many of the district's schools failing to make the necessary changes in instructional practices and systemic redesign to support inclusion of their students with special needs. This problem resulted in a flood of students with disabilities and their families looking for something different, and they came to Clark Street in significant numbers. As noted earlier, while the district's proportion of students with disabilities was in the 10–12% range, Clark Street consistently hovered just above 40% and sometimes neared 50% of our student population.

Unfortunately, many of these families did not come with an understanding of our model or our approach. They had simply been told by

Shawn had an impact on us as soon as he arrived. He possessed an absolutely magnetic personality and was willing to step in and serve in any way possible. It didn't take long, however, for it to become clear that he was using these amazing social skills to mask some very deep insecurities about himself as a learner and to compensate for some very real mental health struggles. When we talked to Shawn in 9th and 10th grade, he would tell us matter-of-factly that he simply didn't write, and he seemed to have very little desire to change the status quo. This mindset presented a bit of a problem in a school that is competency-based and where graduation is totally dependent on the creation of artifacts to demonstrate learning. He would also fall into patterns of attendance where he would miss large chunks of school and then have to struggle to reconnect academically after extended periods of absences. Often, the snowball would get too big, and his team would be triaging to get him stable again.

For Shawn, things began to change when he got deeply involved in a seminar on biking and entrepreneurship. Shawn was part of a team that dreamed of having a functioning bike shop at our school where students could repair bikes. This ragtag team worked to develop their viable product and grabbed any spot they could find within the building to set up shop. Then someone planted a seed of the possibility of building an actual bike shed behind the school, and Shawn and company set out to figure out how to make this happen. Their idea was given a huge boost when the district leadership listened and committed several thousand dollars to the construction of the shed. Shawn and a small committed group were on a mission to get their dream built.

As Shawn found his passion in this project, something else was changing as well. The project provided a spark for Shawn to see a personal reason for digging into writing and other academic skills he had been avoiding. Just as we had seen other students find a spark and use it to power their way through the completion of their graduation requirements at a rapid pace, Shawn thoughtfully and confidently chose to spend an additional year with us in order to continue to learn how to be successful as a learner. In his final 2 years with us, Shawn became one of our best ambassadors. It was incredibly validating to hear him talk about his transformation as a learner and confidently explain to anyone who would listen how enjoyable it was to engage in the hard work of learning once you were receiving the support you needed and were able to work from your strengths and passions.

Shawn left his mark because of the power of his story and his journey of becoming an independent learner. Seeing the superb bike shed he worked so hard to make a reality in the school's backyard is a powerful reminder of how far every learner can come with the right conditions.

well-meaning staff members at other schools that they should go to Clark Street because it is small and students get a lot of attention. This message set the students, their families, and our staff up for struggle from the time students arrived. These students had deeply internalized a message that they were not capable of success on their own throughout their elementary and middle school years. They then chose to enroll in our school because they would "get a lot of attention," which was in direct tension with our goal of helping all students become independent learners who deeply knew themselves and had the skills to successfully navigate any system. Consequently, we now had a dual struggle. First, we worked to continue redesigning our system to meet our deep commitment to serving all students and ensuring that all students become independent learners. Second, we faced the challenge of figuring out how to push back on the district-level systemic issues that were perpetuating a message that was directly opposed to the vision that drove our original creation of the school.

One of the most powerful supports for our efforts came from Zaretta Hammond's (2015) book, *Culturally Responsive Teaching and the Brain: Promoting Authentic Engagement and Rigor Among Culturally and Linguistically Diverse Students*. Her work helped clarify how the design of our traditional, compliance-based system was leading to the disparate results we were seeing and the high level of dependency that many of our students were exhibiting. Further, her work on designing systems for the development of learning partnerships helped us come together as a staff around practices that would ensure that we were able to build learning partnerships with all our students.

Our study of Hattie's work (Donohoo et al., 2018; Hattie & Zierer, 2018) on the power of collective efficacy and a strong belief in the ability of all learners had established our driving belief. Hammond's (2015) work gave us the language to maximize our collective efficacy around the goal of learner independence and interdependence. Rooted in this understanding, staff were able to take many of the tools, strategies, and approaches we had been using and greatly accelerate their effectiveness and impact because we now had the consistency of understanding and practice to ensure that students were hearing the same messages from everyone within the community.

First and foremost, the adults in the building now had a shared understanding of why our efforts to help students form strong, empowering relationships with us and with each other was so critical to deep learning. Hammond's (2015) formula of "Rapport + Alliance leading to Cognitive Insight" helped us move out of the false dichotomy of staff being either likable or rigorous. If we were going to ensure that all students developed a strong sense of personal cognitive insight, they needed to trust us, and once we had that trust, we could walk alongside them as they engaged in the cognitive struggle that was necessary to learn deeply. For many of our students with disabilities, there was simply no way they were going to take the risks needed to learn deeply and improve their confidence and their skills if they didn't have a strong, supportive, empowering relationship with an adult.

As the adults got more consistent with this approach, another even more powerful change began to take place. Once students were directly taught emotional regulation, communication, and problem-solving skills, they began to use those skills with one another. Nothing has been more powerful in shifting our culture than getting to the point where we had a critical mass of students who understood the collective power they had to create a deeply engaged learning community. The community agreements, which we had always had; the circles we had been using; and the consistent social emotional language and curriculum we had recently adopted—all of that now all had a clear connection to our goal of creating a system where deep learning was expected for all and by all. Table 6.1 demonstrates those approaches and their impacts on students with disabilities.

## Developing Clear, Consistent Practices

In ways that likely would have seemed counterintuitive when we started this journey, it became crystal-clear that the path to learner independence and interdependence through personalization was paved by being as consistent as possible in many of our key practices. In addition to working to become highly consistent in our development of strong relationships with and between students, we needed to continue to get even more consistent in our instructional approaches. Yes, the idea of personalized learning and students' greater autonomy over path, pace, and outcomes was appealing. But it was also clear that too many options and too much flexibility was a stressor that worked against learning and did so in a disproportionately negative manner for our students who had struggled the most historically.

This realization brought a clarity of focus to our efforts to standardize classroom practices and procedures and to commit to collaboration among staff—all framed around our shared rubrics, feedback, and assessment practices. Our efforts to use these tools and practices much more intentionally, to ensure that learners are getting consistent messages and seeing consistent successful practices, have led to a clarity about who we are and what we believe as a community. As a leader, this goal of consistency has pushed me to lead through a set of explicit guiding beliefs, creating space to regularly review our practices and support tools, and ensuring that staff have meaningful time to talk, plan, create, and assess together. We must all be very clear about the individual and collective "why" for our work, and we must also have the skills and strategies to challenge and support one another when we see someone behaving in a manner that does not align with these beliefs.

**Table 6.1. Clark Street Strategies for Success for All Learners**

| Universal strategy | Application and impact for students with disabilities |
|---|---|
| Designing for full inclusion: Everyone belongs and is encouraged to bring their full self to school every day. | Students are part of a community that supports all learners in knowing and advocating for themselves while honoring the needs, passions, and lived experiences of others. This creates the space for students with disabilities to see their gifts and understand their limitations. Special needs students are fully integrated in seminars (classes) and all aspects of the curriculum and school culture. Differentiated instruction in all seminars (classes) allows multiple entry points for students. Our certified special education teachers serve as resources to all of our educators to help ensure that instruction is designed in a manner that is accessible to all learners when it is delivered. All special educators serve in a combination of co-teaching, consulting, and direct service roles throughout their day. |
| Fostering the development of learner agency: Know your needs and ask for what you need. | Supporting our learners with disabilities in developing a deep sense of self and the skills needed to advocate for themselves is a significant part of our work. It is our goal that the student will lead their team meetings before they leave us. |
| Collective adult efficacy: By working to our collective strengths, we best serve *all* learners. | While a case manager holds the ultimate responsibility for ensuring that a student is receiving the appropriate services and supports, students know that every adult is a resource, and all adults know that they are supported by a team of committed individuals. |
| Standard operating procedures: Making many things routine and predictable in all environments in the school frees up learning capacity for all. | Predictable routines, clear instructional goals, and systems and practices that are the same in all settings help students with disabilities focus their energy and attention on learning. |
| Asset-based approach/ emphasis on feedback and revision: Highlight what learners can do, and use this to support them in the productive struggle required for learning. | All of our learners are recognized first and foremost for what they *can* do and what they bring to our community. For students with disabilities, keeping the emphasis on their strengths and making the fact transparent that everyone has struggles of some sort helps them to see their potential. |

*(continued)*

**Table 6.1. Clark Street Strategies for Success for All Learners (*continued*)**

| Universal strategy | Application and impact for students with disabilities |
| --- | --- |
|  | Formative assessments provide focus on strengths and paths to improvement. |
| Learning happens everywhere and should be shared: We learn best when the learning matters to us and those we care about. | Taking down the limitations of the traditional school experience opens up so many more opportunities for learners with disabilities to find their passions and their strengths. Our place-based, community-oriented model gives students the opportunity to experience learning in new ways and to share what they have learned in authentic, impactful ways. |

When we reach a critical level of clarity and consistency in these areas, we can then empower each person within our community to make the decisions and ask for the support they need in order to thrive as a learner. Nowhere is this more critical than with our students with disabilities who have rarely experienced the system as something that could empower them as learners.

## CONCLUSION

Each of the students highlighted here, along with so many others, grew and ultimately thrived at Clark Street Community School. In so doing, they taught themselves about the power of ideas and learning, and they taught school staff that their challenges are our challenges. We believe that the students who attend Clark Street are better for the experience, but perhaps just as importantly we are a better school because of what we learn from each student who gives us a chance. A school thrives when it is centered around student engagement and dedicated to student growth through personalized learning, place-based learning, and democratic education.

As we enter year 11, we are now seeing the results of our efforts even in the metrics of standardized testing. Two years ago, our average ACT score for students with disabilities was higher than the average of the students without disabilities in our school. In the 2020–2021 school year, when our students took the ACT on their first day of returning to in-person instruction, our percentage of students reaching the college and career readiness benchmark for reading far exceeded the state average. We are excited to be sharing what we have learned with others in our district and beyond. Clark Street Community School proves the transformative power of trusting student voices and choices and demonstrates the transformative learning that such opportunities provide to student and staff alike. With thoughtful, inclusive instructional design, we truly can create schools in which everyone thrives.

## NOTES

1. Clark Street is what Wisconsin calls an "Instrumentality Charter School," which involves a closer connection to the authorizing school district than is seen with noninstrumentality charters. For instance, Clark Street staff are employed by our school district and are eligible for the state retirement system. The district also shares our responsibility to provide special education services and auxiliary aides.

2. At Clark Street, we recognize that students, as well as their parents and society, also ask schools to address needs around other areas, such as safety, health, morality, kindness, citizenship, and socioemotional development. But we still find the Christensen Institute idea to be helpful.

## REFERENCES

Best, M., MacGregor, D., & Price, D. (2017). Designing for diverse learning: Case study of place-based learning in design and technologies pre-service teacher education. *Australian Journal of Teacher Education, 42*(3), 91–106. https://ro.ecu.edu.au/ajte/vol42/iss3/6/

Capper, C. A., & Frattura, E. M. (2008). Meeting the needs of students of all abilities: How leaders go beyond inclusion. Corwin.

Christensen Institute. (n.d.). *Jobs to be done.* https://www.christenseninstitute.org/jobs-to-be-done/?gclid=Cj0KCQiAs5eCBhCBARIsAEhk4r60-UcTs6y9hfX72tQdFrXL_vil_MtfP9XVXwls3davfyIyPtO77F4aAqNOEALw_wcB

Dewey, J. (1916). *Democracy and education.* Free Press.

Donohoo, J., Hattie, J. A. C., & Eells, R. (2018). The power of collective efficacy. *Educational Leadership, 75*(6), 40–44.

Hammond, Z. (2015). *Culturally responsive teaching and the brain: Promoting authentic engagement and rigor among culturally and linguistically diverse students.* Corwin.

Hattie, J. A. C., & Zierer, K. (2018). *Ten mindframes for visible learning: Teaching for success.* Routledge.

Israel, M., Ray, M. J., Maa, W. C., Jeong, G. K., Lee, C. E., Lash, T., & Do, V. (2018). School-embedded and district-wide instructional coaching in K-8 computer science: Implications for including students with disabilities. *Journal of Technology and Teacher Education, 26*(3), 471–501.

Kauffman, J. M., & Landrum, T. J. (2007). Educational service interventions and reforms. In J. W. Jacobson, J. A. Mulick, & J. Rojahn (Eds.), *Handbook of intellectual and developmental disabilities: Issues on clinical child* psychology (pp. 173–188). Springer. https://doi.org/10.1007/0-387-32931-5_9

Kennedy, A. M., & Haydon, T. (2021). Forming and sustaining high-quality student-teacher relationships to reduce minor behavioral incidents. *Intervention in School and Clinic, 56*(3), 141–147. http://doi.org/10.1177/1053451220942197

Kiely, M. T. (2018). Exemplary teachers' understandings of writing instruction for students with disabilities included in secondary language arts classes: It's a beautiful struggle. *Exceptionality Education International, 28*(3), 122–141.

Kleinert, J. O., Harrison, E. M., Fisher, T. L., & Kleinert, H. L. (2010). "I can" and "I did"—Self-advocacy for young students with developmental disabilities. *Teaching Exceptional Children, 43*(2), 16–26.

Lindstrom, L., Paskey, J., Dickinson, J., Doren, B., Zane, C., & Johnson, P. (2007). Voices from the field: Recommended transition strategies for students and school staff. *Journal for Vocational Special Needs Education, 29*(2), 4–15.

Long, L., MacBlain, S., & MacBlain, M. (2007). Supporting students with dyslexia at the secondary level: An emotional model of literacy. *Journal of Adolescent & Adult Literacy, 51*(2), 124–134.

Martinez, M. (2001). Key design considerations for personalized learning on the web. *Educational Technology & Society, 4*(1), 26–40.

Murray, C., & Naranjo, J. (2008). Poor, black, learning disabled, and graduating: An investigation of factors and processes associated with school completion among high-risk urban youth. *Remedial and Special Education, 29*, 145–160.

Murray, C., & Pianta, R. C. (2007). The importance of teacher-student relationships for adolescents with high incidence disabilities. *Theory Into Practice, 46*(2), 105–112. http://doi.org/10.1080/00405840701232943

Reeves, D. B. (2006). *The learning leader: How to focus school improvement for better results.* ASCD.

Sanderson, K. A., & Goldman, S. E. (2020). A systematic review and meta-analysis of interventions used to increase adolescent IEP meeting participation. *Career Development and Transition for Exceptional Individuals, 43*(3), 157–168. https://doi.org/10.1177%2F2165143420922552

Schlechty, P. (2011). *Engaging students: The next level of working on the work.* Wiley.

Sethi, J., & Scales, P. D. (2020). Developmental relationships and school success: How teachers, parents and friends affect educational outcomes and what actions students say matter most. *Contemporary Educational Psychology, 63*, 101904.

Smith, G. A. (2002). Place-based education: Learning to be where we are. *Phi Delta Kappan, 83*(8), 584–594.

Test, D. W., Bartholomew, A., & Bethune, L. (2015). What high school administrators need to know about secondary transition evidence-based practices and predictors for students with disabilities. *NASSP Bulletin, 99*(3), 254–273. http://doi.org/10.1177/0192636515602329

Zeldin, S., Bestul, L., & Powers, J. (2012). *Youth-adult partnerships in evaluation (Y-AP/E): A resource guide for translating research into practice.* ACT for Youth Center of Excellence, Cornell University.

# CHAPTER 7

# A Holistic Approach to Learning and Development

## Shifting Paradigms One School at a Time

*Kristen P. Goessling, Kate Somerville,*
*Adam York, and Kimberly Grayson*

Criterion 7: Provide Students With Needed Additional Services and
Supports, Including Mental and Physical Health Services

The Schools of Opportunity recognition program includes a criterion designed to assess the types of additional services and supports a school offers, such as those targeting mental and physical health. Our understanding of the criterion description builds on research showing that learning and emotional well-being are deeply related, and there are things schools can do to mitigate the negative impacts of trauma and adverse experiences (Craig, 2015; Plumb et al., 2016; Teicher et al., 2003; Terrasi & De Galarce, 2017).

Unfortunately, many schools in the United States fail to provide students and families with access to essential supports and services to ensure that all students have what they need to learn and thrive. Some schools do not have basic support services such as counselors or nurses. Often, even in schools considered adequate with support personnel in place, those staff are overstretched in their duties and unable to serve all students. In contrast, well-resourced schools have enough support staff to meet students' physical and mental health concerns and to address pressing needs.

This criterion points to schools that go above and beyond "adequate" as they integrate supports and services into the ethos of the schooling experience by providing comprehensive resources to the entire school community to ensure that everyone has what they need to survive and thrive. This chapter features a School of Opportunity, Dr. Martin Luther King, Jr. Early College (DMLK) in Denver, Colorado, that offers students an array

CRITERION 7: PROVIDE STUDENTS WITH ADDITIONAL NEEDED SERVICES AND
SUPPORTS, INCLUDING MENTAL AND PHYSICAL HEALTH SERVICES

"The [exemplary] school has a comprehensive program that meets the physical and mental health, eye care, dental care and nutrition needs of the students and/or their families. Many services are delivered within the school.

"Accessing offsite services is also seamless, with transportation and communication between staff and external providers. Teams who provide such services meet regularly to develop comprehensive plans to address student needs. This might also include connections to other public and/or social service organizations that provide housing, legal, or clothing assistance."

of integrated services and practices as an exemplar of Criterion 7. DMLK's work illustrates the transformative possibilities of schools that place the care of students, as whole people, at the center of education and schooling.

In this volume we highlight two criteria that we argue are closely interwoven: (1) comprehensive services, including mental health; and (2) culturally sustaining and humanizing curriculum and pedagogy. This chapter explores why robust services and especially professional mental health care are so necessary in today's schools, what can be done to improve these services, and how the team at DMLK has answered that call. The next chapter describes what it means to enact a humanizing approach to curriculum and pedagogy using DMLK as an illustrative example.

We begin this chapter by introducing DMLK's holistic approach to education and by providing an overview of the school community and some of its services. Next, we situate DMLK's work in contemporary context and national trends. Finally, we present DMLK's holistic approach in three sections organized by additional categories of supports and targeted services provided to students: (1) oppression and mental health, (2) climate and culture, and (3) community partnerships. Each section integrates relevant research with the stories and examples from the school. We conclude with a brief summary and transition to the next chapter that extends this conversation with attention to DMLK's ongoing culturally relevant curricular and pedagogical work.

## TAKING A HOLISTIC APPROACH

In the last several decades, there has been a significant shift in education away from a myopic focus on students' mind/cognitive development toward a more encompassing and holistic view of students. This broader view considers all aspects of the student's individual health and development as interrelated with the contextual layers in which they are embedded, such as family, peer groups, school, neighborhood, culture, and institutions. This perspective considers students' learning and development as situated in a particular sociocultural context and mediated by social relationships. In other words, education and schooling do not begin and end with academics or learning objectives; instead, they also include relationships with students who understand how they come to be learners in their particular learning spaces and within their communities (Osher et al., 2020).

A holistic approach requires a paradigm shift away from thinking about the purpose of education as academic achievement toward thinking about students holistically, with academic growth as one critical piece. Questions to spark this paradigm shift might include: What does it feel like when a school treats students as family? What community assets and supports could enhance our school? What do students enjoy, need, and want for their schooling experience? What aren't we addressing? Which people and programs can help students thrive in and beyond the classroom? Principal Kimberly Grayson coauthored this chapter with researchers who investigate the role and impact of physical and mental services for students. When Grayson considers the above questions in consultation with students and staff, she does so with a limited discretionary budget. Yet she has designed a school that weaves vital supports throughout the diverse student and school community.

DMLK serves students in grades 6–12 composed of 61.2% Hispanic/Latinx students and 25% Black students, with 80% of students receiving free or reduced-price lunch. DMLK is geographically located in far northeast Denver about 15 miles from the city center in the area known as Green Valley Ranch, which is separated from other parts of the city by major freeways. While it is part of Denver Public Schools (DPS), the distance from Denver's central core means that students at DMLK are on an island relative to their peers in DPS. That is especially true for access to social service providers and resources, which are more readily accessible across other regions of the city. More specifically, there are no mental health providers who serve children located within a 10-mile radius of DMLK (https://findtreatment.samhsa.gov/locator). The geographic and service void are important contextual factors that illustrate the vital importance of the additional supports DMLK provides its students and school community.

Principal Grayson's lived experiences inspired the development of the whole-child practices at DMLK. When her son was a student at DMLK, he had a significant loss and traumatic experience and there were few resources available to support him. As his principal and his mother, Kimberly witnessed both the emotional and academic impact on her son and began to intimately understand the intricate connections of trauma and learning. As a result, she and school staff began to explore strategies for transforming school practices to better serve all students, including those experiencing trauma, as well as destigmatizing the help-seeking process.

The whole-student approach is readily apparent in DMLK's physical environment. The school's commitment to student well-being includes dedicated student-centered spaces, including a large central lounge for students to relax and socialize during their off periods. The adjacent hallway is lined with large posters featuring school social support staff, which includes two social workers, one trauma-certified social worker, three licensed mental health counselors, one psychologist, one nurse, one health technician, and five academic counselors. These posters help students learn about available services and connect with the people who provide those services. Posters include details about the types of concerns staff can help with and how to get in touch with them.

In addition, there is a therapy dog on campus multiple days a week. A Denver Health Clinic operates on-site to address students' physical health concerns. An elective health and wellness class (Body Works) provides students with an opportunity to learn about the impact of stress and how to mitigate its negative effects, as well as historical and persistent traumatic experiences, through healthy solutions. These features are a backdrop to the school's culture that destigmatizes help-seeking and normalizes the challenges related to the stress of high school as well as the traumatic events that may influence students' lives and learning.

## Centering Relationships

School leaders and staff at DMLK foster a culture of family and prioritize relationships. Transforming opportunities for student wellness began by addressing school climate in ways that brought the students and staff into closer relationships. Every student in the building has a trusted adult to connect with informally and formally through advisement classes when they need to express themselves, vent, and cope with the stresses of high school that extend beyond the walls of the classroom. This ethos of care requires coordination and specific strategies employed by the staff. Teachers are trained to identify signs that a student might be struggling or experiencing trauma and to connect them with available programs. Well-being indicators are tracked to provide a comprehensive snapshot of all DMLK students that goes well beyond academic progress. A unique feature of DMLK's approach is its goal of providing care to all students, not only those experiencing crises. Further, these programs and processes are integral, available to the broader school community, and used in good and challenging times alike.

## CONTEXTUALIZING STUDENT SUCCESS:
## NATIONAL TRENDS AND RESEARCH

Relationships at DMLK bring students, teachers, and administrators together to foster deeper exploration into the ways in which their worlds and broader contextual factors impact personal wellness. Wellness for DMLK students includes acknowledging the individual day-to-day struggles that most middle and high schoolers face as well as intergenerational trauma and the legacies of oppression that shape what students see, hear, and feel in their educational journey.

### Addressing Oppression and Mental Health

Garbarino (1997) described "social toxins" as the social factors such as violence, poverty, economic precarity, mental illness, and social isolation that shape the social worlds in which young people live and grow that are "poisonous" to young people's development. We conceptualize all manifestations of oppression, or social toxins, as forms of trauma that may impact students' lived experiences (Goessling, 2020).

We wrote this chapter as the twin public health crises of anti-Black racism and the COVID-19 pandemic were devastating communities across the nation, including the DMLK community of Denver. The uprisings were a response to the persistent collective trauma and grief of COVID-19 and marked a significant epoch of anti-Black racism and police brutality in the United States. The pandemic and racial injustice—viewed as persistent, complex collective traumas—ripple through students' lives and communities, disproportionately impacting students of color and students experiencing poverty (Goessling, 2020) like so many DMLK students.

These crises spotlighted the consequences of historical disinvestment and structural racism within the contemporary context in a way that could not be denied by those in positions of power. The full long-term consequences of this moment on students and schooling remains to be seen, yet we know the significance cannot be overstated. For those at DMLK, this critical moment in time heightened the complexity, challenges, and urgency of providing students with access to supports and services.

Many mental health concerns emerge during the school-age years, and the severity and prevalence of these issues has steadily increased for decades. Researchers estimate that 25% of children in the United States experience mental, emotional, or behavioral issues (Swick & Powers, 2018), with only about 20% receiving care or specialized treatment (Olubiyi et al., 2019). Presidents George W. Bush and Barack Obama both recognized the need to improve young people's health and academic outcomes by enacting initiatives and policies that sought to improve access to school-based mental health services (Lai et al., 2016). No administration or Congress, however, has successfully enacted any federal policy or funding streams necessary to address this gaping hole. A persistent belief held by many educators and administrators is that student mental health is beyond the purview of teachers and schools. Traditionally, students' mental health needs have been viewed through a lens of classroom management and discipline, yet educators are routinely required to address students' socioemotional needs. This contributes to high rates of burnout and turnover within the teaching profession. For most school-aged youth in the United States, schooling is the singular resource where they have access to essential supports and services.

In effect, schools have long functioned as the "de facto mental health system for many children and adolescents" by providing the majority of mental health services to adolescents who need care (Golberstein et al., 2020, p. 819). The expansive unmet needs for child mental health care in the United States are often worse for marginalized and uninsured social groups (Kataoka et al., 2002). Scholars predict substantial learning losses for students of color and poor students due to various factors, including families who are more likely to experience COVID, suffer from economic consequences, and lack access to reliable technology and the Internet necessary for virtual learning (Kuhfeld et al., 2020). Unfortunately, the disparate impacts of COVID on marginalized and vulnerable students' health and well-being is piled on top of the existing "mental health crisis" in the United States that persists due to many systemic failures, including the lack of a national mental health policy and chronic disinvestment in the mental health system (Kataoka et al., 2009).

Unfortunately, exceptional schools and educators providing innovative social emotional supports like DMLK are the exception rather than the rule. The magnitude of this issue and demonstrated need requires a comprehensive approach entailing policy and funding changes that "build[s] on the indigenous resources of schools that that attends to the organizational context of learning, and that applies participatory models for developing and testing school-relevant practices" (Kataoka et al., 2009, p. 1513). DMLK's story illustrates how a holistic approach to education can shift the burden of responsibility from individuals to a school community, thereby creating an environment where students and educators are set up to thrive and grow together. We recognize that mental health, school discipline, climate, and culture are threads of schooling that require a comprehensive approach to effectively address the complex realities facing our students and school communities today.

## STUDENT HEALTH AND WELLNESS AT DMLK

DMLK's approach to education pays explicit attention to the importance of wellness and health for all school community members. The school provides essential resources (time, personnel, programs, and opportunities) for adults in the school community to tend to their needs so that they can show up for young people in the ways that youth need and deserve. The school's practices normalize asking for help by recognizing that over the course of a lifetime, everyone will experience issues, challenges, trauma, and adversity. This awareness is woven through the curriculum, pedagogy, organizational structure, and material conditions that upend deficit and stigmatizing narratives about mental health. Poster-sized photos line the hallway with positive messages and information about existing services. Photos of counselors provide information about areas of expertise and advertise an anonymous hotline, Safe2Tell, for students who need to keep themselves or someone they know safe from harm, dangerous situations, or threats. Photos of school community members have pop-out quote bubbles that say things like "Some days I struggle to get out of bed" and "I feel so much less worried and stressed out after I do yoga with my friends."

DMLK is committed to providing *all* students with access to professional services and supports, and these supports are intended to be used not just when mental health impacts academic performance. While this is a professional ethical standard for school counselors and social workers, the reality is that most schools are grossly understaffed, and mental health professionals deal with oversized caseloads with increasing severity and needs. Teachers and students in Denver and across the country have been demanding access to services and mental health resources for decades (Asmar, 2019). Professional standards recommended a minimum of one counselor and one social worker for every 250 students and at least one nurse and one psychologist for every 750 students and every 700 students respectively (American Civil Liberties Union [ACLU], 2019). The ACLU (2019) found that 90% of students attend public schools that fail to meet these standards, with a national student-to-counselor ratio of 444:1; in Colorado, the ratio is 503:1. Principal Grayson utilized all available resources, striving to move DMLK closer to the recommended ratios, but she recognized that the social workers and school psychologists at DMLK were already at full capacity just serving students with individualized education plans (IEPs). She understood that having her team and specialists working beyond their capacity was not the answer, and resources were not available for additional expansion of the mental health team.

Instead, Grayson turned to the DMLK team to collectively explore what meaningful time per week would look like to address all students' needs. This ongoing conversation led to the creation of the Whole Child Team, described as follows in an internal Whole Child Team report:

> The DMLK Early College promotes the social, emotional, physical and academic well-being of individual students through the identification and implementation of programs, supports and services, collaboration

with the greater school community, and the creation of a supportive and engaging learning environment to ensure student success in current and future endeavors.

As of 2021, the Whole Child Team included three mental health counselors, three social workers, one school psychologist, one nurse, and one health technician. Recognizing the need for this work to be done well and within professional boundaries of competence, all mental health professionals are licensed social work or counseling professionals. A trauma-certified social worker serves the general education student population and provides services separate from the IEP process. During the summer of 2020, Principal Grayson hired a Latinx social worker to focus on serving the predominantly Latinx student population. Having culturally competent staff and professionals who reflect the students and community they serve is an important step in reducing barriers to access of care. DMLK's designation as an Innovation School under Colorado law helped the principal with autonomy and decision-making power over the hiring and staffing decisions as she and her team reallocated resources to implement the whole-child vision.

The school's holistic approach situates mental health and socioemotional development within a framework of relationships. Humanization is at the core of this relational ethos and applies to everyone within the school community. Empathy and trust are prioritized through policy and practice. For example, the critical issue of time in accessing mental health supports can have a significant impact on outcomes. Principal Grayson believes that if students need to talk to someone, they need to talk to someone *now*. DMLK has removed traditional barriers that delay access to services. Students do not need a referral to see a counselor or social worker; they complete a self-referral form to see a counselor or school social worker. Students can speak with their teacher and request to see a mental health team member as situations emerge. To ensure that students have access to services as needed, mental health providers at DMLK have 24 hours to meet with students from the time of the initial referral.

DMLK uses the Behavioral and Emotional Screening System (BESS) to identify immediate risks and the different levels of support each student needs. The different levels range from Extremely Elevated Risk, Elevated Risk, and Normal Risk. Assessments answer the following questions for the team: Who do we need to focus on individually right now? Who would benefit from focused small groups? Who are we keeping an eye on? Monthly Child Study Team (CST) meetings provide "need to know" information within each department that includes Discipline, Special Education, Mental Health, Attendance, and OTTG (Off Track to Graduate). CST meetings are a time where the team comes up with "immediate" next steps on how to best support students as well as making sure that everyone is in the know about what challenges students are facing.

All students in grades 6–12 receive a Signs of Suicide (SOS) presentation, whereas other DPS schools provide these presentations to 6th and 9th grade only. Mindfulness practices are recognized as valuable for everyone, with weekly after-school yoga for students, and wellness sessions for staff. The yoga class targets students based on interactions with teachers and the screening tool. Additional students are included if they are identified as potentially benefiting from breathing practices or meditation.

The school offers a space for students and families called a Place of Peace, the trauma specialist's home base. The space includes a white noise machine, aromatherapy, beautiful art, miniature Zen gardens, and comforting, tactile pillows. The large number of other mental health employees in the building give the trauma specialist time to form meaningful and deep connections with students. She rolls out trauma support to teachers first to make sure they know what supports are available and what to look for in identifying students who need support. A referral sheet for teachers outlines the different specialties of the mental health team and a variety of "look-fors" that remind teachers how perceived discipline problems can often be better addressed with mental health care. A Strengthening Families program encourages healthy home relationships for students and family members experiencing current or past trauma. Facilitated conversations over a shared meal aim to strengthen parenting skills, youth life skills, and refusal skills. With a diverse group of families in the program, parents are able to help each other in culturally relevant ways.

In addition, DMLK is using a third-party transformative social–emotional academic learning (TSEAL) curriculum (Mosaic by ACT) with the screening tool of BESS (mentioned above) to bolster students' social-emotional competencies. This programming is delivered in Social Emotional Learning/Advisement class every morning. During the COVID-19 pandemic, Principal Grayson and the Whole Child Team pivoted to maintain continuity of care for the school community. The American Psychological Association (2020) called for robust screening and supports to address student mental health needs, which they anticipate as greatly exceeding the pre-COVID rate of 15%–20% of students who qualified for support and services. DMLK and schools across the country struggled to support school communities through school closures, toxic stress, grief, racism, and the trickle-down effects of the economic downturn, such as adult mental health and employment and child maltreatment (Golberstein et al., 2020).

At the outset of the pandemic, the primary objective was to ensure that all students' basic needs were met. To adapt their whole-child approach to the virtual/remote learning environment and increased socioemotional needs and challenges, DMLK implemented a three-pronged approach. The school organized students based on high, moderate, and low risk, and provided the high-risk group with daily contact, the moderate group 2–3 contact times a week, and the low-risk once-a-week contact. DMLK supported families by offering on-site food/meal distribution, school supply distribution, and drive-through community events where they passed out gloves, food, and other essentials. Additional support was provided to families that experienced positive COVID diagnoses.

## Student Success Through a Restorative Climate and Culture

Creating a healthy school climate and culture is not an add-on or the responsibility of a single department or person at DMLK. Instead, it is the foundation from which all else builds. Relationships across students, staff, educators, administrators, families, and the broader community are central to the educational ethos of DMLK, where a sense of belonging and connection are integral to learning and development. Further, DMLK has implemented affinity groups for Black males and young women of color focused on self-esteem, advocacy, and life skills. This approach is supported by extensive research on resiliency that demonstrates how relationships are one of the most singular powerful protective factors against adversity, even a single meaningful positive relationship with an adult (Osher et al., 2020; Sciaraffa et al., 2018).

Restorative justice (RJ) emerged as an alternative to punitive approaches for addressing crime, violence, and misconduct with a process that centers accountability. RJ aims to resolve conflict, repair harm, and restore relationships (Morrison & Ahmed, 2006). It assumes that behaviors are driven by basic needs—identified by Zehr (2002) as coalescing around relatedness, autonomy, and order—thus, RJ begins by meeting students' needs. It is a preventive approach to discipline that addresses the sociocultural conditions in which students are embedded by creating spaces of learning that center and support relationships at all levels: student–student, school–community, student–teacher, and teacher–teacher (Suvall, 2009). DMLK embraced RJ in 2013 as a relationship-centered approach to discipline.

RJ has been held up as an alternative to school policing practices and zero-tolerance policies. Those harsh and punitive approaches were a direct response to the first mass school shootings in the United States in the late 1990s. School policing has steadily increased over the past couple decades. The most recent report from the National Center for Education Statistics indicated that 57% of public schools used some form of security staff, and the numbers increased based on school characteristics, including enrollment size, location, and minority students (Musu-Gillette et al., 2018). School policing has disproportionately impacted Black and Latinx students, leading to the expansion of the school-to-prison-pipeline/nexus.

Since spring 2020 in Denver and across the nation, there have been student-led campaigns for police-free schools and calls to eliminate laws and policies that criminalize youth. Generally, police-free-schools campaigns call for districts to divest from school policing and invest funds in other school staff, programs, and alternative school safety plans. In the summer of 2020, Denver's Board of Education (BoE) approved a resolution to end all School Resource Officer (SRO) contracts with the Denver Police Department. The District's transition plan states that

> Cancelling the SRO contract provides funds to hire approximately 7 additional mental health staff who are focused on safety issues and alternative measures for conflict resolution. It is important to note that, because of the previous partnership with the Denver Police Department, the school district did not have to pay the full cost of the SRO program in our schools, so there is no 1:1 salary match for these positions. For example, eliminating one SRO does not free up the entire salary for a DPS mental health team member. (https://www.dpsk12.org/sro-transition)

DMLK's disciplinary practices center on restorative approaches to justice and positive relationships, including cultivating and maintaining a positive healthy relationship with their School Resource Officer. The spirit of the divest/invest approach is reflected in DMLK's whole-child philosophy, which is grounded in abundant mental health services and resources for the school community and a relationship-centered ethos. Taking this further, the school hires graduates who have roots in the community and deep connections with students and families for different roles in the school. Principal Grayson has implemented a preventive prosocial intervention that involves hiring team members from the community with shared lived experiences with students who are particularly effective in deescalating situations. Thus, students see themselves in the school staff and professionals who are working toward a shared goal of creating a school that fosters learning and development.

The two positions primarily responsible for discipline at DMLK are the Dean of Students and the Restorative Justice Coordinator, both of whom are trained and certified restorative justice practitioners. DMLK's Dean of Students supports school operations in the areas of attendance, behavioral, and disciplinary prevention and intervention services with an emphasis on restorative justice, including violence prevention and ensuring school safety. The Restorative Justice Coordinator is responsible for developing strong cultural systems as well as restorative practices and interventions to support students' holistic development, including connecting with students in unique ways that often garner novel insights that aid in student success. All DMLK staff receive professional development training in RJ. Holistic training outcomes include (a) understanding the DMLK discipline ladder, (b) how to use the DMLK restorative justice process, and (c) how to properly deescalate conflict in the classroom.

## Supporting Students and Families Through Community Partnerships

While DMLK is not a formal community school, it demonstrates many of the traditional hallmarks. Community schools are not a new phenomenon and exemplify a social ecological framework in practice. In fact, they stem from the 19th- and early-20th-century social and education reformers, including Jane Addams and John Dewey. Community schools are those that emphasize partnerships between the school and other community resources, such as health and social services, as well as youth and community development, with an aim toward integrating these resources and serving as a community hub for support.

At the heart of this approach is the understanding that to ensure all students thrive, schools must provide essential resources and services to address students, families, and community needs (Comer, 2013; Dryfoos, 2002; Epstein, 2010). Most community school models provide extended learning time that connects students and families to a variety of opportunities such as vocational training, adult education, sports, journalism, travel, technology, mentoring, tutoring, and volunteering (Oakes et al., 2017). Community schools target the school-community nexus with access to opportunities aimed to improve persistent disparate social and educational outcomes (Diamond & Freudenberg, 2016). While this is not a radical approach to transforming the structures and systems of oppression that contribute to inequity, it reflects a more expansive view of students, learning, and schooling as socioculturally situated (Goessling et al., 2020).

Extensive partnerships with community groups offer DMLK students and their families other programs that address health, education, vocation and workforce, economic, and cultural issues. In addition to on-site health services, DMLK provides students with many college preparatory programs, including summer college courses and campus stays from local and national universities through a partnership with the Colorado Student Leadership Institute. DMLK partners with Minds Matter (college prep for low-income families), has a Senior Counselor from the Denver Scholarship Foundation, and offers 21st Century College Readiness Afterschool Programming in partnership with Metro State University of Denver. Student Pathways are classes that prepare students for a certification or internship in engineering, manufacturing, information technology, and education. Some of the additional opportunities and programs offered at DMLK are Alternative Cooperative Education (or ACEConnect individualized college and career coaching), concurrent enrollment, career, technical education classes, trade classes, paid apprenticeships, internships, English classes for Spanish-speaking parents, family workshops, affinity student groups, and a sensory room.

The positive impact of DMLK's innovative and strategic efforts is leading to significant beneficial outcomes for students. These markers reflect changes during the 3 years from 2018 to 2021:

- 89% of DMLK students feel safe while at school, an increase of 3%.
- 84% of DMLK students have a positive response to DMLK discipline, an increase of 7%.
- 82% of DMLK students enjoy going to school, an increase of 14%.
- 87% of students believe DMLK encourages their family to be involved, an increase of 16%.

This evidence provides a compelling case of the power of a school-community culture that prioritizes relationships and wellness for improving academic and social outcomes. DMLK's holistic approach to student wellness is integrated into daily academic learning. It is based on the idea that supporting students' positive identity formation, wellness, and healing go far beyond nonacademic student supports. The next chapter describes DMLK's academic approach to provide a comprehensive view of its whole-child approach that weaves together student well-being and health *with* critical revision of curriculum and pedagogy.

## CONCLUSION

The stories and practices shared here demonstrate the power of a holistic approach to schooling that provides additional supports and services to students and the broader school community. The relational approach underpinning the school's family metaphor is evidenced in the policies and practices that begin with care, connection, and wellness. All students, parents, families, communities, and educators deserve such humanizing and healing schools.

The positive long-term implications and outcomes of this approach cross the spectrum from traditional academic indicators of individual achievement to school-level programmatic innovations, all the way to nationally recognized student-led work on policy and curriculum changes.

## REFERENCES

American Civil Liberties Union (ACLU). (2019). *Cops and no counselors: How the lack of school mental health staff is harming students.* https://www.aclu.org/report/cops-and-no-counselors

American Psychological Association. (2020, September, 22). *Student mental health during and after COVID-19: How can schools identify youth who need support?* American Psychological Association. https://www.apa.org/topics/covid-19/student-mental-health

Asmar, M. (2019, April 19). Student and parent groups pushing Denver schools to hire "counselors, not cops." *Chalk Beat.* https://co.chalkbeat.org/2019/4/19/21108031/student-and-parent-groups-pushing-denver-schools-to-hire-counselors-not-cops

Comer, J. P. (2013). School and moral justice: The school development program as a case study. *Journal of Research in Character Education, 9*(2), 91–106.

Craig, S. E. (2015). *Trauma-sensitive schools: Learning communities transforming children's lives, K–5*. Teachers College Press.

Diamond, C., & Freudenberg, N. (2016). Community schools: A public health opportunity to reverse urban cycles of disadvantage. *Journal of Urban Health: Bulletin of the New York Academy of Medicine, 93*(6), 923–939. http://doi.org/10.1007/s11524-016-0082-5

Dryfoos, J. (2002). Full-service community schools: Creating new institutions. *The Phi Delta Kappan, 83*(5), 393–399.

Epstein, J. L. (2010). *School, family, and community partnerships: preparing educators and improving schools*. ProQuest Ebook Central. http://ebookcentral.proquest.com

Garbarino, J. (1997). Educating children in a socially toxic environment. *Educational Leadership, 54*, 12–16.

Goessling, K. P. (2020). Youth participatory action research, trauma, and the arts: Designing youthspaces for equity and healing. *International Journal of Qualitative Studies in Education, 33*(1), 12–31. http://doi.org/10.1080/09518398.2019.1678783

Goessling, K. P., Selvaraj, S., Fritz, C., & Felton, P. (2020). Accountability "from the ground up": Uncovering the limitations and possibilities of community schools in Philadelphia. *Urban Education.* https://doi.org/10.1177/0042085920959134

Golberstein, E., Wen, H., & Miller, B. F. (2020). Coronavirus disease 2019 (COVID-19) and mental health for children and adolescents. *JAMA Pediatrics, 174*(9), 819–820. http://doi.org/10.1001/jamapediatrics.2020.1456

Kataoka, S., Rowan, B., & Hoagwood, K. E. (2009). Bridging the divide: In search of common ground in mental health and education research and policy. *Psychiatric Services, 60*(11), 1510–1515.

Kataoka, S., Zhang L., & Wells K. B. (2002). Unmet need for mental health care among US children: Variation by ethnicity and insurance status. *American Journal of Psychiatry, 159*, 1548–1555.

Kuhfeld, M., Soland, J., Tarasawa, B., Johnson, A., Ruzek, E., & Liu, J. (2020). Projecting the potential impacts of COVID-19 school closures on academic achievement. *Educational Researcher.* http://doi.org/10.26300/cdrv-yw05

Lai, K., Guo, S., Ijadi-Maghsoodi, R., Puffer, M., & Kataoka, S. H. (2016). Bringing wellness to schools: Opportunities for and challenges to mental health integration in school-based health centers. *Psychiatric Services, 67*(12), 1328–1333.

Morrison, B., & Ahmed, E. (2006). Restorative justice and civil society: Emerging practice, theory, and evidence. *Journal of Social Issues, 62*(2), 209–215.

Musu-Gillette, L., Zhang, A., Wang, K., Zhang, J., Kemp, J., Diliberti, M., & Oudekerk, B. A. (2018). *Indicators of school crime and safety: 2017* (NCES 2018-036/NCJ 251413). National Center for Education Statistics, U.S. Department of Education, and Bureau of Justice Statistics, Office of Justice Programs, U.S. Department of Justice.

Oakes, J., Maier, A., & Daniel, J. (2017). *Community schools: An evidence-based strategy for equitable school improvement*. National Education Policy Center. https://nepc.colorado.edu/publication/equitable-community-schools

Olubiyi, O., Futterer, A., & Kang-Yi, C. D. (2019). Mental health care provided through community school models. *The Journal of Mental Health Training, Education and Practice, 14*(5), 297–314. doi: 10.1108/JMHTEP-01-2019-0006

Osher, D., Cantor, P., Berg, J., Steyer, L., & Rose, T. (2020). Drivers of human development: How relationships and context shape learning and development. *Applied Developmental Science, 24*(1), 6–36. http://doi.org/10.1080/10888691.2017.1398650

Plumb, J., Bush, K., & Kersevich, S. (2016). Trauma-sensitive schools: An evidence-based approach. *School Social Work Journal, 40*(2), 37–60.

Sciaraffa, M. A., Zeanah, P. D., & Zeanah, C. H. (2018). Understanding and promoting resilience in the context of adverse childhood experiences. *Early Childhood Education Journal, 46*(3), 343–353.

Suvall, C. (2009). Restorative justice in schools: Learning from Jena High School. *Harvard Civil Rights-Civil Liberties Law Review, 44*, 547–569.

Swick, D., & Powers, J. D. (2018). Increasing access to care by delivering mental health services in schools: The school-based support program. *School Community Journal, 28*(1), 129–144. https://www.adi.org/journal/2018ss/SwickPowers Spring2018.pdf

Teicher, M. H., Andersen, S. L., Polcari, A., Anderson, C. M., Navalta, C. P., & Kim, D. M. (2003). The neurobiological consequences of early stress and childhood maltreatment. *Neuroscience & Biobehavioral Reviews, 27*(1–2), 33–44.

Terrasi, S., & De Galarce, P. C. (2017). Trauma and learning in America's classrooms. *Phi Delta Kappan, 98*(6), 35–41.

Zehr, H. (2002). Journey to belonging. In E. G. M. Weitekamp & H. Kerner (Eds.), *Restorative justice: Theoretical foundations* (pp. 21–31). Willan.

# CHAPTER 8

# Student Organizing and Leadership for Education Justice

## Curriculum as a Site for Healing and Wellness

*Kate Somerville, Kristen P. Goessling,*
*Adam York, and Kimberly Grayson*

Criterion 8: Enact a Challenging and Supported Culturally Relevant
Curriculum

This chapter expands upon the last chapter outlining Dr. Martin Luther King, Jr. Early College's (DMLK) holistic approach by discussing student organizing and curricular changes. We discuss how DMLK leaders and students work together to examine and change oppressive within-school educational structures that perpetuate harm and trauma. We provide an example to illustrate how this collaborative approach can lead to an overhaul of curriculum. While the previous chapter focused on DMLK's approach to student wellness through largely nonacademic supports and services, this chapter illuminates how DMLK weaves this holistic approach through their curriculum and pedagogy toward transformational aims.

The Schools of Opportunity recognition process does not ask schools to specify explicit *connections* between multiple criteria when they are submitting materials for review. However, the connection between DMLK's holistic approach to student well-being and their culture-centered curriculum is clearly visible across their materials, site visits, and subsequent conversations at the school. Criterion 8, as defined below, includes multiple key practices that are directly reflected in the culturally sustaining work happening at DMLK. We share a story based on recent experiences that begins with important field trips and that grows into a curriculum revision that respected student demands for content to accurately reflect Black history and the lived experiences of Black students. DMLK's initial transformative moves contributed to a broader movement rippling across the Denver Public Schools (DPS) district. We draw connections illustrating how these

**CRITERION 8: ENACT A CHALLENGING AND SUPPORTED CULTURALLY RELEVANT CURRICULUM**

Throughout the school, [exemplary] curricular and pedagogical approaches consciously build on the interests, strengths, and home cultures of the school's students. Instructional practices and content are aligned with students' experiences. There are ample examples of deliberate decisions to infuse culturally relevant pedagogy into the content of literature, class projects, assignments, events and field trips, ethnic studies courses, connections to families and communities, interventions, and other resources. These curricular experiences are accompanied by strong supports for students and their teachers, to ensure that learners are challenged and successful at a high academic level.

curricular changes are integral to the holistic care for students at DMLK and lead to exciting opportunities for participation in system change.

This chapter tells the story of student-led curriculum change at DMLK. First, we draw on research literature to describe the connection between curriculum and wellness. Then we describe the student-led effort for change at DMLK, highlighting how the school's environment made this change possible and connecting the students' change efforts to important elements of radical healing, like critical consciousness and envisioning new realities. We link this student-led movement to healing in two ways: (a) to the learning and wellness benefits that students likely experienced by participating in activism that resulted in success, and (b) to the positive change in the school environment—driven by a change in curriculum—that is likely to sustain and support student wellness and learning going forward.

Education scholars have debated the most appropriate terms to describe curriculum that best supports the racial identities and cultural practices of students, and whether attempts at "culturally relevant curriculum" go far enough to meet evolving student needs (Paris & Alim, 2014). As a Schools of Opportunity criterion, it is difficult to compare culturally sustaining practices directly across schools, as they are tightly bound to context and the intersections of identities in any given school. In the case of DMLK, we find the vision of "culturally sustaining pedagogy" to be an appropriate description, as the practices observed meet the call to understand "culture as dynamic and fluid, while allowing for the past and present to be seen as merging" (Paris & Alim, 2017, p. 8). Additionally, the support for student activism and resulting curricular changes at DMLK address fundamental questions about teaching and learning, such as who gets to decide what content is ex/included and what the role is of students in the (re)creation of schooling. While the work of expanding culturally sustaining practices in the teaching and learning at DMLK is a work in progress, we believe the narrative presented in this chapter contains valuable lessons regarding how vast changes can begin and grow, with school leaders and students working in partnership.

The work highlighted in this chapter took place between 2019 and 2022, a distinct political moment in U.S. public education defined by discourse and policy changes to erase key historical events, including racism, slavery, and genocide, intentionally designed to create a revisionist "whitewashed" history, delegitimize marginalized groups, and maintain the power status quo (López et al., 2021). The significance of the current sociopolitical context provides two key motivators for this chapter. The first is to highlight the immensity of the challenges educators and students face when designing and delivering educational content that is truthful, accurate, and culturally sustaining. New challenges include state and local government leaders banning books or setting up anonymous tip lines to report teachers who are not compliant with critical race theory (CRT) bans. Second is an ethical imperative to amplify and celebrate the courageous work of DMLK students and leaders as a crucial response to uphold the values of public education through this political climate. This chapter provides an example of one (of many) viable pathways for educators, leaders, students, and communities to fight back against the revision of our painful, yet critically important history.

## HEALING THROUGH CURRICULUM-FOCUSED
## STUDENT ORGANIZING

DMLK's holistic approach reflects the understanding that by supporting students' positive identity formation, wellness and healing are simultaneously educational interventions that can enhance and improve traditional educational outcomes, as well as socioemotional development (Diamond & Freudenberg, 2016; Coalition for Community Schools, n.d.). Wellness at DMLK is prioritized through relationships and mental health support, and the leadership at DMLK tangibly enacts these features through a curriculum and decision-making model that puts into practice the school's values of student voice, perspective, and agency.

Until the 2019 school year, the history curriculum at DMLK was the same as it was across all high schools in DPS. Like many history curricula across the United States, Denver's curriculum was whitewashed; it presented the history of Black and African American people as separate from American history. The messages students got from the curriculum did not honor the assets that are a central part of Black and African American culture and history in the United States. Students learned a surface-level version of Black history, consisting mostly of their ancestors' oppression. It did not include anything substantial about their ancestors' contributions and achievements in the United States or elsewhere. Thanks to student organizers at DMLK, that curriculum changed in November 2019 and was soon followed by the rest of Denver Public Schools (Brundin, 2020).

## HEALING AND HUMANIZING CURRICULUM AND PEDAGOGY

Dehumanizing curriculum is defined as "discriminatory practices that strip students of the cultural, linguistic, and familial aspects that make them unique, self-possessed individuals" (del Carmen Salazar, 2013, p. 130). Curriculum that does not honor the histories of students, especially historically marginalized students, compounds histories of oppression and marginalization and further dehumanizes students. Mainstream academic content privileges Whiteness and encourages assimilation, instead of honoring and sustaining non-White ways of being and knowing (del Carmen Salazar, 2013). Kumashiro (2001) points out that Whiteness, maleness, and heterosexuality are commonly privileged in each of the four main subject areas in the United States: language arts, math, science, and social studies.

This can lead to disengagements, tensions, and misunderstandings. Del Carmen Salazar (2013) suggests that student resistance to "practices that exclude their native language and culture from their learning" can result in behaviors that could be perceived by teachers as defiant, disruptive, or disrespectful (p. 123). Meanwhile, lack of representation in curriculum is often understood by students as a teacher's misunderstanding of their world and identity (Warikoo & Carter, 2009). Humanizing pedagogy, on the other hand, "values the students' background knowledge, culture, and life experiences, and creates learning contexts where power is shared by students and teachers" (Bartolomé, 1994, p. 11). Humanizing curriculum promotes more authentic feelings of belonging for students who have been historically marginalized by educational institutions.

Curriculum and pedagogy are therefore connected to student mental health and well-being and have the potential to perpetuate trauma. As a hopeful contrast, curriculum and pedagogy, inherently political parts of schooling, can also promote healing—especially when considering the sociopolitical nature of trauma. We draw on Goessling's (2020) work on politicized trauma to understand the healing potential of student organizing for humanizing curriculum and education policy. A politicized view of trauma understands trauma as always an individual *and* collective experience, which is a departure from traditional trauma frameworks that focus on individuals through a pathologizing and deficit lens (Goessling, 2020). Trauma is widely understood as an individual's response to an adverse or stressful event, rather than the event itself. A politicized view of trauma is grounded in several key assumptions, that (a) trauma is pervasive, socioculturally situated, relational, and intergenerational; (b) consequences and effects of traumas are passed down through communal lines; and (c) oppression and injustice are forms of trauma (Ginwright & Cammarota, 2002; Goessling, 2020; Prilleltensky, 2008). This politicized approach to trauma allows us to better understand the daily lived experiences of young people living in an oppressive, Western White-supremacist patriarchal capitalist society as a form of trauma.

Kirkland's (2021) view of the system of education as oppressive particularly for Black students aligns with this politicized trauma framework. He argued that schooling is "weaponized against Black children through false lessons of Black worthlessness" and the education system as a whole "is a situation of perpetual and deep oppression" for Black children (2021, p. 63). Kirkland advocates for an expanded version of Ladson-Billings's (1995) culturally relevant pedagogy with a curriculum that explicitly names race and racism, especially for Black students. According to Kirkland, "neither education nor the socio-historical school experiences of Black people are neutral or universal" (p. 61), which points to the idea that our school policies that inform curriculum cannot be effective in combating a long history of anti-Blackness in schools if they are presented as "neutral." Even well-intentioned attempts at promoting culturally relevant curriculum have morphed into tools for oppression when curriculum is presented as apolitical in an attempt to appease those who demand we keep politics out of the classroom. The naming of race in culturally relevant curriculum is essential for curriculum to promote belonging and healing because of the fact that belonging and healing themselves are sociopolitical and historical in nature.

Ladson-Billings (1995) and Kirkland (2021) both point to the need for Black education to promote what Freire referred to as "*conscientização*," or critical consciousness, that is aimed at cultivating the recognition of oppression characterized by the social, political and economic realities of society (Freire, 2011). Radical frameworks of healing depend on the recognition of the collective and politicized nature of trauma, and often name the development of critical consciousness as an essential first element to collective healing (French et al., 2020). When designed intentionally, curriculum and pedagogy can contribute to collective healing via developing critical consciousness of young people impacted by oppression and injustice. However, when culturally relevant curriculum is watered down and depoliticized, curriculum becomes another part of the schooling apparatus that oppresses and traumatizes Black students.

Today's conversations about trauma for school-age students too often address curriculum as an afterthought. The burgeoning trauma-informed schools movement has caused educators and administrators to consider how contextual factors influence academic and behavioral outcomes. Trauma-informed schools address behavioral issues from a preventive stance through mental health services instead of punitive methods of discipline and punishment. The trauma-informed care movement assumes that "disruptive behavior is the symptom of a deeper harm, rather than willful defiance, or disrespect" (Ginwright, 2018, para. 4). This is a profound and necessary shift, but there must also be an ideological shift in how educators think about wellness and healing in schools and communities (Ginwright, 2018). Most trauma-informed care focuses on individuals and fails to acknowledge structural oppression, as trauma is often experienced collectively. As an alternative to responses centered on individual people, Ginwright's healing-centered engagement centers youths' assets, well-being, and collective healing by working to change conditions and structures that perpetuate trauma (Ginwright, 2018).

Black and racialized students experienced DPS's social studies and Black history curriculum as oppressive and sometimes traumatizing. The glossed-over, deficit-based treatment of Black history in school reproduced the historical and structural marginalization of people of color that has a traumatic impact on individuals. Bartolomé (1994) points out that dehumanizing curriculum has the potential to spark valid resistance from students who don't see themselves valued or reflected in the curriculum. To some, resistance may be recognized as problem behavior that needs to be fixed. To others, like Principal Kimberly Grayson, student resistance indicated that something about her school needed to change.

## Radical Healing Through Student-Led Change

In the fall of 2019, Principal Grayson took a group of students to visit the National Museum of African American History and Culture in Washington, DC, to enrich and supplement students' classroom learning. The museum paints a complex and unflinching picture of the experiences of formerly enslaved peoples in the United States, which students identified as vastly different from what they learned in their own history and social studies courses. In the middle of the trip, students approached their principal with concerns about the history curriculum at DMLK. Students were disappointed that they had to fly halfway across the country to learn what they should have learned in school. A testament to the close and trusting relationships with students, Grayson recalled that one night on the trip after the day at the museum, a senior called her to task: "Grayson, you're Black. How are you as a Black leader not making sure we have more Black representation in our school?" All Grayson could say was, "You're right." That trip began a healing process, and the student's pointed question catalyzed a deep political discussion. Grayson was receptive, open, and vulnerable with the students. She explained that "we were broken together . . . and we were able to rebuild together."

The students recognized the harmful impact of the curriculum on their own community, communities of color across the district, and across the country. And they wanted it to change. The students, whom Grayson refers to as "a force to be reckoned with," asked that the school let them lead the way in creating a necessary change in their school community. Their goal was to change their history curriculum to reflect what they had learned about their own histories in a way that centered the richness, wealth, and assets that define Black history. They asked for her support, but they made it clear that their voices were the ones that needed to be heard. Grayson agreed to play a supportive role in the students' quest to change the school's curriculum.

The students started working almost as soon as they returned home from their trip to DC. They began by meeting with DPS district staff. Grayson recalled thinking about the power of the group of students and wondered how the conversation would go as she took a back seat. The students were persuasive, but when district leaders thanked Grayson after the conversation she was shocked. A door had been opened into transformative potential, with students driving the process backed by committed adult allies.

The students then continued this process with their history teachers, all of whom were White. They asked Grayson to send the entire history department to the National Museum of African American History and Culture (NMAAHC) in Washington, DC, and Grayson agreed. Two days later, the students gave a presentation to the history department on what they learned and what was possible to remedy long-standing problems in the curriculum. A couple weeks later the entire department headed to the nation's capital to immerse themselves in the NMAAHC for the weekend. While in DC, the teachers began rewriting DMLK's history curriculum from their hotel and shared a Google Doc to collaborate with Grayson immediately. Once back in Denver, the history department gave a presentation to the students about how they *thought* they had been teaching history and shared ideas for how they would *change* moving forward. Afterward, the students and history teachers presented the forthcoming curriculum changes to the rest of the faculty. The change process was characterized by authentic relationships, humanizing interactions, and student-adult partnership.

The entire DMLK community engaged in healing from the first spark of the student-led movement for change. French and colleagues' (2020) framework of radical healing for people of color in the United States names the following essential elements of healing: critical consciousness; strength and resistance; cultural authenticity and self-knowledge; radical hope; and emotional and social support. The authors name how racism "can operate as daily mini-traumas" on individual, systemic, and cultural levels (p. 18). Central to this radical healing framework is the idea that healing should move past simply coping with oppressive realities toward recognizing when people of color "gain critical consciousness about their oppression and seek to resist the associated racial trauma" as healing (p. 19).

Relatedly, Ballard and Ozer (2016) link youth activism and positive mental health outcomes. In telling the story of changes taking place at

DMLK, we call attention to the multiple layers of transformative practice. Yes, the curriculum change was under way and that would constitute a visible indicator of transformation. However, learning opportunities embedded in the experience of critical investigation, leadership, and guiding the adults around them can be transformative in themselves, beyond any singular outcome. Participation in youth-led campaigns for change can give youth a beneficial sense of control and empowerment over oppressive and stressful environments (Ballard & Ozer, 2016). Systemic changes resulting from youth activism have the potential to create feedback loops that support and sustain the well-being of youth, for both those involved in making change who experience a changed environment and those who benefit from the changed environment in the future (Ballard & Ozer, 2016). Also central to radical healing is acknowledging existing interlocking systems of oppression while simultaneously committing to visions of justice and liberation about how things *could* be (French et al., 2018; Goessling, 2020), which is closely aligned with Solorzano and Bernal's (2001) concept of transformational resistance, defined as "student behavior that illustrates both a critique of oppression and a desire for social justice" (p. 319).

Without an understanding that resistance and vision are central to radical healing, the student resistance at DMLK—resistance to a curriculum that was not supporting their wellness—may have been perceived as negative by the school's educators. While youth activism can be linked to positive mental health outcomes, the same outcomes can be negative when youth face significant barriers in changing stressful or oppressive situations (Ballard & Ozer, 2016). All too often, students' feelings of dissatisfaction with the status quo are interpreted by school personnel as disrespectful or problematic. Grayson could have brushed off the student who called her out on the whitewashed curriculum, deferred to district guidance, asked students to focus on the positives of the trip, or discouraged them from trying to change the way things were. Instead she recognized that students were bringing forward a valid critique of oppressive school policy and had a vision for how the policy could be changed to promote justice—aligned with the idea of transformational resistance. The fact that students felt comfortable enough to call attention to issues that needed to change and had the support of Grayson—a person with institutional power—is reflective of the environment and relationships that generated the possibility of change.

A traditional approach to wellness that considers student mental health from a clinical perspective will often address resistance to oppressive structures as a problem that resides within the individual, and is best solved with one-on-one counseling interventions. While individual social-emotional supports are integral to a comprehensive system of care for students, a system characterized by individualized interventions alone is incomplete at best and oppressive at worst. The individualistic deficit-focused perspective that aims to help students *cope* with oppression ignores the reality that mental health is sociopolitically situated and fails to address the oppressive structures that perpetuate collective trauma both in and outside of schools. Alternative systems, like the one at DMLK, recognize students as the experts that they are in their own experience of schooling and racialized experiences in society. This not only promotes a sense of agency and healing but also results in changes that are more culturally sustaining than they would be without the authentic engagement of youth.

## Driving District-Level Change

The healing environment at DMLK is based on the premise that students are agents in their own wellness and healing. This chapter's story demonstrates the space and support provided for students to recognize dehumanizing schooling practices and change those practices. The student leaders, with support from their school, did not stop with curriculum change at DMLK. In January 2020, DMLK students met with the Denver School Board to advocate for curricular changes that would center the histories of Black, Latino, Indigenous and other peoples of color in district wide curriculum. Unfortunately, COVID-19 ground everything to a halt. In May, students grappled with the murder of George Floyd and the calls for racial justice that followed. Protective measures like remote schooling and social distancing made safe physical gatherings nearly impossible. Student organizers at DMLK had to find a different way to continue their campaign. They started a podcast called "Know Justice Know Peace: The Take," where they discussed youths' perspectives on racial justice issues. The students' podcast received attention from local, national, and international news outlets like CBS, *The Today Show*, and NPR, among many others.

The podcast gave students a platform to tackle important topics—like the history of policing in communities of color, the future of culturally responsive policy in DPS, and why Whiteness is centered in school curriculum—from their own perspectives, which helped to fuel a broader campaign to change curriculum across the district. Supporting and promoting this form of expanded outreach for the voices of students is another feature of the culturally sustaining work at DMLK. For the student organizers at DMLK, the movement to change district wide curriculum policy became an enactment of the curriculum itself. Such opportunities are reflective of academic calls for scaffolded approaches that emphasize student learning about what it means to be active participants in civic life by taking action on an issue (Kirshner & Middaugh, 2014). Action-oriented civic learning frameworks encourage learning by doing and early involvement in political and social change (Flanagan & Levine, 2010; Youniss, 2011). The student-led podcast and campaign to change curriculum across the district gave students a chance to apply their knowledge and learning by fighting for a change that was important to them and reaching a broad audience under challenging circumstances.

The podcast and the curricular changes at DLMK were supported by DPS's school board, which paved the way for curriculum change across the entire district. The students involved with the podcast collaborated with a school board member, the deputy superintendent of academics, and the executive director of culturally sustaining curriculum and instruction to write the resolution. On October 22, 2020, the Denver Public Schools Board passed the Know Justice Know Peace Resolution, which credited the student organizers at DMLK. The resolution enacted policy to transform and humanize DPS's curriculum by considering the impact of learning materials that are used across course areas. It directed the district to continually engage in curriculum revisions to ensure that learning materials are promoting antiracism and using asset-based resources. Further, the resolution charged the district with developing mechanisms for feedback about student academic growth and growth in cultural responsiveness. Additionally, DPS committed to an external review of courses in civics, economics, and elementary social studies and literacy to ensure that materials are promoting asset-based truths about historically marginalized communities. Finally, the resolution directed the district to provide professional learning opportunities for social studies and literacy teachers to ensure effective implementation of the new curriculum.

## CONCLUSION

Since passage of the Know Justice Know Peace Resolution in Denver Public Schools, Principal Grayson, the student activists at DMLK, and their teachers have continued their important work. They produced an additional curriculum that honors and centers the histories of Latino American students, which, along with the curriculum that centers Black history, is used as the primary source of curricular materials at DMLK. DPS is working to adopt the Black history curriculum in all schools. A documentary, *Power in Our Voices*, was created about the students who host the "Know Justice Know Peace: The Take" podcast. They have also been invited to speak at a state-level education meeting and advocate for history standards to be changed.

During a time when multiple states across the country have adopted or proposed legislation that forbids conversations about race, equity, and privilege in public schools, DMLK showed how embracing the difficulty, the pain, and the beauty of these conversations honors the whole histories of their students of color. Additionally, this story illustrates how resistance to dehumanizing curriculum can spark movements for change that contribute to healing and co-created school environments that sustain the wellness of students.

DMLK demonstrates what it means and what is possible when schools see and honor students' full selves by directly supporting student mental health; investing in wellness through comprehensive supports and services; and *attending to the student-wellness implications of the academic curriculum.* DMLK's story provides other school leaders, educators, and administrators with conceptual and strategic pathways for engaging students and designing educational environments that enhance student and community well-being. This story, of how this work expanded throughout the district, also clearly illustrates one of the central beliefs at the foundation of the Schools of Opportunity recognition project and this book: that examples like DMLK might guide us toward a system that humanizes and cares for all students.

## REFERENCES

Ballard, P. J., & Ozer, E. J. (2016). The implications of youth activism for health & wellbeing. In J. Conner & S. M. Rosen (Eds.), *Contemporary youth activism: Advancing social justice in the United States.* ABC-CLIO, LLC.

Bartolomé, L. I. (1994). Beyond the methods fetish: Toward a humanizing pedagogy. *Harvard Educational Review, 64(2),* 173–194. https://doi.org/10.17763/haer.64 .2.58q5m5744t325730

Brundin, J. (2020, September 18). Student-led initiative will incorporate more Black, Indigenous and Latino voices into DPS' curriculum. *Denverite.* https:// denverite.com/2020/09/18/student-led-initiative-will-incorporate-more-black -indigenous-and-latino-voices-into-dps-curriculum/

Coalition for Community Schools. (n.d.). *What is a community school?* Coalition for Community Schools. http://76.227.216.38/aboutschools/what_is_a_community _school.aspx

del Carmen Salazar, M. (2013). A humanizing pedagogy: Reinventing the principles and practice of education as a journey toward liberation. *Review of Research in Education, 37*(1), 121–148. https://doi.org/10.3102/0091732X12464032

Diamond, C., & Freudenberg, N. (2016). Community schools: A public health opportunity to reverse urban cycles of disadvantage. *Journal of Urban Health: Bulletin of the New York Academy of Medicine, 93*(6), 923–939. https://doi.org/10 .1007/s11524-016-0082-5

Flanagan, C., & Levine, P. (2010). Civic engagement and the transition to adulthood. *The Future of Children, 20*(1), 159–179. https://doi.org/10.1353/foc.0.0043

Freire, P. (2011). The banking concept of education. In E. B. Hilty (Ed.), *Thinking about schools* (pp. 117–127). Routledge.

French, B. H., Lewis, J. A., Mosley, D. V., Adames, H. Y., Chavez-Dueñas, N. Y., Chen, G. A., & Neville, H. A. (2020). Toward a psychological framework of radical healing in communities of color. *The Counseling Psychologist, 48*(1), 14–46. https://doi.org/10.1177/0011000019843506

Ginwright, S. (2018, May 31). The future of healing: Shifting from trauma informed care to healing centered engagement. *Medium.* https://ginwright.medium.com /the-future-of-healing-shifting-from-trauma-informed-care-to-healing-centered -engagement-634f557ce69c

Ginwright, S., & Cammarota, J. (2002). New terrain in youth development: The promise of a social justice approach. *Social Justice, 29*(4), 82–95. http://www.jstor.org/stable/29768150

Goessling, K. P. (2020). Youth participatory action research, trauma, and the arts: Designing youthspaces for equity and healing. *International Journal of Qualitative Studies in Education, 33*(1), 12–31. https://doi.org/10.1080/09518398.2019.1678783

Kirkland, D. (2021). A pedagogy for black people: Why naming race matters. *Equity & Excellence in Education, 54*(1), 60–67. https://doi.org/10.1080/10665684.2020.1867018

Kirshner, B., & Middaugh, E. (2014). *#youthaction: Becoming political in the digital age.* Information Age Publishing.

Kumashiro, K. K. (2001). "Posts" perspectives on anti-oppressive education in social studies, english, mathematics, and science classrooms. *Educational Researcher, 30*(3), 3–12. https://doi.org/10.3102/0013189X030003003

Ladson-Billings, G. (1995). Culturally relevant teaching. *Theory Into Practice, 34*(3), 159–165.

López, F., Molnar, A., Johnson, R., Patterson, A., Ward, L., & Kumashiro, K. (2021). *Understanding the attacks on critical race theory.* National Education Policy Center. http://nepc.colorado.edu/publication/crt

Paris, D., & Alim, H. S. (2014). What are we seeking to sustain through culturally sustaining pedagogy? A loving critique forward. *Harvard Educational Review, 84*(1), 85–100.

Paris, D., & Alim, H. S. (2017). *Culturally sustaining pedagogies: Teaching and learning for justice in a changing world.* Teachers College Press.

Prilleltensky, I. (2008). The role of power in wellness, oppression, and liberation: The promise of psychopolitical validity. *Journal of Community Psychology, 36*, 116–136. https://doi.org/10.1002/jcop.20225

Solórzano, D. G., & Bernal, D. D. (2001). Examining transformational resistance through a critical race and LatCrit theory framework: Chicana and Chicano students in an urban context. *Urban Education, 36*(3), 308–342. https://doi.org/10.1177/0042085901363002

Warikoo, N., & Carter, P. (2009). Cultural explanations for racial and ethnic stratification in academic achievement: A call for a new and improved theory. *Review of Educational Research, 79*(1), 366–394. http://www.jstor.org/stable/40071169

Youniss, J. (2011). Civic education: What schools can do to encourage civic identity and action. *Applied Developmental Science, 15*(2), 98–103. https://doi.org/10.1080/10888691.2011.560814

# The High School in the Middle of Everywhere
## Nebraska's Lincoln High

*Edmund T. Hamann, Janet Eckerson, and Mark Larson*

Criterion 9: Build on the Strengths of Language-Minority Students and
Correctly Identify Their Needs

In 2002, world-renowned author Mary Pipher published a book about her home city, Lincoln, Nebraska, playfully titled *The Middle of Everywhere*, a tongue-in-cheek rejoinder to the idea that Nebraska is "the middle of nowhere." But wordplay aside, her title was empirically apt, as her volume documented how immigration and refugee resettlement were demographically transforming Nebraska's capital city. As in other cities, resettlement was concentrated in some areas of Lincoln, placing differential burdens on different parts of the community's institutional infrastructure. Of interest to readers of this volume, Lincoln's refugees and immigrants were concentrated in the city's oldest high school. This account shares how that school embraced the challenge of demographic change by valuing the knowledge, skills, and experience of students and their families.

Founded in 1871 and in its current building since 1915, Lincoln High School (LHS), home of the Links, is the oldest public comprehensive high school in Lincoln, Nebraska, and the most centrally located. With marble stairs, detailed moldings, and stone columns, the school has the classic Greek temple appearance of many turn-of-the-20th-century urban high schools. Yet with students speaking 30 different first languages and claiming heritages from Africa, Southeast Asia, Latin America, the Middle East, and Europe, as well as Indigenous identities, the current enrollment is clearly a 21st-century demographic. It is currently one of six comprehensive high schools in fast-growing Lincoln Public Schools (LPS) and soon to be one of eight, with construction under way on a seventh and eighth comprehensive high school on the city's northwestern and southern edges.

Since the 1990s, Nebraska has allowed choice enrollment. That means, with few exceptions, that as long as there is space and a means for a student to get there, a student can choose to attend a public school outside their home catchment zone, even outside their home district. When the fifth and sixth comprehensive high schools (Lincoln North Star and Lincoln Southwest) opened in the early 2000s, LHS increasingly was pejoratively labeled the "Ghetto High School," a term that was profoundly problematic and consequential, but also in many ways what precipitated the transformations that led to LHS's exemplary practices of today. This chapter primarily focuses on the ninth Schools of Opportunity criterion, which pertains to the importance of building on the strengths of students whose first language is other than English; in doing so, however, we place LHS's work in the context of other school practices that more broadly embrace and support the school's students. Framing that one element of LHS's practice in isolation would be misleading without a broader characterization of both the context and intended ethos of the whole school.

This chapter is coauthored by LHS's principal; by a former Spanish teacher and department chair who rejuvenated its lapsed Spanish as a Heritage Language course sequence before accepting a teacher education position in 2020 at the University of Nebraska at Kearney (UNK); and by a professor of education policy and practice at the nearby University of Nebraska-Lincoln (UNL). The remainder of the chapter is presented in nine parts:

(I)   Demographics and history of the building
(II)  Adding supports to address opportunity
(III) Diversity, inequality, and the pandemic
(IV)  Heritage Language Program
(V)   English Language Program and Curriculum

---

**CRITERION 9: BUILD ON THE STRENGTHS OF LANGUAGE-MINORITY STUDENTS AND CORRECTLY IDENTIFY THEIR NEEDS**

The [exemplary] school excels in approaching its bilingual students as emerging bilinguals, building on the language strengths they bring to school and engaging them equitably across their programs. The school has programs explicitly designed to serve EB students that is research based and implemented thoroughly. The school implements strategies that provide students with access to multi- or bilingual supports as needed in core content classes, supporting students at all levels of fluency.

Professional development is designed to equip teachers with the skills necessary to serve EB students, and there is meaningful communication between the school and EB families.

(VI)    Cultural Ambassadors and Student Clubs
(VII)   Bilingual Liaisons
(VIII)  The Bilingual Career and Education Fair
(IX)    Final Thoughts

When we began crafting this chapter in 2019, prior to the COVID-19 pandemic and the renewed Black Lives Matter mobilization that was precipitated by the racist killings of George Floyd, Breonna Taylor, Ahmaud Arbery, and others, we did not anticipate crafting the third segment at all. But an account that excludes those factors would not only immediately feel dated, it would ignore how supporting students from various language backgrounds, as well as diverse cultural and racial backgrounds, has necessitated attending to these recent momentous events. Additionally, as one would both hope and expect, programs continue to be refined, adapted, and expanded, so the descriptions here reflect realities and goals circa January 2022, when this chapter was finished. Segments II–VI below each describe building-specific efforts, while segment VII references districtwide programs that pertain to LHS. Segment VIII—about a new Language Career Fair—is saved for last because it describes a previously tiny initiative begun by the Latino Caucus (a student club) at Lincoln Southwest that LHS imported and was able to scale into an event that now operates districtwide.

## I. LINCOLN HIGH'S HISTORY AND DEMOGRAPHICS

For the first 55 years of its existence, LHS was the capital city's only high school. That changed in 1926 when the growing city annexed University Place, and the former University Place High School became Jackson High School, which later became part of the Northeast High School in 1941. Even as suburban development grew the population and pushed the city south and east, only slowly did LPS add new high schools—Lincoln Southeast in 1955 and Lincoln East in 1967. That status quo of four high schools held until the beginning of this century, when the city's fifth and sixth comprehensive high schools—Southwest and North Star—opened a year apart in 2002 and 2003. Those school openings combined with previous state legislation in the 1990s that permitted "public school choice" (enrollment outside of one's catchment zone) and a change in the 1970s in which the U.S. government identified Lincoln as a "refugee-friendly" city. Each had bearing on the challenges and opportunities LHS educators and students have negotiated over the last 20 years.

When Lincoln Public Schools (LPS) opened Southwest and North Star High Schools, enrollment at LHS predictably declined, but it declined more than it should have. Changing LHS from a 10–12-grade building to a 9–12-grade building (which happened at the same time) should have checked most of the decline, but Lincoln High went from 2,169 students as a three-grade school in 2000–2001; to 1,988 students in 2003–2004, the first year it had four grades; and after both new high schools had opened, to a low of 1,555 in 2006–2007. From *esprit de corps* and resources stand-points, a 25% decline was hard. For the next 4 years, the enrollment grew only very slightly; the 2011–12 student tally was just 1,571.

LHS faced a challenge: How could it reverse its demographic decline? Yet that question was not asked in isolation. As one of two (and now three) LPS high schools with a program for English learners, as one of two LPS high schools with a nursery and day-care facility for the children of teen-age parents, and as the school with the catchment zone in the city's oldest and poorest neighborhoods, growing/rebuilding enrollment could not come at the expense of no longer meeting the needs of LHS's traditional popula-tions. The task was to keep LHS attractive and responsive to its then-current enrollment while also making it an exciting environment for students from elsewhere in the city. The solution was to conceptualize its diversity as a re-source. While that remains a work in progress (perhaps inevitably given that LHS cannot and should not isolate itself from national social dynamics of xenophobia, inequality, and racism), it is a struggle to be better that we hope others can learn from. Here, therefore, we attempt to explicate the structures, strategies, and real successes that mark progress in LHS's ongo-ing quest to be a School of Opportunity for all its constituents.

LHS's enrollment has grown, from 1,571 in 2011–2012 to 2,356 stu-dents in 2020–2021. Corresponding with that growth, the school has seen renewed interest from all groups that form its larger community. Also, more than a third of the school's enrollment chooses to come to LHS from other high schools' catchment zones. LHS also remains Lincoln Public School's only majority non-White high school, and it has the highest free and reduced-price lunch (FRL)-eligible student enrollment of any district high school. It is one of three high schools with an ESL program. And it is one of two with sup-port facilities (e.g., day care) for teenage parents.

With over 30 languages other than English spoken by its students, LHS's strategy for assuring robust enrollment includes assuring strong supports for its students whose first language is other than English. Counting the number of identified English learners (ELs) is more fraught than counting race and ethnicity, because EL status can change when a student's mastery of English is recognized (see Hamann & Reeves, 2013). We can nonetheless see the growth in the percentage of ELs served at LHS following the low point in 2015–2016. In fact, the recent slippage in the percentage of ELs enrolled at LHS is mainly due to the denominator, the school's rising total enrollments. Moreover, the school district's total EL population fell during this same period more dramatically, from 8.1% to 7.1%. So LHS enrolled a higher proportion of the district's identified ELs than it had previously.

As Catalano and Hamann (2016) have noted, Ruíz (1984) famously cate-gorized approaches to language in schools as either "language as a problem,"

"language as a right," or "language as a resource." There is a parallel termi-
nology in the United States around teaching students whose first language is
other than English. Most governmental bodies currently use "English learners" (ELs), which implies a deficit—that the students have a problem that
schools need to remediate or address. The Schools of Opportunity project
initially used the term "language-minority students," which arises out of the
idea that these students have—or should have—legally protected rights. The
project now uses the term "emergent bilinguals" (or "emerging bilinguals")
to emphasize that these students are bringing an additional resource that
schools can build upon and value.

We (the coauthors) of this chapter echo this sentiment and note that
many LHS students should even be categorized as "emergent multilinguals"
because they bring familiarity with more than language to LHS. Many African
students (born in Africa or born to Africa-born parents) know a colonial language (e.g., French) and a religion-related language (e.g., Arabic), as well
as Indigenous African languages (e.g., Swahili), while Guatemalan-origin
students often have familiarity with an Indigenous language (e.g., K'iche') as
well as the dominant colonial one (i.e., Spanish). Honoring this background
knowledge describes practices and beliefs by many at LHS, yet reflecting district and state practice, the language development program for identified
EBs continues to be called the ELL program. Referencing the School of
Opportunity project stance, we use EB here when not referring to governmental policies or datasets, but when referring to students in the designated
English acquisition programs. That allows us to distinguish EBs (those in
the program) from the bigger, more heterogeneous category of LHS students
with heritage language backgrounds whose cognition, learning habits, and
cosmologies are all influenced by these additional linguistic capabilities.

## II. ADDING SUPPORTS TO ADDRESS OPPORTUNITY

Being equitably responsive to LHS's recent enrollment has required supports
for all students that may be more valuable for multilingual LHS students than
for some of their peers. In 2016, LHS extended its media center hours into
the evening. Though previously open until 5 P.M., through the help of grants
and The Lighthouse, a nonprofit community organization whose goal is to
provide middle and high school students with supports that will increase the
probability of graduation, LHS was able to stay open until 8 P.M. Monday
through Thursday, 5 P.M. on Fridays, and from 8 to 11 A.M. on Saturdays.
Keeping the space open for extended hours in the evenings has made it easier
for low-income students to access the Internet and technology necessary for
them complete their schoolwork and, additionally, to become more familiar with technology they may or may not have access to outside the school
walls. Library staff have noted that parents appreciate having a safe place

for students to stay after school while they are still at work. Hundreds of students have taken advantage of these extended hours in order to complete schoolwork, meet with other students for group projects, wait for parents or rides home, or pass time between after-school activities in a safe, stimulating environment.

During these extended library hours, tutors and school staff are available to students. Through this partnership, The Lighthouse provided volunteers who work with students, most of whom help students with schoolwork as well as applications for jobs, finding information about other programs or scholarships, receiving help with other work, and having access to resources they do not have at home. Teachers are also available to help with tutoring during this time, as are individuals who are working with students through other organizations like Upward Bound, Life After High School, and College Club. More recently, the after-school program was split into two parts: quiet hour studying and tutor opportunities in the library and a community-learning-center (CLC) partnership with Civic Nebraska that offers more than 30 after-school clubs.

LHS also supports students, including EBs, through its Academic Resource Center (ARC). This after-school support is curriculum-specific; ARC ensures that teachers for each curricular area are available Monday through Friday after school. Times are dependent on each curricular area, but teachers can assign ARC to students or students can walk in to talk to and work with a teacher in the curricular area in which they need support. Finally, LHS offers a Saturday school. It is the only school in the district to offer weekend hours for students to work on and complete schoolwork. On Saturdays from 8 A.M. to 11 A.M., students who have fallen behind due to attendance issues, athletic or theater involvement, or other factors can work on missing and late work with the help of teachers and administrators.

## III. DIVERSITY, INEQUALITY, AND THE PANDEMIC

Before looking more directly at strategies with/for EB students, it is worth pointing out that LHS has hardly been immune from the three pandemics that emerged in 2020—COVID-19, the economic contraction that came with the resulting shutdown, and the renewed racial justice awakening catalyzed by the brutal killings of George Floyd, Breonna Taylor, Ahmaud Arbery, and others at the hands of police and vigilantes. Because of how broadly consequential these pandemics have been for schooling, they need to be accounted for if one is to claim (as we do) that LHS still embraces the practices and values that led to its recognition as a School of Opportunity. The senses of dislocation, worry, anger, exhaustion, and vulnerability (among others) that the pandemics precipitated have mattered for more than just EB students—indeed for more than just students. And the soul-searching, honest, community-oriented, and sometimes trepidatious responses have also mattered to more than just EB students. Having all students feel welcome, safe, and successful at LHS is more than an issue of particular pedagogical design and curricula for EL courses and heritage language education; it is also connected to the broader patterns of welcome and inclusion that are intended to encompass everyone in the building.

As with schools across the country, in March 2020 LHS closed to in-person instruction because of COVID and operated for the remainder of the 2019–2020 academic year remotely. As elsewhere, some students negotiated the transition nearly seamlessly, but for others it was much more of a challenge, as at-home access to the Internet was limited and/or expensive and/or they were needed for domestic labor (like watching younger siblings who were also no longer in school). EB students were more likely to have these kinds of challenges than some of their student peers, but not all did. In turn, EB students were more likely to have their parents declared essential workers (who needed to stay on the job) in their employment, particularly in the food industry such as supermarkets and meatpacking.

Just after the school year ended, George Floyd was murdered in Minneapolis, and that precipitated a local reaction in Lincoln. Given youth mobilization for marches, this included students from all local high schools and from all backgrounds, but with the relatively intense response from Black, Indigenous, and people of color (BIPOC) youth, involvement by LHS students may have been greater than from other schools since LHS has more BIPOC students. The Floyd murder was consequential for the LHS community even though school was no longer in session. We share an email below from the principal to LHS staff in early June 2020 (edited for length) that does two things: It depicts a specific effort to bring together any students and staff who wanted to process events through Zoom conversations, and it more generally illustrates the inclusive, communitarian, and transparent ways LHS leadership has tried to live out the goal of LHS serving as a welcoming resource and safe space:

> To: "lhsstaff"
> Sent: Tuesday, June 2, 2020 11:22:10 AM
> Subject: Reflections and one next step—Lincoln High Community
> Connection Circle
>
> Staff—
> Since the death of George Floyd at the hands of a Minneapolis police officer, I have, I assume like many of you, struggled to find the words to articulate what I am thinking and feeling. The conversation around race, police brutality, and systemic racism has taken center stage in our country and in our city.

Over the last couple of days and nights I have seen the faces of the students we've committed to serve and they are sad, tired, and angry. But I've also been inspired by our current and former students' action and voice in this conversation. I have seen [student name] standing on the steps of the Capitol holding a sign that said "I Can't Breathe," practically alone before an organized protest happened. I have seen [another student name] kneeling in protest. I have seen former students [four former students named] speak with passion and anger. I have seen kids like [three more names] attempt to speak and lead.

This is a tough time for us to not be in school. Many times in situations like these, our students depend on us to give them the time and space to process hard things. Some of our students have already reached out, searching not necessarily for answers, but just to talk and to process. They want to be seen, heard, and valued and many of them are used to getting that from us. I'm missing not being with our students and with you all because we see education as our way to make our world a better place, so in the midst of all of this mess, we feel kind of helpless.

I also have to admit that right now, I'm uncomfortable. I'm a White man at a school where I'm trying to educate young people who have experienced a very different life than me. And if I'm honest, the more I become aware of how much I don't understand, and the more I see the weight of how racism, injustice, and inequality has affected people different from me, the more uncomfortable I become. I worry about saying the wrong thing, I worry about responding the wrong way. I'm not sure I'm able to articulate all of my feelings and thoughts. But ultimately, that has to be okay. I have to learn to lean into that. Sometimes as educators we're used to having the answers and when we don't we're uneasy.

So I don't know if this is the right thing, or the best thing, but we're going to take a step tomorrow. Tomorrow afternoon we are going to invite students and staff to a *Lincoln High Community Connection Circle from 2pm-3pm via Zoom.* We'll be sending a call and an email to parents and students this afternoon with an invitation. In the interest of safety, students will fill out a Google Form to indicate their interest in being a part of the Connection/Restorative Circle and we'll send a Zoom link to their school email address closer to the meeting tomorrow afternoon. This will be an opportunity for us (students and staff) to begin to process all that we're experiencing. . . . We've worked with a few staff members and some students to help facilitate these circles, but we want to invite all of you to participate and be a part. *If this is something that you're interested in and available for, please indicate that on [hyperlink] so that we know who to send the Zoom link to.* School isn't in session and most of us are not on contract, so there isn't pressure coming from me and this isn't a test measuring what kind of person you are. So if you're not ready, or the time simply doesn't work for you, that's okay. This needs to be the first of many steps we need to take as a community.

I love you all, miss you, and am proud to do this really important work alongside you. Mark

The principal also sent a shorter invitation than the one to staff to LHS families and students, which explained:

The recent events that have taken place in Minneapolis, as well as other cities in our country, have caused pain, anger, sadness, and confusion. We believe that our role as educators at Lincoln High is to not only educate our students, but to also love them, care for them, and provide a safe space and welcoming space for them to process their emotions. Tomorrow, at 2 p.m., we will be holding a Lincoln High Community Connection Circle, via Zoom, for our staff and students, focused on these events. While this is only a very small step in the work that needs to be done to bring justice and equality in our country, we hope it serves as a place for voices to be shared and heard . . .

These Community Connection Circles helped set a tone of inclusion, seriousness, and purposeful listening. In early July, in another email to LHS staff, the principal observed (italic text in the original):

Our Community Conversation on June 3rd and other conversations with students and staff have caused me to reflect on my personal biases and my place within a system that has helped some students rise but has oppressed others.

I would guess that on some level all of us chose to work at Lincoln High because we view education as an act of social justice and our way to give back to our community and our world. I believe that because that common thread exists, it makes Lincoln High a great place to work. It's invigorating to work alongside people who see the work they do as more than just a job, but as a mission. But that doesn't mean we don't have work to do. I want to be vulnerable and apologize that sometimes I think because I work at Lincoln High, where we have so much diversity, that it somehow by osmosis makes me culturally competent. Being around students and others who are different from me has caused me to learn a lot over my time at LHS, but this summer has made me realize that it's not enough.

. . . Over the last month, I've begun meeting with a group of staff members to plan our learning and goals and I'm really excited about this work. I'm going to outline a few next steps that we'll be asking teachers to take leading up to August to prepare us for this work, but first I want to clearly communicate a few things:

—At Lincoln High, Black Lives Matter
—This work won't be something that is here today and gone tomorrow. We are committing to this work for the long haul.
—This work and these conversations may make you feel uncomfortable . . . we're going to move forward. We all chose to work here and with our students, and talking about race, injustice, and our own personal biases needs to be part of the gig, but especially at Lincoln High. I hope you choose to continue on this journey with us.

Our Staff Committee that I've been meeting with has laid out a statement as a goal for this work. It's heavy and aspirational, but I want you to read it and commit to being a part of it:

*To build awareness, understanding, and to challenge individual, collective, and systemic racism present at LHS. To require teachers to actionably improve daily classroom practice to create equitable opportunities and outcomes—with student supports—for all students. To change policies and systems that create inequities within our school.*

We believe that this is in alignment with our school mission statement:

*Lincoln High School is committed to preparing each student to use multiple perspectives and individual talents to live, learn, and work in a diverse society . . .*

The long email then finished with a segment called "Next Steps" that included a survey link for staff to indicate professional development desires and that shared links to two articles, one an op-ed by Kareem Abdul-Jabbar reflecting on the death of George Floyd and the Black Lives Matter movement, the other a piece that considered the many ways racism can exist and be consequential at schools. The email ended with a request that staff think about how they had witnessed or experienced racism at LHS, whether intentional or unintentional, and an invitation to think about how their work was or could be antiracist.

A month later, staff came back together for several professional development days before the 2020–2021 academic year launched. Those meetings referenced the work of the summer, included the needed optimism that usually characterizes coming back to start a new year (albeit with the social distancing expectations and only half of the enrollment physically in the building at a time on alternating days), and then included a tough examination of inequities by race, gender, FRL status, and EL status and enrollment in honors-level courses. A review of the honors course enrollment was followed by a review, with a similar demographic breakdown, of course failure rates. Opposite of the honors course data, this lens showed that American Indian, Black, Hispanic, Two or More Races, English learners, and FRL-eligible students all had above-average course failure rates. Reflective of the above emails, staff considered three key points: (1) LHS is a great place, with most students feeling welcomed; (2) LHS staff have chosen to work at the school because they see education as a form of social justice; and (3) school data nonetheless show that staff make decisions and operate within a system that advantages some students and disadvantages others, so the school must work to change this. From this arose two commitments from the school's teachers:

1. They would be ready to acknowledge that students would return to school changed because of recent events and personal experiences with racism and would need encouragement to use their words and confidence to articulate it.
2. They would embark on a collaborative journey to better understand and respond to students.

Staff subsequently committed to ongoing group book study as part of their professional learning as well as monthly equity-focused discussions in small-group faculty meetings. Topics included how to have hard conversations about race with students, how to increase diversity in the curriculum, and how to identify inequities in teachers' own classrooms.

These 2020–2021 academic year themes illuminate that even though LHS had been honored to be recognized as a School of Opportunity (before the three pandemics), building staff and leaders insisted that there remained much work to do. This recent activity also helps contextualize how the school's commitments to better support EB and other multilingual students was part of its broader consideration of advantage and disadvantaged through acts of commission and omission.

## IV. HERITAGE LANGUAGE PROGRAM

A key mechanism to reducing disparities is to recognize and build on the assets (what Norma González et al. [2005] and others have called "funds of knowledge") that students bring with them to school. In 2014 Dr. Janet Eckerson helped to create LHS's and LPS's Spanish for Heritage Learners (SHL) coursework, after moving to the district from Crete Public Schools, a school district serving a nearby meatpacking community where approximately 50% of students are of Latinx backgrounds. In Crete she had launched one of Nebraska's first SHL programs at a time when they were so unusual that she wrote her dissertation in part about helping different SHL teachers in different schools and districts find one another to compare notes on how they were trying to support students with prior familial and community backgrounds with Spanish (Eckerson, 2015).

SHL programs acknowledge that students with some background in Spanish but little or no formal academic experience with it bring a different profile to the *Spanish as a world language* classroom than do their peers who encounter Spanish as a foreign language. In the sequence that Dr. Eckerson led through the beginning of the COVID pandemic, which enrolls many former EBs and even a few still-identified EBs, heritage learners study Spanish with an emphasis on building upon what they know and reconciling it with the academic Spanish encountered in world language programs and the Advanced Placement (AP) test.

"Correcting" the Spanish of a Spanish speaker is, at minimum, a fraught exercise and prospectively comes intertwined with issues of judging dialects as inferior or superior to each other and upsetting a student's sense of identity (Flores & Rosa, 2015). A premise of SHL classes is to avoid these hazards by, among other things, engaging students in consideration of the multiple "Spanishes" spoken around the world and encountered in Lincoln. The program at LHS was run by coauthor Dr. Eckerson (a classroom teacher), who has worked with the Nebraska Department of Education and LPS leaders to create professional development support for teachers of this specialized topic area. Like the *Cultural Ambassadors* described later, the SHLs program sees students' first language as an asset.

While Spanish is not the first language of all of LHS's current and former ELs, it is the only world language taught in Lincoln Public Schools for which there is a significant heritage learner enrollment. There are large Karen-, Arabic-, and Vietnamese-speaking populations at LHS, but those languages are not taught as world languages in LPS, so creating a heritage language (HL) class for them would be much more complicated. There is also a modest French-as-first-language-speaking population at LHS, mainly composed of students from Francophone African backgrounds, but their numbers are small enough that a French for HLs strand has not yet been attempted. LHS has also been working with the district, state, and university to explore the prospect of Arabic as both a world and heritage language, but as of this writing those have not advanced beyond conversations.

## V. ENGLISH LANGUAGE PROGRAM AND CURRICULUM

While recognizing and building on heritage languages is important work, that mainly describes a different portion of LHS's practice and a different student population than the school's efforts directed at identified EBs. Regarding the latter, LHS hosts the district's largest English as a Second Language (ESL) program at the secondary level. Students in this program are placed in one of five levels based on proficiency, with 1 indicating very limited facility in English, and levels 2, 3, and 4 describing increased English proficiency (and more mainstreaming for elective and academic coursework). In turn, level 5 references those who have exited any extra language support but who have not passed the English language proficiency assessment (ELPA). While the ELPA is technically required for a student to no longer be classified as an EL, it is not a gateway to anything and does not block students from earning credits toward graduation.[1] Level 5s are taking an entirely non-ESL load but the ELL Department continues to track their success, which means their progress is more closely monitored than if they formally exited.

Students at Level 1 spend multiple hours a day in ESL classes, with their limited forays beyond either in electives (like PE) or in content coursework (like mathematics) where all of their classmates are also identified EBs. Content teaching at this level has included some co-teaching and more co-teaching remains a department goal, but in the most recent semester (fall 2021) new enrollments of identified EBs forced pulling ELL teachers who were co-teaching in content classrooms back to meet the increased demand for the ESL classes. At level 2, identified EBs begin taking social studies and science courses that can count toward graduation. At levels 3 and 4, identified EBs continue to take one ESL course, but also begin enrolling in language arts classes that count toward graduation. For the EBs with the least developed English skills (i.e., levels 1 and 2), content coursework tends to be with fully identified EB enrollments, allowing content-area teachers to adapt coursework for an ELL enrollment and clarifying to ELL teachers which colleagues and which classes need additional support. For EBs who also are identified for special education, supports from the Special Education program are also leveraged.

One goal is for EL classrooms to feel like a safe space for participating students, but not a separate one. This explains the ELL Department's continued monitoring of EBs even as more/most of their coursework occurs outside of the department. From another perspective, it also explains why the ESL classrooms are located near the cafeteria in a high-volume part of the school (rather than some distant corner).

Given the broad needs and aspirations of its various constituencies, LHS also must be plurally involved with the community. LHS has a full-time parent and community engagement specialist who has both direct and coordinating roles, and the school convenes an EB parent advisory committee.

Until recently, this role was complemented by a second position, an EB student advocate, who did an impressive job as a kind of "counselor lite" to EBs, becoming their first stop for academic support, legal support, and/or mental health support. The academic support included regular monitoring of all identified EBs' grades and intervention with both the student and usually the teacher when an EB was not passing a class. The legal support references when a student or family member need assistance with visas, legal papers, and other documentation that newcomer families regularly need to negotiate and that can be profound distractions for students if not dealt with. The advocate was not a provider of such services, but rather an intermediary connecting an EB to community and advocacy resources where they could find help. Similarly, the advocate was not a provider of mental health services but was often an intermediary connecting an EB in need to counseling support.

When that EB student advocate left LHS, the ELL Department divided the role among its teachers and designated advocates by proficiency level. (That meant a review of all level 1 EBs by a teacher, a review of all level 2 students' grades by a different teacher, and so on.) Mostly these teachers do not take on the multiple advocacy roles directly, except partially the academic one, but, like the former student advocate, they are prepared to support EB students by connecting them to the right resources. More generally, the smaller scale of the ELL Department means EBs are known and advocated for as they make forays into the rest of the school. This helps even level 5s who are no longer taking any designated coursework but whom ELL Department personnel continue to monitor.

ELL faculty often also help students get ready to pass the English reading proficiency test used by Southeast Community College, which, if passed, takes away a key obstacle to students qualifying for a Learn to Dream scholarship that fully funds pursuit of an associate degree. Alignment with Southeast Community College also matters in a second way. Many EBs at the high school level arrive with interrupted schooling and often are older. The Nebraska state constitution allows enrollment in high school up to age 21 for residents who have not yet finished high school. This means some EBs will "time out" before they can earn a high school diploma and that students will need to pursue a GED. While earning a GED is literally a process of taking and passing a multifaceted test, Southeast Community College (like other Nebraska community colleges) offers GED test prep, which includes both content and logistical support for the exam. In this scenario, ELL Department faculty work with EBs to have their high school ESL classes set up students to continue with GED prep at community college.

Expectations to position graduates for further academic success broadly describes a pervasive norm at LHS and does not mean EBs are only expected to be ready for community college. EBs are also supported in planning for 4-year degrees and institutions. One of the most generous scholarships available for public higher education in Nebraska is called the Susie Buffett Scholarship. Typically, identified EBs earn a fifth to a third of all these scholarships that LHS graduates obtain each year. In 2021, a total of 23 LHS graduates earned Susie Buffett Scholarships and EBs earned 7 of those; in 2020, they won 4 of 24; in 2019, they received 8 of 23; and in 2017, they earned 4 of 15.

While the ELL Department takes the lead on assuring that EBs are adequately supported, consistent with Miramontes et al. (2011), support of EBs is not seen as ELL faculty task only. Equitable inclusion of identified EBs and equitable and meaningful parent and community engagement are products of attitude and the culture that school leaders are seeking to build. During job interviews, educators and classified staff alike are asked about their attitudes toward cultural and linguistic diversity. Only candidates who explain that they see home language(s) and cultural background as assets are offered positions.

## VI. CULTURAL AMBASSADORS AND STUDENT CLUBS

As another example of seeing students' bi/multilingualism as an asset, LHS runs a program called Cultural Ambassadors. Students in this group serve as multilingual liaisons to help parents and other visitors with limited English negotiate the school when there are public events. Students are not interpreters for high-stakes and private communication (about an IEP, for example); the school district relies on paid community liaisons for that. Rather, the ambassadors help parents and visitors find out where to go to get from point A to point B and otherwise negotiate the school. While occasionally ambassadors are native English speakers who have developed advanced skills in another language, most of the ambassadors act as interpreters between English and their native languages, among them Arabic, Karen, Kurdish, Russian, and Spanish. While too often first language skills are seen as obstacles or irrelevant by American public schools, here the orientation is intentionally quite the opposite. LHS wants language skills to be visible, helpful, and a point of pride.

This orientation also fits for several of the 42 student clubs that students can join. One day a month is Club Day, and on that day students can miss up to two classes to participate in one or two of the 42 clubs (all of which have faculty or staff sponsors). The themes of the clubs vary, as is implied by titles like Feminists for Change, Cribbage Club, and HOSA (for future health professionals), with several having explicit culture, identity, and language tie-ins. For example, the Joven Noble Latino Leaders Club, operated in partnership with a local Hispanic-serving community organization, targets Latino male students and encourages them to pursue their academic and life goals through interactions with successful male role models and community interactions. Another club, Las Razas Unidas, helps students become involved in LHS activities and does so by affirming Latino/a/x heritage (using both Spanish and English for its formal description of its purpose). Guest speakers, fundraising, and a variety of options encourage students to engage in school and community activities. Another club, the Karen/Zomi/Karenni Club, supports students from Burma and Thailand as they explore the American culture and education system while celebrating the Karen traditions.

Through clubs such as these, LHS endeavors to help all students find multiple and various points to engage and connect. Clubs that affirm backgrounds, identities, and languages and that give means for social connection through service learning or various group activities can be particularly helpful for their welcoming of EB students.

## VII. BILINGUAL LIAISONS

Starting in 2016, LHS teachers and staff have participated in a professional development workshop on how to effectively call students' homes. In many instances those calls (and written communication) need to be in languages other than English, and LHS staff work closely with district-level liaisons for the seven largest language groups in the district (Spanish, Karen, Kurdish, Vietnamese, Arabic, Ukrainian, and Russian). Several of the district's 24 liaisons, however, are multilingual (despite the colloquial label describing their job as "bilingual"). That means that in addition to the "main seven," the district had interpretive capacity in six more languages, among them Farsi and Kurmanji (the language spoken by Yazidis, an ethnic group from Iraq).

The district coordinator of the liaison program has lauded its impact, noting its close work with LHS where some of the liaisons spend the majority of their time. He also noted the increase in permanent funding (versus grant-dependent) for liaison positions. The district is still seeking to expand capacity to support Central American Indigenous languages, since an increasing number of students and families from Guatemala have made their way to LPS and LHS. While the bilingual liaisons and a related districtwide Welcome Center are not, strictly speaking, LHS programs, they do have a substantial impact on LHS and the school's commitments to welcome, support, and include EB students and their families.

## VIII. BILINGUAL CAREER AND EDUCATION FAIR

The LPS Bilingual Career and Education Fair, now in its 6th year at Lincoln High, brings employers, educational institutions, government, and community organizations together to showcase for students and families the opportunities available in Lincoln and across the state for multilingual students. From scholarship opportunities to on-the-spot interviews, the fair connects language-minority students and their families with recruiters and representatives of community institutions that value multilingualism. The event, hosted annually in LHS's cafeteria, now boasts dozens of diverse exhibitors and is visited by hundreds of students and parents from across the city.

To create the fair, teachers involved in the district SHL professional learning community (PLC) seized upon an idea that began in a Latino student club at Lincoln Southwest High School in 2014. The group hosted a small event in which a handful of Latinx professionals talked with students about their careers and the opportunities for Spanish/English bilinguals in their fields. The SHL PLC, then led by Dr. Eckerson, reimagined the event as an opportunity for students in the SHL level 1 courses across the district to use skills they were learning in class to help plan the fair, from writing professional emails to creating promotional materials. LHS was the obvious choice to host the district-level event, with its large multilingual student population, central urban location, and supportive administration.

In the fall of 2015, LHS hosted the first annual LPS Bilingual Career and Education Fair, or *Feria de Educación y Carreras Bilingües*—focusing, at first, on Spanish/English bilinguals. The event exploded and in subsequent years expanded to target multilingual speakers of many other community languages, as well as second language learners of world languages, within LPS. It is now attended by a diverse cross-section of Lincoln's population, mainly but not exclusively LPS students. Students in SHL courses still participate in organizing the event and inviting and thanking the presenters. In fact, the fair is so successful in bringing parents of minority language students to the building that LHS counselors began to offer other services, like college financial planning presentations, in conjunction with the fair.

## IX. FINAL THOUGHTS

As the city's oldest high school and with a current physical plant that includes portions of the school that are over 100 years old, Lincoln High also explicitly if modestly attends to its ties to generations of alumni/ae. In the main hallway outside the Ted Sorensen Theatre (named for President John F. Kennedy's speechwriter, who was an LHS alum), there is a wall of fame with portraits of 100 distinguished alums, including (in addition to Sorensen) former talk show host Dick Cavett and former Lincoln Public Schools Director of Multicultural Education Dr. Thomas Christie (among many others). Past generations can enter the school and still see familiar hallways and even familiar faces on the wall. Lincoln High takes seriously its century-plus role of being a beacon and anchor of the community. That community now speaks multiple languages and represents most of the globe in terms of ethnic origin, and it too finds welcome and embrace at LHS.

## NOTES

1. Rather than the ELPA, the typical test emphasis for advanced EBs is actually the ACT, which students can take for free, and that does double duty by aiding prospective college admission.

## REFERENCES

Catalano, T., & Hamann, E. T. (2016). Multilingual pedagogies and pre-service teachers: The modeling of "language as a resource" orientations in teacher education programs. *Bilingual Research Journal, 39*(3–4), 263–278.

Eckerson, J. (2015). *Teacher perspectives on professional development needs for better serving Nebraska's Spanish heritage language learners* [PhD dissertation, University of Nebraska—Lincoln]. http://digitalcommons.unl.edu/teachlearnstudent/62/

Flores, N., & Rosa, J. (2015). Undoing appropriateness: Raciolinguistic ideologies and language diversity in education. *Harvard Education Review, 85*(2), 149–171.

González, N., Moll, L., & Amanti, C. (2005). *Funds of knowledge: Theorizing practices in households, communities, and classrooms.* Lawrence Erlbaum.

Hamann, E. T., & Reeves, J. (2013). Interrupting the professional schism that allows less successful educational practices with ELLs to persist. *Theory into Practice, 52*(2), 81–88.

Miramontes, O. B., Nadeau, A., & Commins, N. L. (2011). *Restructuring schools for linguistic diversity: Linking decision making to effective programs* (2nd ed.). Teachers College Press.

Pipher, M. (2002). *The middle of everywhere: Helping refugees enter the American community.* Harcourt.

Ruíz, R. (1984). Orientations in language planning. *NABE: The Journal for the National Association for Bilingual Education, 8*(2), 15–34.

# CHAPTER 10

# "Like a Family"

## Sharing Leadership With Teachers, Students, Families, and Community at Rainier Beach High School

*Ann M. Ishimaru and Dwane Chappelle*

Criterion 10: Sustain Equitable and Meaningful Parent and Community Engagement

Beach was like a family. Even if there was an issue outside of the school, the families will come to the school, would circle up and huddle—we'd put our brains around how to support the families and the kids. And teachers and everyone will be involved. Because even if something happens on the weekend it always comes to the school.

—Dwane Chappelle

Ask students, parents, teachers, or community partners to describe Rainier Beach High School, and they will unerringly use the word "family" in their description. That deep sense of ownership and identification with the high school permeates the community of Rainier Beach and its extended network of alumni and community members. Although former principal and coauthor Dwane Chappelle recognizes that he played a key role in the profound shifts that led to the school's recognition as a School of Opportunity, he is quick to emphasize that the story of Beach is not about a heroic individual leader.[1] Rather, it's a story of collaboration and of engaging and listening to community. Dwane describes it as a story of "relentless" and strategic parents, "phenomenal" teachers, and a recognition that trusting the local experts—particularly the teachers and the parents—must mean more than an open door and token gestures. As the principal at the time of the most dramatic changes, Dwane led multiple improvement strategies and leveraged resources to support change at the school, but at the end of the day, his leadership practice prioritized fostering community voice and expertise to enact shared decision-making at the school.

Our aim in this chapter is to highlight specific leadership practices of shared decision-making and collaboration within the so-called "turnaround" of Rainier Beach High School, the only predominantly African American high school in the Seattle Public School district. We aim to share these practices not as panaceas or even decontextualized "best practices" but as potential ways forward toward reimagining schools amidst deeply rooted historical inequities and constantly changing contexts. The demands of top-down accountability-driven policy can make school and district leaders feel they have little choice but to carry out a set of prescribed initiatives narrowly focused on producing short-term test score gains, particularly in the context of pandemic-era dominant narratives of "learning loss." We hope these leadership practices can help illuminate alternatives for leading equity-driven change, even given long-standing racial inequities, deficit-based policies, and ongoing tensions in U.S. education reform. We begin by contextualizing leadership within current educational policy contexts, then describe how the principal worked to trust local expertise, humanize relationships, and integrate racial equity with instructional improvement work within the broader arc of the change-making process at Rainier Beach High School.

## LEADERSHIP WITHIN NEOLIBERAL POLICY REFORM CONTEXTS

The notion of leadership *with* school community members stands in stark contrast to the top-down, technically driven accountability approach typically undertaken in school turnaround strategies. Inspired by for-profit business models, so-called "turnaround" reforms were catalyzed by federal education policy during the No Child Left Behind (NCLB) era, despite a dearth of research on their effectiveness (and even research that suggested more failure than success in industry, where the approach originated [Mathis, 2009]). Turnaround reforms incentivize rapid organizational change instigated by major turnover in leadership as well as teaching staff and a "laser" focus on producing change in the form of standardized achievement test score outcomes (Duke & Jacobson, 2011; Herman et al., 2008).

Although NCLB gave way to the Every Student Succeeds Act (ESSA) and a global pandemic has reshaped the landscape of schooling, technical-rational approaches to decision-making persist. Educational decisions, often made with a great sense of urgency by policymakers and district leaders, are seen as "rational, value neutral, interest free, objective, and reliant only on 'hard facts'" (Khalifa et al., 2014, p. 15). Far from neutral, though, the technical-rational logic embedded in turnaround reforms and the efficient management of conventional schooling often disregards historical power inequities and champions dominant hierarchical leadership to compel change.

In such approaches, those in formal authority (like principals) often consolidate power and control; disregard context, relationships, and nondominant forms of expertise; and seek to shut down local educators and community voice and agency. The all-too-common turnaround story consists of top-down policy mandates and basic skills remediation focused on boosting high-stakes testing outcomes. Ironically, a growing body of research highlights such change as having a disproportionately negative impact on the very working-class, Black and Brown students and communities such reforms are supposedly intended to support (Kirshner & Jefferson, 2015; Trujillo & Renée, 2015).

A growing body of literature has pushed beyond the conventional approaches to school improvement and parent involvement to illuminate nondominant family and community members as educational leaders who drive sustained, equitable school change (Bertrand & Rodela, 2018; Ishimaru, 2018). By moving beyond passive supporters of educator-driven agendas or individual consumers who "choose" between constrained options, collective parent agency has been a force for educational justice in working-class communities of color across the country (Shirley, 2009; Warren & Goodman, 2018). In tandem with educators and formal leaders, these collective family and community leadership efforts suggest that a broader notion of leadership holds potential for re-imagining school "turnarounds" by making community engagement central to the mission, as illustrated by Rainier Beach's exemplary practices tied to this Schools of Opportunity criterion. While the 10th Schools of Opportunity criterion focuses on making the dominant parent engagement strategies more inclusive, the approach at Rainier also takes the next step: shifting power so that leadership is genuinely shared.

Rainier Beach High School's "turnaround" story runs counter to the dynamics of technical-rational school improvement regimes, even if its context of disinvestment and racial inequity sounds all too familiar (Ishimaru,

---

### CRITERION 10: SUSTAIN EQUITABLE AND MEANINGFUL PARENT AND COMMUNITY ENGAGEMENT

Parents and community members are a central part of this [exemplary] school's leadership. Several different structures, programs, and policies formalize these relationships. Teachers and staff receive professional development about how to engage diverse parents and communities.

Parent and community meetings are designed to be convenient for working families. The school has a translator [or community engagement liaison] that can help parents with limited English engage with the school. Several community partnerships bring additional resources to the school.

2018). Rainier Beach is a highly diverse, low-income high school in Seattle Public Schools, a mid-sized urban district in the Pacific Northwest in the heart of a historic African American community. Known nationally for its basketball prowess and prominent alumni who have made it to the NBA, the high school and the neighborhood continue to be home to many African Americans, refugees, and immigrants, though growing gentrification in the city has raised rents and property values and led to an influx of White residents in nearby areas. Constructed in the 1960s, the school enjoys a deep sense of connection with its alumni, many of whom stayed—or returned— to the neighborhood to raise their own children. In 2017–2018, the student population was 97% students of color and over 76% eligible for free and reduced-price lunch, including 50% African Americans, 27.3% Asians, 13.5% Hispanic/Latinos, 0.3% American Indians, 1.6% Pacific Islanders, 3% White, and 4% two or more races.[2]

The threat of closure due to low graduation rates and enrollment in 2008 echoes a familiar cascade of long-standing resource inequities, neighborhood disinvestment, White flight, and the disenfranchisement of low-income African American and other students of Color in the urban secondary school. Efforts to revitalize the school began around 2009, as communities sought to recover from the Great Recession and the federal government invested in incentive-based turnaround reforms. Today, the school's student enrollment has increased dramatically from the low of 300 that triggered closure considerations in 2008, graduation rates have risen to consistently surpass the district average,[3] and the school has been recognized nationally for its academic programs and for opening opportunities to African American and other historically minoritized students from the neighborhood.

The daily reality of the school continues to reflect complexity and struggle, so we in no way mean to suggest an uncomplicated success story. Even so, Rainier Beach represents a very different "turnaround" story, as parents, alumni, community members, teachers, and leaders all rallied around the school to reckon with deep-seated racial inequities, reshape the school's image, leverage new resources, build rigorous learning opportunities, partner with community to foster youth leadership, and navigate contentious politics in the district. As the principal, Dwane sought to leverage the expertise of educators, families, and communities and enable them to "infiltrate the system" by reimagining traditional structures—like turnaround reforms, advanced learning opportunities, the PTA, and student interventions—to disrupt the status quo and foster a more equitable educational environment for students.

In this chapter, we highlight three key leadership practices employed in the Rainier Beach reform to share decision-making and to collaborate in racial equity work with their extended school community. We highlight below how the leadership team's practices illuminated the following principles: (1) Trust the experts to have voice in decisions and action, (2) humanize relationships to foster a familial culture, and (3) integrate racial equity and instructional improvement. These efforts must be understood within the context of a broader set of efforts over time and an infusion of financial, social, and cultural capital as well as new structures and personnel. However, we also recognize that new money, people, and structures are insufficient foundations for leading racially equitable change in schools; such change requires fundamentally reorienting the dominant assumptions and racialized institutional scripts that infuse educational leadership.

## TRUST THE EXPERTS TO HAVE VOICE IN DECISIONS AND ACTION

Prior to Dwane's hiring at Rainier Beach High School, the stage had already been somewhat set by a group of parent and community leaders who successfully mobilized to keep the school open when its enrollment had dropped perilously low and its 48% on-time graduation rate ranked it as one of the lowest-performing schools in the district and state (Washington State Office of Superintendent of Public Instruction, 2008–2009). A self-described "small but mighty" group of predominantly African American parents resolved to "counter the negativity in the media" about Rainier Beach and build a new academic identity to attract students back to the school. At the suggestion of a district leader, parents at the school decided to adopt the International Baccalaureate (IB) program, a rigorous international curriculum originally designed for the children of diplomats. To garner resources, the parents—who by now had formally become the Rainier Beach Parent-Teacher-Student Association (PTSA)—engaged in political advocacy for the school in the district, the neighborhood, the city, and even eventually at the state legislature. This advocacy resulted in, among other things, a $1 million state allocation for the school through the Urban School Turnaround Initiative to support the IB adoption and outreach. Although unsuccessful in its first bid, the school also applied for a federal School Improvement Grant (SIG) and developed a turnaround plan, which included the formation of a SIG team to oversee the transformation.[4] Also sometimes referred to as the design team, the SIG team included several of the PTSA parent leaders, a key community leader, and the district administrator who had first suggested the IB program.

Even though the school was not awarded a SIG grant at that time, the district and school agreed to move ahead with the plan. Members of the SIG team hired Dwane Chappelle, an African American, as the new principal who would oversee planning and implementation of the IB program. Although he was from out of state, Dwane's wife was a Rainier Beach alumna whose family still lived in the area. Dwane brought prior experience with IB and impressed the team with his emphasis on relationships. IB Coordinator

Colin Pierce, who was from Arizona, was also hired around this time and joined the design team. The design team played a major role in Dwane's socialization into the school and the neighborhood, and he perceived their regular meetings as a form of community accountability that he came to value.

One of the first moves Dwane made after his arrival at Rainier Beach was to start by listening to the local "experts" on content (teachers) and on students (families and communities). He quickly realized that teachers, parents, and other groups had ideas and information about how to go about the work. Lip service to "listening" is common in approaches to leadership, especially in the form of symbolic gestures like open-door policies and being visible in the school and at sports events (Auerbach, 2010). Dwane worked to go beyond symbolic gestures and listen to "what's being said underneath the words." He soon recognized that there was an opportunity not just to get input but to incorporate teacher, student, parent, and community voice into the decisions that were being made at the school. He worked to expand decision-making authority to the experts.

Rather than trying to prove his expertise and authority as a new turnaround leader, Dwane listened to teachers. For instance, he relied on his 9th-grade teaching team, taking a calculated risk by empowering them as instructional leaders for the rest of the staff. The 9th-grade team shared the common expectations and assessments they had developed for students schoolwide. The team also shared their practices for engaging families. By listening and trusting their expertise as well as being explicit about his own limitations, Dwane modeled a vulnerability that opened teachers to being reflective about their own areas of growth, and teachers came to realize administration was "not a gotcha" situation.

Sharing vulnerability and inviting others to lead sounds a bit heretical within the context of turnaround reforms premised on the notion of a bold new leader willing to make immediate and dramatic change. Dwane explains that coming in and turning everything upside-down might meet *your* needs as a leader, but that is not the same as meeting the needs of the community.

> You have to understand that it's not about power. It's not about you. It's about doing what's right for our students, and it's about taking what you've learned and making sure that there's a well-rounded approach to it. Some folks step into the position [of principal] with the understanding of what they have learned and experienced and often forget to center themselves on students and families. They think they know what needs to happen. But it's not about me. It's always about the kids and the school and the community. The reality is that oftentimes we forget to trust the experts, especially those in the classroom. It isn't enough to just hear what people say; we need to empower them with decision-making authority.

In school improvement, the test scores and attendance rates are nationally predetermined metrics for success, but the reality according to Dwane is that you have to "unpeel the wallpaper to really understand what's happening in the building before you can know what needs to change." Listening to people recenters expertise on the collective and disrupts the notion that leadership is about the principal's power.

The leadership team of the school also turned to parent leaders as experts. These parent leaders were "relentless" in their advocacy for the school and in their insistence about their role as key, authentic decision-makers. With a rueful laugh, Dwane recalls stumbling over his assumptions about the role of parents in decision-making early in his principalship:

> I remember they got on me! So my first year I had to hire approximately 19, almost 20 teachers that summer, when I was hired right before school started. And they [parents] were like, "When are you having these interviews? And how do we know that the teachers being hired are the best for our students?" And I'm saying, "Oh, I have a great process, I hired a few teachers so far, we screened the apps, and so on . . ." In which the parents pushed my thinking. "Well, that's what you think. We're the parents. Can we have some input on who will be hired?" So those remarks inspired me to look at recruiting teachers and staff differently. Like, oh, I guess that does make sense, right? From there we tried to have as many parents as possible on interview committees and tried to get students to be part of the process. And I think at one point we were like, at almost like 85 to 90 percent of our interviews had some type of parent and or student participation.

Thus, listening and recognizing expertise provided a foundation for sharing decision-making authority with teachers, parents, and community leaders to ensure that any changes would be in the best interests of the school, kids, and community.

Finally, the practice of trusting the experts also required identifying allies, especially among parents and community members, who shared a vision of equity for the school and helped navigate the inevitable power and politics of the school and district. Issues of power can become complicated in seeking to share leadership, especially in relation to the small group of privileged parents in almost any school who feel entitled to dictate decisions because of their fundraising, donations, or other relational privileges and access they may have. In many schools, the PTA can be dominated by privileged, disproportionately White parents, but Dwane quickly realized Rainier Beach's PTA was different. The small and tight-knit network of 6 to 10 parent and community members were mostly African American residents of the neighborhood, many of whom were themselves graduates, employees, or relatives of staff at the school. One of these parents, Carlina Brown-Banks, explained how this group of parents' daily influence for and within the school related to the group's motto, "Not Your Mother's PTA," particularly in response to challenges by formal authorities:

> Rainier Beach PTA was brought up, and she [a former co-principal] says, "I don't understand why they have to be involved in [the] day-to-day practice of the school. They should be going to make cookies to build money for the school . . ." We don't make cookies. We're not here to fund-raise for your school. We're here to be transformative change agents for the school. We need you to deploy us to spaces that you can't get to, like School Board meetings and the Superintendent . . . No, we don't make cookies. We don't make cookies . . . We infiltrate, that's right.

The parent leaders helped Dwane to recognize that they could speak up on behalf of issues that his position in the district made it challenging for him to address directly or alone. As described elsewhere (Ishimaru, 2018), the mostly Black parent leaders refused the institutional scripts of passive "cookie-baking" PTA parents and instead used the conventional parent involvement structure to reshape the role of families as fellow leaders in the core work of the school as well as the broader sociopolitical contexts of school change.

Although this allyship in advocacy was particularly clear in the realm of resource advocacy at the district and state levels, parents were also able to expand the conversation and sense of accountability in the building with regard to teacher practice, sometimes in ways that were more effective than the principal or administrative roles would enable. With the support of teachers who also wanted to dispel the myth of being a "bad" school, school administrators consistently found ways to get parents and community into the building. Inviting parents to do walk-throughs of classrooms and witness the life of the school became a routine practice. For instance, one parent was in the hall and noticed three students getting sent out of a classroom in rapid succession. The parent later approached the teacher to ask what happened and to offer help—*Did the teacher need training? If so, they could help identify people or resources to provide that training. Could parents advocate for personnel funds to provide more classroom support?*

Conversations like this shifted the typical power dynamic between parents, particularly Black mothers, and teachers in ways that were not always comfortable, but because teachers' expertise had been trusted from the start and they had developed relationships with the core group of parent leaders (as discussed below), teachers felt supported by administration. Dwane emphasized that partnerships cannot be about "last-minute" asks "just when you need something." As part of the Building Leadership Team, parent leaders were also part of crafting the budget, master scheduling, and professional development decisions. Thus, engagement was embedded in the daily practice of the school.

In sum, the practice of trusting the experts and sharing leadership with them is not easy, as it challenges dominant conceptions of leadership that vest a single heroic individual with the expertise to turnaround a "troubled" school. In reflecting on leading in schools like Rainier Beach, Dwane pinpointed the challenge of really knowing yourself and being realistic about your capacities and your limitations. Often individuals who take on leadership opportunities are afraid to ask for help because they may see it as weakness—or their superiors and others may see it as a lack of leadership, particularly in the case of leaders of Color who are perceived differently than their White counterparts. But the leadership practice of trusting experts requires you to know your own vulnerabilities and be willing to seek support in those areas. Expecting the leader to have expertise in everything is both unrealistic and unfair. No one person has the key to all the expertise required to transform a school or system. "It isn't about hiding your weaknesses," Dwane explained. "It's about giving other people the opportunity to step up." Trusting the experts to shape decisions and action thus constituted a vital practice for developing leadership across the school.

## HUMANIZE RELATIONSHIPS TO FOSTER A FAMILIAL CULTURE

A second deceptively simple leadership practice enacted in the change-making process at Rainier Beach was to put relationships first in the work and deliberately shift the default culture of the school. Relationships with students, teachers, and parents are at the heart of change, but given the complexities of many transitions and the history of racialized distrust between local communities and the district, those relationships can take time and effort to build and sustain. Dwane and Ivory Brooks, the assistant principal, worked to establish a more relational culture at the school through simple daily routines such as walking the building to bid good morning to every staff member prior to the doors opening, then greeting kids as they entered school to begin their days. This simple act was about seeing and responding to students as individuals, going the extra mile to "build a small family" at the school by humanizing students and adults. When they eventually got parents to come into the building and they realized the principal or assistant principal knew their child, parents would react with concern as though their child were in trouble. But they soon realized that the entire staff worked to know the students, to build a "circle of trust" so they each had a trusted adult to go to in the building, something Ivory Brooks was keen on implementing.

The school's administrators also normalized their presence in classrooms by doing regular 5-minute nonevaluative walk-throughs and periodically

surprising teachers with healthy snacks. Dwane explains how this small routine of appreciation established a positive dynamic with teachers and intentionally modeled humanizing interactions for students:

> Once a month we would go and buy apples, oranges, yogurt, protein
> bars, and put them on a tray with juice and cups, and we would go
> to all of the classes in the building to appreciate our educators. Once
> class would begin, we would go in and say, "Hey, Mrs. Burks, can we
> talk to you for a minute?" And of course the kids will all look! "We
> just want to appreciate you. Would you like some snacks?" We'd get
> them to smile, bringing them some fruit or juice early in the morning.
> We thought it was kind of corny, but our amazing educators really
> appreciated that. And it became a point where staff and students were
> looking forward to it.

These simple routines established an important foundation for the inevitable
challenging dynamics that arose in the course of school interactions.

A practice of "circling back" became a strategy for reaffirming relationships, regardless of the incident. Dwane gave the example of a parent-teacher
conversation that did not go as smoothly as it might have and a teacher who
felt they were not "backed" by Dwane in the meeting:

> We always would circle back—maybe it didn't go as we wanted, as we
> thought it would go, according to plan. We would always circle back
> just to follow up and close the loop to see if anyone needed additional
> clarification on why one of us said what we said. It's a reflective
> moment in those areas of challenge.

Through this practice of "circling back" face to face with students, staff,
and families, the school's administrators kept their relationships in the foreground, even as they sought to resolve challenging dynamics and issues.
These more trusting relationships opened staff to be more creative or innovative and to take calculated risks in changing their practices or offering
leadership beyond their own classrooms or departmental efforts.

With regard to centering relationships with families, two key practices
emerged over time. Even though Rainier Beach was a highly diverse community, events held for the entire school community could still feel exclu-
sive or marginalizing to specific groups within the parent community. For
example, Somali parents would often not attend all-school events; they would
express discomfort with not understanding the language and expectations
in those spaces. With the support of parent leaders, the school's leadership
team instituted events specifically for Somali families. Because gender plays
a significant role, they held Somali Mothers' Night Out and Somali Dads'
Nights. Community-specific activities enabled families with shared language

and cultural backgrounds to build relationships with one another and the school.

Second, after the school received a federal grant, the parents on the design team recommended hiring a parent engagement coordinator to support the work of building relationships and understanding with families. The liaison worked with the PTA to reach out and build capacity among parents, students, and even community members without children at the school through the IB Community Cafes. The school's administrators and parents eventually reimagined the expectation that parents needed to come to the school to be involved. The Community Cafes were gatherings in local restaurants and other community gathering spaces where teachers would offer sample lessons from the IB curriculum, answer questions, and build relationships among teachers, families, and community members. These events established new lines of communication between teachers, parents, and communities, and they engaged families in experiences and conversation about teaching and learning at the core of schooling and improvement work, a distinction that moved relationship-building beyond simply making families "feel welcome" when (or if) they came to the school.

Building relationships and ownership of the school with students, families, and staff may not seem like an instructional leadership move, but Dwane explained that the familial culture cultivated around the school directly linked to the classroom. He gave the example of how families precluded the need for police at football games:

> So we would have football games Friday night. And we wouldn't have any police officers come to the football game. . . . So we . . . huddled up with the families and we just basically took care of our own and not seeing it as we policed people. But we met folks at the gate and just said hello—we're just continuing to model and create an open and welcoming friendly environment. And the same thing we did at the football games, it translated into the classroom and translated into the building.

The shift to a more relational culture provided fertile grounds for collaboration across the school—from families, students, and administrators hiring new staff together, to teachers sharing their data in faculty meetings, and from expanded planning in grade-level professional learning communities (supported by funds to extend the day) to partnering with a youth organizing group in order to support academic interventions and foster social change leadership. The work of humanizing relationships shifted the culture of interactions around the school and the conditions within which the school pursued instructional improvement and racial equity.

## INTEGRATE RACIAL EQUITY AND INSTRUCTIONAL IMPROVEMENT

The implementation of the new IB curriculum was only one of many different instructional and school climate improvement efforts at Rainier Beach in the early years of the "turnaround" effort. Conventional turnaround reforms tend to focus solely on structural and technical changes. But this school's administrative team and its teacher and parent leaders recognized that the shifts to teaching, learning, and schooling necessary at Rainier Beach were intimately tied to the adaptive challenges that underlie behaviors, including the shared assumptions, norms, habits, ways of working, and interacting (Heifetz & Linksy, 2017). While technical changes may draw primarily on people's existing repertoires, adaptive change requires learning new practices, grappling with the uncertainty of change, and reshaping the culture of deliberations and everyday work. Such adaptive changes are implicated in overall instructional improvement reforms. But particularly efforts to address entrenched racial inequities in schooling often entail contentious political and normative aspects of educational change (Renée et al., 2010). What's more, in practice, these two types of reforms are rarely undertaken in tandem with each other—addressing one is often seen as being in the service of addressing the other (e.g., improving instruction for all will result in greater racial equity, or identifying and disrupting racial bias in schooling will improve student learning and outcomes). At Rainier Beach, however, shifts in the culture around explicitly addressing racial inequities happened *simultaneously* over time with efforts to improve instruction. Dwane explained the approach: "Identify racial bias everywhere in the system and engage the school community in changing practices—from the start, not as an afterthought."

Although racial equity work in schools has become more common in recent years, at the time in 2012 or 2013, work to grapple with racial inequities in turnaround efforts was far from the norm in the field. Because of the turnaround reform, Dwane hired nearly 80% of his staff anew, and the hiring committee (which included key parent, community, and student leaders) always ensured that questions of race and equity were part of the interview process. When teachers set out to improve their instruction, the 9th-grade team read Gloria Ladson-Billings's (2009) *Dreamkeepers* and requested outside expertise to work with the entire staff on cultural responsiveness. This ongoing learning helped to infuse into instructional improvement much-needed attention to the racialized dynamics of interactions and schooling. For example, efforts to improve math instruction were a matter of examining not only the technical aspects of teaching mathematics, but also teachers' racial positionalities and biases, how they positioned themselves in the classroom, how they set their class up, and how race related to the outcomes they saw both in a given class and across the school. The math teachers reflected on how those racialized dynamics played out in their grading practices, requested training on standards-based grading, and subsequently provided professional development to shift the entire school to adopt a new grading system. Therefore, the math department started implementing standards-based grading practices.

The school also took up instructional rounds (in which teachers visited each other's classrooms to share their practices [City et al., 2009] in tandem with racial equity work. Most instructional rounds at the time tended to evade discussions of race (Roberts, 2012). Unlike the original instructional improvement model, though, instructional rounds at Rainier Beach were grounded in foundational notions of cultural responsiveness. These visits highlighted not only content-based problems of practice but also the differential experiences of Black males, how teachers engaged some students as opposed to others, and how rules and adult–youth relationships unfolded differently across race and gender. Such efforts spurred instructional changes as well as policy-focused discussions, such as a focus on racialized teacher responses to class tardiness. Students also organized to increase the number of minutes between classes, and the school changed the policy to add time to passing periods even as teachers began to rethink their discipline and explore restorative justice approaches in their practice.

Finally, the school partnered with a youth-focused community organization called Washington Building Leaders of Change (WA-BLOC) to support student academic interventions. WA-BLOC supported students in classroom learning and homework and in developing them as young leaders of social justice in their communities. The group adopted the Freedom Schools model, a summer and after-school enrichment program of the Children's Defense Fund, inspired by the African American Freedom Schools of the civil rights movement. Academic learning support unfolded within a context of building community, change leadership, and social action. In 2015, Rainier Beach students organized and succeeded in winning a major action to get the City of Seattle to provide bus transit cards for low-income students across the district to get to school. In the fall of 2017, students demanded and won School Board commitments to renovate the school, which had long been promised but never delivered. As we write this in late 2021, a design team of students, alumni, and community members are helping to lead the renovation in a process they have dubbed "Build the Beach for Us by Us." Thus, across time, the school's leaders intentionally wove efforts to address deep-seated racial inequities with instructional improvement and student academic supports into an integrated strategy that sought both structural and cultural transformations in the school.

## IMPACTS BEYOND THE NUMBERS

Part of the reason Rainier Beach's story has captured the imagination of so many is that the dramatic improvements in attendance, graduation rates, participation in advanced learning coursework, IB exam scores, and college-going acceptance rates were all evidence of change that flew in the face of expectations and stereotypes of Black and Brown "inner-city" high schools. By 2015, graduation rates at Rainier Beach High School had surpassed the district average; by 2018 it had jumped to 89% and enrollment was surging; and the graduation rate has stayed at over 90% since then (with Black student graduation rates over 94% in 2021 despite the massive impacts of the COVID-19 pandemic). For Dwane and others who played a key role in the changes at Rainier Beach during that time, those statistics are important evidence of change, but the impacts that really stand out are the sense of pride, confidence, and belonging evident among the students, families, and community. The lasting impacts of these shifts are especially notable when they hear from Rainier Beach graduates, many of whom they are still in touch with. For instance, one student, an African American male football player, shared that he was initially placed in a remedial writing class in college based on assumptions about his proficiency, but because he had been taking IB classes in high school, he "blew them away" with his first essay assignment and was immediately moved.

Today, the dynamics of gentrification and displacement in the Rainier Beach neighborhood continue, while superintendent turnover and district politics converge with pandemic impacts on Black and immigrant communities to raise new challenges. The school district has made renewed commitments to Black students and families as those "farthest from educational justice" and the policy language of targeted universalism (powell, 2009). But the story of Rainier Beach High School also raises questions about the resources to sustain programs like IB—and the structures and staff needed to support it—in low-income schools (Brazile, 2019). Many Rainier Beach teachers and parents emphasized that, unlike schools elsewhere in the district, the resources required to sustain the program do not exist in the surrounding neighborhood (Ishimaru, 2018). For instance, the district funding formulas do not cover the additional expenses of IB program and testing fees, additional staff training, and the additional seventh period that allows for adequate collaborative planning (and incurs personnel costs due to union agreements) to make the model possible. Most of the families who were such powerful leaders at the time of the dramatic shifts have now gone onto leadership in other realms, and at least one expressed regret that they had not intentionally cultivated the parent leadership to sustain their efforts at the same level, though student leadership and advocacy have remained strong across the years. Miraftab (2004) argues that neoliberal democracy simultaneously employs processes of symbolic inclusion and material exclusion. It remains to be seen to what extent the "turnaround" at Rainier Beach may constitute symbolic inclusion in tandem with forms of material exclusion that constrain its sustainability over time.

Finally, educational change-making for racially equitable schools continues to be portrayed as the work of a heroic leader who single-handedly rescues a troubled school. Although frank about the messiness and risk of sharing leadership with not only students and teachers but also families and communities, Dwane was clear that the cultural shifts at Rainier Beach would not have been realized via top-down, unilateral authority. He subsequently took the leadership lessons he gleaned at Rainier Beach with him onto a broader stage when he became director of the City of Seattle's Department of Education and Early Learning. In reflecting on how he applies those lessons to his current role, Dwane emphasized the importance of having your community with you as a leader, despite the pressure to make decisions for people without engaging them. Only one voice in decision-making does not make for good decisions; other experts from the community must be part of shaping consequential deliberations.

Even now, years after Dwane's move from Rainier Beach, the familial relationships cultivated at the school sustain through touchpoints with former students, family members, teachers, and community members. Not long ago, Ann bumped into Dwane in the neighborhood standing outside the grocery store on the sidewalk, and a constant stream of former students and community members greeted him with smiles and warmth, like the relative they consider him to still be. He explained:

> One of my old students says, "Hey Unc!" And that's just how they do it. You know, it's like [we're] uncles, aunties, fathers, cousins and . . . there's always a respect.

These relationships and interactions remain a testament to the so-called "turnaround" work at Rainier Beach and the power of those efforts to not simply subvert but to transcend formal roles and top-down policy implementation to reimagine leadership in the journey of equitable school transformation.

## NOTES

1. This chapter is the joint work of the two coauthors. However, because Dwane Chappelle was also central to the reform, we refer to him in the third person throughout. We also quote Dwane based on interviews conducted by Ann Ishimaru. We hope this helps to clearly tell the story of the high school. Dwane began serving as principal in 2011 and continued through 2015, when he took his current position as head of the City of Seattle's Department of Education and

Early Learning. Accordingly, the focus of this chapter is on the 4–5 years of reform from 2011 through 2015.

2. More recent school demographics are similar; we are presenting the older data as more relevant to the reform period.

3. Enrollment in 2020–2021 was 780 students, and the overall 92% graduation rates continued to be higher than the district average of 86%, with 94.1% Black student graduation rate far exceeding the 79.9% Black graduation rate in the district (Washington State Office of Superintendent of Public Instruction, https://washington statereportcard.ospi.k12.wa.us/ReportCard/ViewSchoolOrDistrict/101125).

4. Later, in 2014, the school did receive a federal SIG grant, in the amount of $4.3 million, covering the period from April 2014 to August 31, 2017. The grant was used to, among other things, support the school's IB program and to generally focus on providing updated curriculum, materials, technology, and summer enrichment activities; reducing class sizes; and other factors.

## REFERENCES

Auerbach, S. (2010). Beyond coffee with the principal: Toward leadership for authentic school–family partnerships. *Journal of School Leadership, 20*(6), 728–757.

Bertrand, M., & Rodela, K. C. (2018). A framework for rethinking educational leadership in the margins: Implications for social justice leadership preparation. *Journal of Research on Leadership Education, 13*(1), 10–37.

Brazile, L. (2019, September 23). Some Rainier Beach High School students won't get a full year of history class due to budget cuts. *Crosscut.* https://crosscut.com /2019/09/some-rainier-beach-high-school-students-wont-get-full-year-history -class-due-budget-cuts

City, E. A., Elmore, R. F., Fiarman, S. E., & Teitel, L. (2009). *Instructional rounds in education* (Vol. 30). Harvard Education Press.

Duke, D. L., & Jacobson, M. (2011). Tackling the toughest turnaround—low-performing high schools. *Phi Delta Kappan, 92*(5), 34–38.

Heifetz, R., & Linsky, M. (2017). *Leadership on the line, with a new preface: Staying alive through the dangers of change.* Harvard Business Press.

Herman, R., Dawson, P., Dee, T., Greene, J., Maynard, R., Redding, S., & Darwin, M. (2008). *Turning around chronically low-performing schools: A practice guide* (NCEE #2008-4020). National Center for Education Evaluation and Regional Assistance.

Ishimaru, A. M. (2018). Re-imagining turnaround: Families and communities leading educational justice. *Journal of Educational Administration, 56*(5). https:// doi.org/10.1108/JEA-01-2018-0013

Khalifa, M. A., Jennings, M. E., Briscoe, F., Oleszweski, A. M., & Abdi, N. (2014). Racism? Administrative and community perspectives in data-driven decision making: Systemic perspectives versus technical-rational perspectives. *Urban Education, 49*(2), 147–181.

Kirshner, B., & Jefferson, A. (2015). Participatory democracy and struggling schools: Making space for youth in school turnarounds. *Teachers College Record, 117*(6), 1–26.

Ladson-Billings, G. (2009). *The dreamkeepers: Successful teachers of African American children* (2nd ed.). Jossey-Bass.

Mathis, W. J. (2009). *NCLB's ultimate restructuring alternatives: Do they improve the quality of education?* Education and the Public Interest Center & Education Policy Research Unit.

Miraftab, F. (2004). Making neo-liberal governance: The disempowering work of empowerment. *International Planning Studies, 9*(4), 239–259.

powell, j. a. (2009). Post-racialism or targeted universalism. *Denver University Law Review, 86*(3), 785–806.

Renée, M., Welner, K., & Oakes, J. (2010). Social movement organizing and equity-focused educational change: Shifting the zone of mediation. In A. Hargreaves, A. Lieberman, M. Fullan, & D. Hopkins (Eds.), *Second international handbook of educational change* (pp. 153–168). Springer.

Roberts, J. E. (2012). *Instructional rounds in action*. Harvard Education Press.

Shirley, D. (2009). Community organizing and educational change: A reconnaissance. *Journal of Educational Change, 10*(2–3), 229–237.

Trujillo, T., & Renée, M. (2015). Irrational exuberance for market-based reform: How federal turnaround policies thwart democratic schooling. *Teachers College Record, 117*(6), 1–34.

Warren, M. R., & Goodman, D. (2018). *Lift us up, don't push us out!: Voices from the front lines of the educational justice movement*. Beacon Press.

# Conclusion

## From Schools of Opportunity to Systems of Opportunity[1]

*Jeannie Oakes and Kevin Welner*

It can be done. Even in the midst of insidious underfunding and wrongheaded federal and state policies, schools can embrace policies and practices that close opportunity gaps.

The schools profiled in this book are existence proofs, and they exemplify practices that we hope many more schools will take up. But these schools and many of their practices are rare, and we need to address the reasons. What are the obstacles that make it difficult for excellence and equity to coexist—for schools to initiate and maintain research-based practices that provide so many benefits for students?

In this chapter, we take a step back from these specific schools, thinking broadly about how a system might facilitate and sustain the practices outlined by the Schools of Opportunity criteria. In doing so, we place individual schools within their broader contexts, recognizing that exceptional schools will always be just that—*exceptions*—if the policy context favors practices that are less effective and less equitable.

Further, we recognize that the students served by our schools exist in a context, as do school systems statewide and nationally. This societal context determines school funding. It encompasses families' poverty and wealth, along with associated hardships and advantages. It establishes neighborhood safety and community resources. It defines racial privilege and racist oppression. In short, societal context profoundly controls the resources and opportunities available to children inside and outside of schools.

From these realities, we can appreciate the limitations of school centric reform. Opportunity gaps are created through the cumulative impact of unequal opportunities to learn and thrive arising in schools and in larger society (Carter & Welner, 2013). Accordingly, opportunities to learn for students attending high-poverty schools are harmed by inequities at the school level and by inadequate and inequitable state funding systems. But these opportunities are also undermined, especially for Black, Native American, and Latinx children, by unaddressed barriers to learning that stem from adverse out-of-school conditions associated with concentrated poverty. A principal in a North Carolina rural high-poverty elementary school explained how several of the school's teachers "came back after delivering food and broke down in tears telling me what they saw. A student was living in a home with no roof; they've got a tarp for a roof kept on by bricks and tires. Homes didn't have doors" (Oakes et al., 2021, p. 11.)

Such communities of concentrated poverty expose children to a compilation of adverse out-of-school conditions that pose barriers to learning: lack of high-quality care for young children, food insecurity, substandard housing or homelessness, unsafe neighborhoods with limited youth development services and activities, reduced employment opportunities, policing and the carceral state, lack of access to social and health services, and an array of traumatic experiences. Opportunity gaps arising from these harms, even more than in-school inequities, drive the measured achievement gaps (Welner & LaCour, 2020). For the child living in the roofless home described above, poverty impacts learning more than school-level factors such as teacher inexperience. And because poverty in the United States is highly racialized, these burdens fall most heavily on Black, Latinx, and Native American children—those who also face direct, individualized racism.

Sixteen percent of U.S. children (11.6 million children) lived in poverty in 2019 (National Center for Education Statistics [NCES], 2021a). But this poverty is not distributed randomly. The number is 23% for Hispanic children and 37% for Black children. Because of residential and school segregation, the numbers become even starker at the school level. In 2017, a total of 45% Black and 44% Hispanic public school students attended high-poverty schools (NCES, 2021b). This compares to just 8% for White public school students. A review of research conducted in 2002 determined that the negative effects of concentrated poverty, on any child in a school, are found once poverty rates exceed 20%, and they grow rapidly before leveling off around 40% (Galster, 2012). Whatever the exact percentages and tipping points, the reality of childhood poverty is stark, and it is felt as individual poverty and at the level of schooling opportunities. Moreover, because poverty is often concentrated and often racialized, academic outcomes and their racially disparate patterns can be predicted at the school-district level (based on average socioeconomic characteristics of the district) with shocking accuracy (Stanford Education Data Archive, n.d.).

A humane and wise society would address societal harms associated with poverty and racism by directly reducing poverty and racism themselves. But the United States generally tries to "educationalize the welfare state" (Kantor & Lowe, 2013), asking its schools to play the role of "great equalizer" (Mann, 1848). Setting aside the judiciousness of this policy choice, it is true that well-resourced schools can offset some of the harms of concentrated poverty by, for instance, providing high-quality prekindergarten programs, using inclusive whole-child approaches to K–12 schooling, connecting child well-being wraparound services to schools, building respectful connections to community members and institutions, providing school support personnel at levels that meet national standards, and offering additional learning time and opportunities beyond the regular school day. Although frequently not as well-resourced as schools in wealthier districts, the Schools of Opportunity presented in this book manage to do these things by creatively shifting their priorities and resource allocations (and they could do much more if they had more resources to work with!).

So schools can help close opportunity gaps when they embrace research-based policies and practices. And such Schools of Opportunity could do more if they had more resources. But is a great-equalizer school *system* possible, even with well-resourced and extraordinary schools? Citing research that apportions test-score variance, Welner (2022) notes that the range for attributing that variance to school-level factors, including teaching quality, is only 20% to 40%—leaving approximately 70% to factors beyond schools' immediate control. Students' academic performance is powerfully driven by outside-school inequities—which is a central reason why the Schools of Opportunity recognition focuses on inputs, not outcomes.

Welner (2022) describes what the outside-school dominance in the variance breakdown studies means for a school centric approach for lifting up all children:

> Imagine a task whereby you are given a heavy vehicle with two engines that work in concert, one of which provides 70 percent of the horsepower. Your task is to double the power of the vehicle's combined engines, but you are told to leave the larger engine alone and tinker only with the smaller engine—the one accounting for the remaining 30 percent of the horsepower. To get that 100 percent increase, you will have to increase that smaller engine's power by 433 percent. In a nutshell, that is the irrational challenge of "Great Equalizer" thinking: when we fail to address larger societal inequalities, we place unreasonable demands on our schools. Nonetheless, that is the challenge framed by the nation's long-standing policy approach. (pp. 86–87)

With that challenge in mind, this chapter outlines a *school-improvement plus reciprocal accountability* approach with the strength to facilitate and support many more Schools of Opportunity and with the versatility to reach beyond formal schooling and improve students' larger opportunities to learn and thrive. School practices make a difference, but on a national scale they appear to have little effect on overall trends linking poverty and race to educational outcomes. This means one of two things. Either too few schools are breaking the mold in beneficial ways, or our system asks far too much of schools and far too little of larger society. Or both.

In this final chapter, we describe large-scale reforms with the potential to address these possibilities, creating a system within which schools like those described in this volume will thrive and multiply—where continuous improvement is systemically sustained. We also consider how educational policy can be combined with national and state policies that broadly support children and their families and communities.[2]

We first propose a system of reciprocal accountability, designed to ensure that all key participants in the schooling process meet their responsibilities. This includes the responsibility to ensure that schools have sufficient resources. We then propose a system of opportunity-to-learn standards, akin to the Schools of Opportunity criteria. This system would provide the foundation for a virtuous cycle—for the feedback process necessary for continuous, research-based improvement. Finally, we explain the important federal role in driving and sustaining these reforms as well as broader policy reforms that would address opportunity gaps that arise outside of schools.

## ACCOUNTABILITY REFORM

The accountability approaches set forth in the federal No Child Left Behind Act of 2001 (NCLB) and related policies were poorly conceived and not successful (Baker et al., 2010; Dorn, 2007; Hout & Elliott, 2011; Koretz, 2017). But done correctly, accountability can and should be in the service of an educationally just system. It can press for and inform policies and practices that can make schools work well for all children by providing sufficient resources, supports that mitigate the in- and out-of-school disparities in children's learning opportunities, and daily practices in which adults cultivate all children's ability to learn and thrive.

To play this critical role, accountability systems must be anchored by goals and standards that signal the broad, multiple, and complex outcomes we desire for all students, including preparation for postsecondary and college programs, careers, and civic life. Accountability must also be reciprocal in that it involves every level of the educational system, from schools and classrooms to the state agencies whose responsibility is to translate policy into effective, well-resourced, and fair practices. Finally, to be equitable, common, and sustainable, accountability must be national, grounded in federal policy.

This type of accountability framework starts with the classroom and builds up through the school and district, and then to the state and federal government. At the classroom and school levels, the focus is on closing opportunity gaps that are within the control of school-based educators and their community partners, as exemplified by the Schools of Opportunity practices described in previous chapters. At the district and state levels, the focus is on the provision of resources and other inputs that are under the control of local and state policymakers. The state and federal focus is also on school-level opportunities to learn, as well as opportunity gaps that arise at the societal level. Most of the capacity-building and funding needed by schools cannot arise within the schools or even at the district level; these essentials depend on a societal commitment.

## The Limits of Unidirectional Accountability

For the past 2 decades, policymakers adopted an outcomes-focused, test-based approach to accountability. In compliance with NCLB, policymakers in every state used test-based accountability policies to hold schools accountable for student performance. The approach set performance targets for each school, publicized their results, and specified sanctions and interventions (such as closing schools or firing educators) for schools not meeting their targets. It was grounded in the view that past policy had provided few or no consequences for good or poor performance and that states had not been clear about their expectations for schools and had not provided good information about how well schools were doing (Mathis & Trujillo, 2016). The NCLB approach would, supporters argued, lead to equity, since achievement gaps among student subgroups would be made concrete and public. It assumed that schools could and would improve under three conditions: (1) if there were clear expectations for student performance; (2) if educators and students had reliable information, disaggregated by (among other categories) racial and ethnic subgroups, about how well or how poorly they were doing overall; and (3) if educators were motivated to do better by the rewards or shame that would come from having the public watching and demanding improvement and from having the state poised to act if things did not go well (Shepard, 2008).

This test-based approach reflected a misapplied understanding of behavioral psychology and organizational change (Koretz, 2017). It assumed that motivation for educators would and should come through the shaming and blaming likely to follow unsatisfactory results as schools' test scores were publicized and as schools were given ratings or "grades." The approach rested on the confidence that standardized tests would measure what is important and could thereby drive the desired beneficial change—rather than promoting superficial or even fraudulent changes (Nichols & Berliner, 2007). It also rested on the belief that these tests would communicate clear standards and expectations for performance and that they offered fair and scientific metrics to determine who performed up to expectations. In doing so, the approach eschewed the idea that any failure might be the result of insufficient resources and capacity or of policies that undermine equitable student access or limit educators' opportunities to teach or develop their knowledge and skills.

## Accountability and Continuous Improvement

Two decades later, we know that the punitive approach of NCLB failed to bring significant improvement either in students' performance overall or in the gaps between demographic groups (Hout & Elliott, 2011; Koretz, 2017). But encouraged by increased flexibility in the Every Student Succeeds Act (ESSA), which replaced NCLB, many states have been working to reconstruct their accountability systems so that they provide more comprehensive data and support to increase stakeholders' knowledge and skills to make their schools better (Darling-Hammond et al., 2016; Forsyth et al., 2017). In this way, ESSA was a step in the right direction. Rather than simply relying on standardized test scores, some states are using ESSA's flexibility to pursue the goal of providing parents, educators, and policymakers with a more complete package of the information and the support they need to make progress toward state performance goals, such as college- and career-readiness for every student (Hargreaves & Braun, 2013).

Reflecting management scholar Edward Deming's (1993) findings that organizations improve when people within them have opportunities to gain knowledge and skills as they work with others to achieve quality, this more supportive accountability approach is designed to collect comprehensive data that can be used to pinpoint real-time problems and inform solutions that are consistent with long-term goals. The underlying assumption is that continuous improvement requires comprehensive and diagnostic data beyond test scores, along with support that engages educators and policymakers (at all levels) in understanding and using these data to make the education system better. Such continuous improvement involves a cyclical process intended to help groups of people at many levels of the education system—from parents and schools to state agencies—identify shortcomings, set goals, detect ways to improve, and evaluate change. All participants in the system must engage, learn from, and act on diagnostic and summative data provided by the accountability system rather than awaiting judgment in the form of annual scorecards or grades designed to make schools, teachers, and students try harder (Elmore, 2002).

In a comprehensive improvement system, outcome indicators should provide timely and actionable feedback and should reflect the full set of basic education goals, knowing that conventional achievement test scores are insufficient. Moving beyond test scores, these broader systems do collect comprehensive outcome data, but they also assess the performance of the system. And they focus on the underlying conditions and opportunities that are the barriers to or facilitators of improvement, such as the inputs and processes that produce student learning. They do not presume that measures of student outcomes are sufficient to make judgments and inform improvement.

Accordingly, a comprehensive system eschews a focus only on the extent to which a limited set of student outcome goals are being met, as past systems have done. Instead, a comprehensive system focuses on continuous learning and gathers information about resources being provided and how students are experiencing learning—the same sort of criteria used in the process of recognizing Schools of Opportunity. In addition, a comprehensive

**Figure 11.1. Key Elements of a Supportive Accountability System**

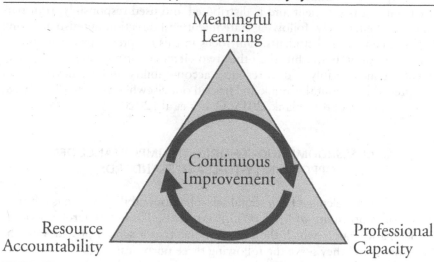

*Source*: Darling-Hammond, L., & Plank, D. N. (2015). *Supporting continuous improvement in California's education system*. Policy Analysis for California Education and Stanford Center for Opportunity Policy in Education. Used by permission.

system considers students' *progress* toward a broad set of outcomes. These measures help educators and policymakers assess how the school is working and how well students are learning. They help identify what actions are needed to ensure that students have sufficient learning opportunities and that the system is operating effectively and equitably. According to Darling-Hammond and her colleagues, these broader systems set expectations for performance, collect data, and provide adequate support in three key, related domains: (1) meaningful learning, (2) enabled by professionally skilled and committed educators, and (3) supported by adequate and appropriate resources (Darling-Hammond et al., 2014).

These three elements are intertwined (see Figure 11.1). Preparing college- and career-ready graduates requires deep and meaningful learning, which comes about through the development of the knowledge and skills that students need to thrive in today's world: problem solving, collaboration, communication, independent inquiry and learning, relationship-building, and resilience and resourcefulness (Darling-Hammond & Plank, 2015). This, in turn, requires professionally skilled educators. These educators must be prepared in ways that enable such meaningful learning and college and career readiness for all students, placing in the forefront students who have generally been minoritized and marginalized by society and by schools—those who are diverse in their culture, language, and home-based resources and supports.

Preparing these graduates also requires resource accountability to ensure that funding is sufficient and is distributed and used responsibly, transparently, and effectively, following state intent and direction but also adapting to local context and students. Our focus in this chapter is primarily on resource accountability, but the other two elements of continuous improvement are inextricably tied to resource accountability and are developed in chapters throughout this book and fleshed out elsewhere as well (Bae, 2018; Darling-Hammond & Plank, 2015; Oakes et al., 2020).

## CLASSROOMS AND SCHOOLS: THE IMPORTANCE OF OPPORTUNITY-TO-LEARN STANDARDS

A foundational element for a sound school accountability system is a framework of opportunity-to-learn (OTL) standards. These standards provide a benchmark against which the opportunities that a school provides can be measured, and they serve the following three purposes:

- Telling parents, students, community members, and public officials whether schools and the education system are working equitably for all
- Focusing attention on what education officials and other policymakers can do to improve the quality of schools and to make sure that all schools have basic opportunities in place
- Focusing attention on the conditions in the school system and not just on measured outcomes

Using OTL standards as a guide, we can measure whether students have a realistic shot at learning the subjects the state requires and whether they will have a fair chance of college success. OTL standards can also help students, parents, communities, and school officials discover and correct needs and problems in schools.

These input standards also identify and specify the resources and opportunities needed to meet the state's comprehensive goals. Standards (and goals) would likely include areas such as those addressed in the 10 Schools of Opportunity criteria, plus clean and safe facilities, and pre-high-school supports such as high-quality early childhood education and intensive early interventions in math and reading (Bae, 2018; Carter & Welner, 2013; Darling-Hammond et al., 2014; Oakes, 1989).

Some schools provide students with enriching opportunities to learn while other schools offer very few opportunities. In other words, these opportunities are not equal throughout most states' school systems, and many schools would have trouble meeting basic OTL standards. For example, an overwhelming body of research shows that schools enrolling the highest numbers of Latinx and African American students have the biggest shortages of curriculum materials and the lowest numbers of qualified and experienced teachers (Carter & Welner, 2013; Darling-Hammond, 2010; Oakes, 1990).

By measuring and reporting the presence or absence of learning opportunities against a set of standards, OTL can bring to light examples of unfair conditions—within and across schools—that limit students' equal access to a high-quality education. And this process would highlight schools, like those profiled in this volume, that are closing opportunity gaps.

## DISTRICTS AND STATES: DESIGNING AN EFFECTIVE SYSTEM OF RECIPROCAL ACCOUNTABILITY

Opportunities to learn are felt at the level of the school, so they should be reported at that level. But schools themselves have circumscribed control over the opportunities they provide students. As Oakes and colleagues (2004) have explained, a true accountability system is reciprocal; it cannot stop with students, parents, teachers, and principals. Policymakers in state capitol buildings and school districts can either support the success of educators and families, or they can undermine that success. Those policymakers are a key part of the educational system, but current accountability systems generally fail to incorporate them and their influence.

Accordingly, Oakes and her colleagues (2004), and subsequently Bill Koski (2007), outlined an approach for "reciprocal accountability," based in part on the work of Richard Elmore (2002). Reciprocal accountability means holding each level of the system accountable for the contributions it must make to produce the desired results. Such a system would continue to hold schools and educators accountable—albeit with holistic measures that go beyond test scores (see Schneider, 2018)—but would also look to ensure that all pieces are in place for those schools and educators to meet both opportunity-to-learn and performance standards. Accordingly, federal, state, and local education agencies must be equally accountable for meeting certain standards of delivery, providing schools and educators with the resources and support that those schools and educators need in order to meet the performance goals that the policymakers put in place (Adams et al., 2017; Elmore, 2000, 2002).

In addition to collecting data about opportunities and outcomes at schools, an accountability system that provides sufficient information to guide improvement must address and involve multiple levels of the system, recognizing that simply focusing on schools gives very limited information or prospects for broad improvement. A reciprocal accountability system would collect and report information about resources and support at the district and state levels that share responsibility for creating a system that supports schools in meeting policy goals effectively and equitably.

For example, while valued educational outcomes are positively linked to having a well-qualified, stable, and diverse educator workforce at a school (Cardichon et al., 2020; Philip & Brown, 2020), the preparation, supply, and distribution of teachers among schools are largely determined by state policies and local district practices. Therefore, in addition to reporting teacher-quality indicators for each school (e.g., years of experience, induction and mentoring programs, and working conditions), comparable indicators of quality and distribution should be reported at the district level and statewide—not simply aggregating school-level data, but describing how well the school districts and states are supporting those schools. Similarly, moving from high-quality standards and high expectations to high-quality teaching and learning requires high-quality curriculum materials and assessment tools, including curriculum-embedded assessments that provide formative data. Teaching for meaningful learning also requires state support for student assessments that include authentic performance tasks (e.g., classroom-based projects) that assess and encourage development of a full range of higher-order skills (Darling-Hammond et al., 2014), such as those used in Fannie Lou Hamer Freedom High School (see Chapter 4).

These district- and state-level indicators are critical to fostering systems change (at the district, state, and federal levels) in order to create a context where improvements take hold in the form of better opportunities to learn in schools and classrooms.

As Koski (2007) notes, however, accountability systems that work in this way must provide parents and local community members with tools and the legitimacy to report to a state oversight agency when such resources and conditions are not provided in schools and classrooms. Complaints, he argues, must be promptly investigated and findings issued, accompanied by an order for corrective action. The goal is that a finding of noncompliance and an order for corrective action will compel the relevant provider—the state or local school district—to ensure that every child has the necessary educational resources and opportunities.

Yet it is not difficult to find examples of recalcitrant legislatures (and governors) that have failed to meet court-mandated obligations to increase funding for their states' schools (Burns, 2014). While various means could be used to flag OTL problems, a linchpin for an effective reciprocal-accountability system lies in ensuring that resources will be available to educators. Few enforceable policy levers are practically available to pry loose resources, even when the funding duty is not in serious dispute. With that in mind, we note here two possibilities that might be considered by state lawmakers attempting to bind their successors to resource-accountability obligations.

One option would be to put in place a trigger mechanism enforceable through a private right of action (a lawsuit). The wording might be something like, "In the event of a determination through the reciprocal accountability process, as described in [provision X], that the state is not meeting its resource-accountability obligations, a necessary percentage of funding will be cut from all discretionary budget items and moved to fund the needs identified through the process described in [provision X]. If the legislature does not carry through in moving this funding, a private right of action shall be available to any state taxpayer to enforce this requirement." While such a law may be effective, it is also possible to imagine that the legislature would ignore a resulting court order, thus simply creating a new separation of powers confrontation.

The second, and possibly more effective, option would be a different sort of trigger mechanism, whereby results-based accountability can only be exerted if the resource accountability is met. The state legislation would allow a school district or the parent of a child in an impacted school to seek a court order that places any school-level accountability repercussions in abeyance until the state comes into compliance. Imagine, for example, that the results-based accountability system included a requirement that a school enter into a restructuring process because outcome measures are low and not improving. If state lawmakers have not met their resource obligations, the school district or a parent could seek a court order relieving the school of its obligations concerning the restructuring process. The goal of such an approach would not be to eliminate all accountability; rather, the goal would be for the enforcement mechanism to pressure the state to meet its obligations within a functioning reciprocal accountability system.

## OTL Indicators

Many of the policy components included in frameworks of Koski (2007) and of Oakes et al. (2004) are built upon OTL indicators that provide data about the uneven conditions, resources, and supports that can underlie persistent gaps in achievement. Supportive accountability systems, in addition to being more comprehensive and more reciprocal, are focused on capacity-building. They include elements that are internal-facing as well as external-facing and that are adaptable to variations among districts and schools in ways that support local improvement.

To develop and use OTL indicators requires five steps, each of which requires the engagement of key K–12 education stakeholders (see Figure 11.2).

**Step 1.** The first step is to construct an explicit, simplified model of the entire K–12 public education system that represents the *theory of action* about how the system can achieve its goals effectively and equitably. That theory includes the goals that the system has set for students. It also includes the key features of the system that enable students to meet those goals effectively and equitably. All accountability systems are based on models, but

**Figure 11.2. Steps of Development and Use of OTL Indicators**

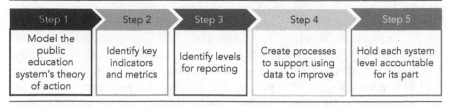

**Figure 11.3. Example Theory of Change**

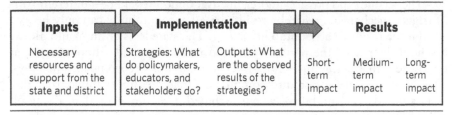

they are often incomplete and do not move beyond the implicit. The goals and the key system features of the explicit model should be revealed in, and enforced through, statutes and other policies. The resulting model, such as a fleshed-out version of the one depicted in Figure 11.3, can guide education stakeholders to select indicators and collect data that can be used to monitor the system's progress and provide information necessary to improve.

*Step 2.* Identify OTL indicators of key system elements and outcomes. An indicator is a single or composite statistic that reveals something about performance or health. For example, a key input element is a well-qualified, stable, and diverse educator workforce. Expansive OTL indicators could include statistics that assess the percentage of educators who are fully certified, calculate the educator turnover rate, or compare the racial composition of the workforce to that of the student population. Many of the categories that could inform a set of system indicators are found in the 10 Schools of Opportunity criteria and scoring rubric. Such indicators can reveal improvement or challenges and lead to further investigation. A reading from a thermometer can be thought of as an indicator of whether a person may be ill. If the temperature is high, the goal is not to simply lower it (perhaps by throwing cold water on the person's face) but to detect and heal the condition the thermometer and temperature helped to reveal. Indicators must be verified as evidence based (that is, research confirms that they are linked to the outcomes the system seeks to achieve). They also must be feasible, in that existing or newly developed measures can produce valid and reliable data about them (see Marion, 2020). Students' scores on standardized tests are the best-known indicator, but they measure primarily outcomes, not opportunities; they also measure only a slice of the overall goals of schooling. Together, the indicators, when measured well, can assess the health of the entire K–12 education system and inform its improvement.

**Step 3.** Determine how to report and communicate the indicators to maximize their usefulness. Accountability systems have generally focused on the school as the level at which data should be reported, with those school data disaggregated into subgroups of students. A more useful approach would report some indicators at multiple levels of the system—the school, the district, and the state (and nationally, as explained in the next section of this chapter)—emphasizing responsibility and capacity to make improvements. Returning to the example noted above, having a well-qualified, stable, and diverse educator workforce at a school is positively linked with valued outcomes. However, state policies and local district practices largely determine the supply and distribution of teachers among schools. Therefore, in addition to reporting teacher quality indicators for each school, indicators of quality and distribution should be reported at the district level and statewide.

**Step 4.** Create supportive and ongoing data-use processes to make effective use of collected indicators. Unless data are used, the whole accountability system will become a superficial exercise in compliance. Systemic improvement requires that people at many levels of the education system—from parents and schools to districts and state agencies—use the indicator data to identify shortcomings, set goals, detect ways to improve, and evaluate change. It requires also that they work to realize the state's ambitious goals and remove barriers that inhibit equitable access to high-quality learning opportunities. These improvement efforts might, for example, include processes such as strategic planning, informed by comprehensive data and data dashboards. Creating and sustaining such improvement processes requires support from the state to help people learn to use the data and to set up mechanisms that make this an ongoing process at districts and schools. While some states have some elements of an effective data-use system, none comes close to a complete and fully integrated system.

**Step 5.** Hold each level of the system accountable for the contributions it must make to produce the desired results. As Koski (2007) noted, in addition to the state having mechanisms for holding schools accountable, others such as local communities, parents, and students need the tools and roles to hold the system accountable for providing educational resources at the classroom level. These tools must include monitoring and enforcement mechanisms, accompanied by the procedural rights to redress educational deprivations through simple and inexpensive complaint mechanisms. Many of the recognized Schools of Opportunity were able to accomplish their reforms and sustain their practices in spite of—not because of—their district and state contexts. Scaling up will require this to change.

## Federal Roles

The focus for Oakes et al. (2004) and for Koski (2007) was on the state level—specifically, the state of California. Given the federalist approach taken in the U.S. Constitution, and given in particular the lack of any formal role provided to the federal government in the Constitution, one might reasonably contend that an educational accountability system should stop at the state level, not extending to the federal government. This contention is buttressed by the failure of the plaintiffs in *San Antonio Independent School District v. Rodriguez* (1973), with the U.S. Supreme Court holding that there is no fundamental federal right to an education.

But compelling reasons also support a substantial federal role in any effective and comprehensive accountability system. Accordingly, we provide here an outline of an expanded federal role, designed in particular to ensure that states provide necessary resources and supports. Such capacity-building would greatly facilitate the efforts of school-based educators seeking to create schools of opportunity.

The seminal work in this realm has been conducted by law professor Kimberly Jenkins Robinson, who contends that federalism in education is a historical relic and should, in fact, be even further diminished (Robinson, 2016, 2018). Note in this regard that if we went back 150 years, we would observe most authority residing with school boards, followed in the 20th century by a shift of authority to state governments, which accompanied a corresponding shift in funding responsibility (Tyack, 1974). Even later, federal involvement in K–12 education began ramping up after the Soviet Union's launch of Sputnik in 1957. In short, the respective roles of districts, states, and the federal government are ever-evolving.

In this context, Robinson's work details how the balance of power between federal, state, and local governments currently still emphasizes substantial state authority over education. Yet the federal government's role has steadily increased, even with the slightly less heavy hand exerted through ESSA. Moreover, Robinson and others have made a strong argument for a major increase in federal funding for education, accompanied by conditions placed on states to improve the adequacy and equity of school funding and opportunities to learn. This has two important implications for the state-level reciprocal accountability system we have described: (1) additional resources to help states meet their resource-accountability obligations, and (2) pressure applied uniformly to all states, prompting them to meet those obligations.

Using the Spending Clause (Article I, Section 8, Clause 1) of the U.S. Constitution, the federal government can attach conditions to the receipt of federal funding. Existing examples include the antidiscrimination provisions of Title VI and Title IX and the various requirements included in the Individuals with Disabilities Education Act (IDEA). The federal government can also use funded programs as incentives to prod states and districts in a given direction. The $4.35 billion Race to the Top Fund during the Obama administration offers a recent example of how incentives can be used to shift state policies.

Several scholars have considered the potential for the federal government to increase the equity and adequacy of school funding. Houck and DeBray (2015) suggest policies using competitive grants, which are one form of incentive. They build their proposal on a similar suggestion by Smith (2011), who pointed to the success of Race to the Top in driving state policy reforms.

> We conceptualize . . . a competitive grant to provide states with the incentives to undertake the difficult work of school finance reform in exchange for priority consideration in a grant competition designed to provide substantial federal funds for work in developing integrated and successful schools in supportive communities across the P–12 spectrum. This approach privileges finance equity as a value in exchange for providing students with greater opportunities to learn. Our supposition is that states will be willing to do the former in exchange for funding and flexibility to implement the latter. (Houck & DeBray, 2015, p. 157)

Robinson (2016) also suggests using a grant program to prompt state-level reform—but she rejects the idea of competitive grants, saying that one lesson from Race to the Top "is that federal grants should avoid the winners-losers paradigm of competitive grant funding," since states that "most need the assistance [often] lose in a competitive grant program." Instead, "any state that meets the established criteria should be rewarded for taking this important initial step" (p. 224).

Specifically, "funding should be available to all states that design and implement comprehensive plans" for "a state funding system that promotes equal access to an excellent education" (Robinson, 2016, p. 224). These plans must be "supported by rigorous research and expert analysis" and must do the following:

> . . . provide such analyses as: how the current funding approach benefits and harms children; how harmful aspects of the system will be reformed to reduce inequities and promote educational achievement and excellence; how the proposed funding reforms are linked to desired educational outcomes, including how funding is linked to standards; research supporting the effectiveness of the

proposed reforms; a roadmap for raising any additional necessary funding; and, accountability measures to help ensure that the money under the revised system is well spent. (p. 223)

The roadmap would include interim benchmarks for the state to meet. This federal incentive program should, Robinson stresses, be combined with federal research and technical assistance. These are all parts of what she describes as a collaborative and incrementalist model of change. In a subsequent article, she explains that such incentive programs should be separate from the Elementary and Secondary Education Act (ESEA) but "can encourage the laboratory of the states to try reforms before they are included as federal conditions for the entire nation through ESEA" (Robinson, 2018, p. 980). These states would also voluntarily work with one another, with federally supported assistance from experts, to adopt a uniform set of opportunity-to-learn standards.

In Robinson's vision, this new theory of education federalism makes the federal government "the ultimate guarantor of equal access to an excellent education" (2016, p. 205). Her approach "embraces federal policymaking strengths in education, such as federal research, technical, and financial assistance, that support state and local reforms to promote equity and excellence" (p. 205).

The Biden administration's proposed budget for fiscal year 2022 included a program that was apparently influenced by Robinson's (2016) approach: "States would set goals, interim targets, and timelines for closing identified gaps and would need to demonstrate progress in improving the equity and adequacy of their funding systems to be eligible for future increases in funding under this program" (U.S. Department of Education, 2021, p. A-23). However, the proposal was not included in congressional budget plans.

Goodwin Liu (2006) proposes a very different type of incentive, which he describes as a "modified form of 'power equalizing' whereby the federal government would guarantee each state a minimum amount per weighted pupil for a given level of state effort" (pp. 2118–2119). This idea builds on a seldom-used type of state school-financing system, called "district power equalization" (DPE) formulas. These approaches allow all districts in the state to act as if they have the same tax base per student. In this way, DPE systems seek to guarantee equal revenue yield for tax effort regardless of assessed property wealth. More specifically, under a DPE plan, the state would choose a uniform (fictitious) tax base per student. When a district then sets a specific tax rate, it will raise a given amount (rate multiplied by actual local tax base) from local sources. It would then receive state aid to equalize pursuant to the uniform tax base. That is, any given district tax rate will result in the same total revenue as the same tax rate in another district, since the state makes up the difference using a formula tied to the rate and the local tax base. For instance, the state may set a uniform tax base per student of $300,000. If the district's actual base is only $200,000 per student, then a given rate will raise only two-thirds of the equalized amount. The state would then provide the remaining third.

The modified power equalization idea proposed by Liu uses, as its baseline, the average fiscal capacity among all states. The federal government would incentivize higher and more equitable funding through a national foundation aid program that would subsume Title I and would assure, for each state that exerts at least a required minimal level of effort, "an amount per weighted pupil at least equal to what the state would have raised had it applied its tax effort against" that baseline (Liu, 2006, p. 2119). This approach would provide substantially more federal support for states with less fiscal capacity, and it would provide those states with a strong incentive to increase the adequacy of their school funding. Liu also suggests using this approach to drive equitable state-level funding policies:

> To participate in the program, each state should be required to use federal aid not only to bring all districts up to at least the foundation level but also to narrow both interdistrict and intradistrict resource disparities. One approach would be to require each state to use federal aid to reduce its coefficient of interdistrict variation by a minimum percentage, while offering small increases in the federal matching rate to states that reduce interdistrict disparities by more than the minimum percentage. (pp. 2120–2121, internal footnotes omitted)

Using a different mechanism, a similar idea was proposed by Derek Black (2015), who suggests heavily weighting Title I funding, to distribute among states according to effort and progressivity. That is, states that increase the adequacy and equity of their systems would receive more Title I funding, essentially building conditions into the federal distribution formula. In addition, he suggests that the Title I formulas be changed, in order to provide more funding for poorer states. (Black is also one of several scholars who have stressed the importance of the federal government more strongly enforcing the comparability and supplement-not-supplant provisions of Title I.)

As an alternative to, or as a companion to, such incentive approaches, several researchers have argued for using federal funding to compel state-level reforms. As noted earlier, Robinson (2016) advocates for a *both-and* approach, with conditions attached to sufficiently high levels of funding, such that states would feel strongly incentivized (compelled) to accept the funding even with the strings attached.

The report of the U.S. Department of Education's Equity and Excellence Commission (2013) includes a similar suggestion, for the federal government to "direct states, with appropriate incentives, to adopt and implement school finance systems that will (1) provide a meaningful educational opportunity for all students, along with appropriate budgetary and other frameworks to ensure the effective and efficient use of all funds to enable all students to achieve state content and performance standards as outlined above, and (2) demonstrate progress toward implementing such a school finance system" (p. 19).

Also thinking in terms of conditioning Title I funding, Arocho (2014) returns to the idea of a guaranteed tax base. Arocho suggests conditioning Title I funds on states adopting a guaranteed tax base approach in their school-finance laws. More modestly, Kristine Bowman (2010) proposes conditioning Title I funding on states adopting policies to monitor school districts' fiscal health and to intervene when needed.

Robinson (2016) also offers the possibility of a federal funding stream separate from Title I, to which conditions regarding state school-finance systems would be attached. She does note, however, that the funding would have to be substantial in order for the approach to be successful. "It is impossible to estimate the dollar amount of such funding, but for impactful reforms of state funding systems to occur the amount would likely need to rival, or even exceed, the funding within Title I, which in fiscal year 2015 was $14.4 billion" (Robinson, 2016, p. 227).

Almost all of these proposals for federal incentives and conditions focus narrowly on states' school finance systems, or at least on resources and opportunities centered at the school level. The one exception is the competitive-grant proposal from Houck and DeBray (2015). Since opportunity gaps primarily arise because of societal-level inequalities, they suggest using the competition to incentivize reforms that address opportunity gaps no matter their source—whether they arise inside or outside schools. "State applications should specify the particular interventions (desegregation, community interventions, improving or expanding early childhood education) they seek to develop, in which districts, and should submit relevant documentation of support from district leadership" (Houck & DeBray, 2015, p. 160). They also point to areas such as housing and community development.

This approach of bringing additional provisions into an otherwise education-focused policy is unwieldy and, in some ways, difficult. But we agree with Houck and DeBray on the need to address opportunity gaps arising at a societal level, since it would be even more difficult to create a school system that alone could counteract those larger inequalities.

## PROPOSED COMPREHENSIVE SYSTEM

The following skeletal proposal for a comprehensive accountability system brings together many of these earlier ideas. Our proposal is for an aligned and overlapping package of incentives and conditions that seeks to leverage federal education funding to overcome intransigent policies and persistent inequities in states' school-finance systems. It then combines those proposals with reciprocal accountability proposals and the foundational OTL standards. And it explains how larger societal opportunity gaps can be addressed as part of such an approach. The goal of this accountability system is to create a context wherein schools of opportunity could thrive—a context where all students in all classrooms in all states have relatively equal opportunities to learn and therefore relatively equal chances for academic success.

At the federal level, we propose two major new noncompetitive grant programs. The first would be a foundation-aid program similar to the one outlined by Liu (2006), using a power-equalizing approach to incentivize and help states toward adequate and equitable finance systems. The second would be similar to the funding and innovation grant program outlined by Robinson (2016), along with the research and technical assistance that she suggests.

As part of the foundation-aid program suggested by Liu, our proposal would add Arocho's (2014) proposal to link eligibility to a state's adoption of a guaranteed tax base (or district power equalization) approach in the state's own school-finance system. This is consistent with Liu's own suggestion to make participation dependent on the state taking steps "to narrow both interdistrict and intradistrict resource disparities" (Liu, 2006, p. 2121).

As a modification to the funding and innovation grant program approach outlined by Robinson (2016), we think it important to add Houck and DeBray's (2015) idea of including outside-school reforms. Schools alone cannot realistically be expected to close opportunity gaps that arise because of racialized poverty and discrimination in far-reaching areas such as housing, employment, nutrition, health care, transportation, and the carceral state. Houck and DeBray mention a few such reform areas, and other researchers and advocates have pointed to others. For instance, the Schott Foundation's (2020) "Loving Cities" project identifies 25 indicators covering issues of care, commitment, stability and capacity. These sorts of outside-school considerations fit well within a grant program; they would fit less well as a condition to the receipt of education-focused funding, such as Title I.

These two grant programs would work in concert, with the foundation aid program focused specifically on the nuts and bolts of getting federal funding to states according to need as well as on the states' school-finance formulas, while the funding and innovation grant program would include a broader set of considerations and criteria. These would include the equity and adequacy of states' funding systems. They would also include, for instance, innovations (inside and outside of schools) designed to close opportunity gaps and "accountability measures to help ensure that the money under the revised system is well spent" (Robinson, 2016, p. 223). We propose in particular that the funding and innovation grant program reward states for putting in place key elements of a reciprocal accountability system.

Many of these same ideas and goals can and should also be pursued through placing conditions on states' receipt of Title I funding. Derek Black's (2015) proposal to use weights within the Title I allocation formula—rewarding effort and progressivity—is a way to do this and should be thought of as an alternative to Liu's (2006) grant-proposal suggestion, with each approach accomplishing similar goals.

An ESEA reauthorization should include other conditions, however. Most importantly, any grant (incentive) program should only be thought of as a predecessor to placing new conditions on ESEA funding. As Robinson (2016) explains, the incentive program allows for state innovations and for Congress to learn from those innovations. Subsequently, "adopting and maintaining a progressive funding system should be an essential condition for any new ESEA program or for a modification to Title I" (p. 229). As a related condition on Title I funding, Rebell and Wolff (2008) propose requiring states to demonstrate that they are addressing a variety of key OTL indicators, such as "effective teachers, principals and other personnel," "adequate school facilities," and "instrumentalities of learning, including, but not limited to, up-to-date textbooks, libraries, laboratories, and computers" (p. 157).

These federal incentives and conditions, along with additional federal funding, should increase state resources and should result in state funding systems with greater adequacy and equity. This buttresses states' financial capacity in a comprehensive and supportive system of reciprocal accountability. And that in turn changes the context for school-district leaders and school-level educators, increasing their ability to close opportunity gaps.

States' new accountability systems would, under this proposal, be built upon OTL standards and indicators, as designed through the five-step process we outlined. The resulting system would hold schools, teachers, and principals accountable for providing rich opportunities to learn. And it would hold state and local education agencies accountable for providing schools and educators with needed resources and supports—with ensuring that all pieces are in place for schools to meet opportunity-to-learn standards.

We caution, however, that resources and accountability focused only on formal schooling will have to grapple with the *smaller engine* problem described earlier in this chapter. Policymakers cannot realistically expect even the best schools to consistently overcome the harms of racialized and concentrated poverty.

## CONCLUSION

The Schools of Opportunity described in this book have sometimes been aided by their school districts. Other times, they succeeded in spite of their district and state contexts. The same is true of many other extraordinary schools across the country. Moreover, all schools that strive to provide well-rounded, deep, and individualized instruction have been swimming upstream against the 2-decade-long federal push for standards-based testing and accountability.

Looking to the future, we contend that this context can become much more supportive. But comprehensively reforming systems involves changing a wide range of factors, including curriculum, finance, accountability, school culture, within-school supports and stratification, connections to the community, teaching, teacher preparation, and teacher professionalization. It also involves addressing opportunity gaps that arise from outside-school inequities tied to poverty and racism. Through wraparound services and connections to the community, schools like those profiled in this volume have shown the powerful impact of providing expansive services. But their stories only reinforce the conclusion that they should not alone be asked to do this. Schools can mitigate the harms of poverty and racism, but schools cannot mandate that the community's employers pay a living wage. They cannot reform police forces and carceral systems. They cannot provide housing. Until we see greater investment in young people societywide, schools will often sit as the primary resource filling these gaps—leaving us to seek isolated examples of amazing, overextended schools.

The policy shifts concerning incentives, resources, and accountability that we propose in this chapter require a corresponding political and cultural shift in how policymakers conceptualize the problem. In particular, the approach that we set forth moves away from the belief that schools will improve if policies simply make the desired outcomes clear and impose serious consequences of not achieving them. Instead, policymakers must recognize that data about learning *opportunities*, together with support from states and districts, can enable systems to build the capacity and invest wisely in equitable resources and practices. For this to happen in a consistent and widespread way will require federal leadership and resources.

Systemic and effective school improvement is adaptive and includes elements that face externally as well as internally. External-facing accountability requires that system leaders assure parents and the public—through transparency, monitoring, and selective intervention—that their system aligns with societal expectations and requirements (Darling-Hammond et al., 2014). Supportive systems also simultaneously build accountability that faces internally by developing a culture in districts and schools wherein individuals and groups willingly take on personal, professional, and collective responsibility for continuous improvement and success for all students. This requires supporting individual and collective efficacy, promoting collaborative cultures, and creating a team like environment where members press one another to improve (Fullan et al., 2015; Hargreaves & Shirley, 2009).

The schools we celebrate in this book have implemented practices rooted in core ideas of antiracism, equity, engagement, challenge, and supports. These values and commitments carry across specific practices, such that we often see an interplay between different Schools of Opportunity criteria. By extending those values and commitments to the larger U.S. educational system and buttressing them with the necessary resources, it follows that the practices themselves will correspondingly scale up. Changed policy context facilitates changed policies (Welner, 2001). Until then, we'll celebrate the exceptional even while we look forward to the day when they're longer exceptions.

## NOTES

1. The two authors contributed equally to this chapter.
2. This chapter draws heavily upon a paper titled "Infusing Education Justice into Standards and Accountability Policies," which the authors presented at the Edmund W. Gordon Centennial Conference, held remotely by Teachers College, Columbia University on June 2–3, 2021.

## REFERENCES

Adams, C. M., Ford, T. G., Forsyth, P. B., Ware, J. K., Olsen, J. J., Lepine, J. A. Sr., Barnes, L. L. B., Khojasteh, J., & Mwavita, M. (2017). *Next generation accountability: A vision for school improvement under ESSA*. Learning Policy Institute.

Arocho, J. (2014). Inhibiting intrastate inequalities: A congressional approach to ensuring equal opportunity to finance public education. *Michigan Law Review, 112*(8), 1479–1505.

Bae, S. (2018). Redesigning systems of school accountability: A multiple measures approach to accountability and support. *Education Policy Analysis Archives, 26*(8). https://doi.org/10.14507/epaa.26.2920

Baker, E. L., Barton, P. E., Darling-Hammond, L., Haertel, E., Ladd, H. F., Linn, R. L., Ravitch, D., Rothstein, R., Shavelson, R. J., & Shepard, L. A. (2010). *Problems with the use of student test scores to evaluate teachers* (EPI Briefing Paper #278). Economic Policy Institute.

Black, D. (2015). Leveraging federal funding for equity and integration. In C. Ogletree & K. Robinson (Eds.), *The enduring legacy of Rodriguez: Exploring new paths to equal educational opportunity* (pp. 227–248). Harvard Education Press.

Bowman, K. L. (2010). Before school districts go broke: A proposal for federal reform. *University of Cincinnati Law Review, 79*, 895–966.

Burns, J. R. (2014). Public school funding and *McCleary v. State of Washington*—A violation of the separation of powers doctrine or a legitimate exercise of judicial autonomy. *Seattle University Law Review, 38*, 1437–1462.

Cardichon, J., Darling-Hammond, L., Yang, M., Scott, C., Shields, P. M., & Burns, D. (2020). *Inequitable opportunity to learn: Student access to certified and experienced teachers*. Learning Policy Institute.

Carter, P. L., & Welner, K. G. (2013). *Closing the opportunity gap: What America must do to give every child an even chance*. Oxford University Press.

Darling-Hammond, L. (2010). *The flat world and education*. Teachers College Press.

Darling-Hammond, L., Bae, S., Cook-Harvey, C. M., Lam, L., Mercer, C., Podolsky, A., & Stosich, E. L. (2016). *Pathways to new accountability through the Every Student Succeeds Act*. Learning Policy Institute.

Darling-Hammond, L., & Plank, D. N. (2015). *Supporting continuous improvement in California's education system*. Policy Analysis for California Education and Stanford Center for Opportunity Policy in Education.

Darling-Hammond, L., Wilhoit, G., & Pittenger, L. (2014). Accountability for college and career readiness: Developing a new paradigm. *Education Policy Analysis Archives, 22*, 86.

Deming, W. E. (1993). *The new economics for industry, government, and education*. MIT Press.

Dorn, S. (2007). *Accountability Frankenstein: Understanding and taming the monster*. Information Age Publishing.

Elmore, R. F. (2000). *Building a new structure for school leadership*. Albert Shanker Institute.

Elmore, R. F. (2002). *Bridging the gap between standards and achievement*. Albert Shanker Institute.

Forsyth, P. B., Ware, J. K., Olsen, J. J., Lepine, J. A. Sr., Barnes, L. L. B., Khojasteh, J., & Mwavita, M. (2017). *Next generation accountability: A vision for school improvement under ESSA*. Learning Policy Institute.

Fullan, M., Rincón-Gallardo, S., & Hargreaves, A. (2015). Professional capital as accountability. *Education Policy Analysis Archives, 23*(15).

Galster, G. C. (2012). The mechanism(s) of neighbourhood effects: Theory, evidence, and policy implications. In M. van Ham, D. Manley, N. Bailey, L. Simpson, & D. Maclennan (Eds.), *Neighbourhood effects research: New perspectives* (pp. 25–56). https://doi.org/10.1007/978-94-007-2309-2

Hargreaves, A., & Braun, H. (2013). *Data-driven improvement and accountability*. National Education Policy Center. https://nepc.colorado.edu/publication/data-driven-improvement-accountability

Hargreaves, A., & Shirley, D. (2009). *The fourth way: The inspiring future for educational change*. Corwin Press.

Houck, E. A., & DeBray, E. (2015). The shift from adequacy to equity in federal education policymaking: A proposal for how ESEA could reshape the state role in education finance. *RSF: The Russell Sage Foundation Journal of the Social Sciences, 1*(3), 148–167.

Hout, M., & Elliott, S. W. (Eds.) (2011). *Incentives and test-based accountability in education*. National Academies Press.

Kantor, H., & Lowe, R. (2013). Educationalizing the welfare state and privatizing education. In P. Carter & K. Welner (Eds.), *Closing the opportunity gap: What America must do to give every child an even chance* (pp. 25–39). Oxford University Press.

Koretz, D. (2017). *The testing charade: Pretending to make schools better*. University of Chicago Press.

Koski, W. S. (2007). Ensuring an "adequate" education for our nation's youth: How can we overcome the barriers? *Boston College Third World Law Journal, 27*, 13–44.

Liu, G. (2006). Education, equality, and national citizenship. *Yale Law Journal*, *116*, 330–411.

Mann, H. (1848). *Twelfth Annual Report to the Massachusetts State Board of Education*.

Marion, S. (2020). *Using opportunity-to-learn data to support educational equity*. National Center for the Improvement of Educational Assessment.

Mathis, W. J., & Trujillo, T. M. (Eds.). (2016). *Learning from the federal market-based reforms: Lessons for ESSA*. Information Age Publishing.

National Center for Education Statistics. (2021a). *Characteristics of children's families*. https://nces.ed.gov/programs/coe/indicator_cce.asp

National Center for Education Statistics. (2021b). *Concentration of public school students eligible for free or reduced-price lunch*. https://nces.ed.gov/programs/coe/indicator_clb.asp

Nichols, S. L., & Berliner, D. C. (2007). *Collateral damage: How high-stakes testing corrupts America's schools*. Harvard Education Press.

Oakes, J. (1989). What education indicators? The case for assessing school context. *Educational Evaluation and Policy Analysis*, *11*(2), 181–199.

Oakes, J. (1990). *Multiplying inequalities: The effects of race, social class, and tracking on opportunities to learn mathematics and science*. RAND.

Oakes, J., Blasi, G., & Rogers, J. (2004). Accountability for adequate and equitable opportunities to learn. In K. A. Sirotnik (Ed.), *Holding accountability accountable* (pp., 82–99). Teachers College Press.

Oakes, J., Cookson, P., George, J., Levin, S., Carver-Thomas, D., Frelow, F., & Berry, B. (2021). *Adequate and equitable education in high-poverty schools: Barriers and opportunities in North Carolina*. Learning Policy Institute.

Oakes, J., Espinoza, D., Darling-Hammond, L., Gonzales, C., DePaoli, J., Kini, T., Hoachlander, G., Burns, D., Griffith, M., & Leung, M. (2020). *Improving education the New Mexico way: An evidence-based approach*. Learning Policy Institute.

Philip, T. M., & Brown, A. L. (2020). *We all want more teachers of color, right?: Concerns and considerations about the emergent consensus*. National Education Policy Center. https://nepc.colorado.edu/publication/diversity

Rebell, M., & Wolff, J. (2008). *Moving every child ahead: From NCLB hype to meaningful educational opportunity*. Teachers College Press.

Robinson, K. J. (2016). No quick fix for equity and excellence: The virtues of incremental shifts in education federalism. *Stanford Law and Policy Review*, *27*, 201–249.

Robinson, K. J. (2018). Restructuring the Elementary and Secondary Education Act's approach to equity. *Minnesota Law Review*, *103*, 915–998.

*San Antonio Independent School District v. Rodriguez*, 411 U.S. 1 (1973).

Schneider, J. (2018). *Beyond test scores: A better way to measure school quality*. Harvard University Press.

Schott Foundation. (2020). *Creating loving systems across communities to provide all students an opportunity to thrive*. http://schottfoundation.org/sites/default/files/loving-cities-2020.pdf

Shepard, L. A. (2008). A brief history of accountability testing, 1965–2007. In K. E. Ryan, & L. A. Shepard (Eds.), *The future of test-based educational accountability* (pp. 25–46). Routledge.

Smith, M. S. (2011). Rethinking ESEA: A zero-base reauthorization. In F. Hess & A. Kelly (Eds.), *Carrots, sticks, and the bully pulpit: Lessons from a half century of federal efforts to improve America's schools* (pp. 231–252). Harvard Education Press.

Stanford Education Data Archive. (n.d.). *Educational opportunity in the U.S.* https://edopportunity.org/explorer/#/map/none/districts/avg/ses/all/3.5/38/-97/

Tyack, D. B. (1974). *The one best system: A history of American urban education.* Harvard University Press.

U.S. Department of Education. (2013). *For each and every child: A strategy for education equity and excellence.* https://oese.ed.gov/resources/oese-technical-assistance-centers/state-support-network/resources/every-child-strategy-education-equity-excellence/

U.S. Department of Education. (2021). Congressional budget justification, education for the disadvantaged. https://www2.ed.gov/about/overview/budget/budget22/justifications/a-ed.pdf

Welner, K. G. (2001). *Legal rights, local wrongs: When community control collides with educational equity.* State University of New York Press.

Welner, K. G. (2022). The mythical great equalizer school system: Exploring the potential to make it real. In D. C. Berliner & C. Hermanns (Eds.), *Public education: Defending a cornerstone of American democracy* (pp. 84–93). Teachers College Press.

Welner, K. G., & LaCour, S. (2020). Education in context: Schools and their connections to societal inequalities. In K. L. Bowman (Ed.), *The Oxford handbook of U.S. education law* (pp. 23–47). Oxford University Press.

# Index

21st Century College Readiness Afterschool Programming, 142

Abdi, N., 177
Ability grouping versus heterogeneous grouping, 7–8, 19. *See also* South Side High School (SSHS)
Academic achievement
and data analysis, 109
Dr. Martin Luther King, Jr., Early College, 128
Fannie Lou Hamer Freedom High School, 67, 81–82, 87
Rainier Beach High School, 189
Revere High School, 35–36, 37, 45
South Side High School, 23–24, 31–32
and tracking, 20–21
Access to education, 23, 64, 168. *See also* Universal access
Accountability. *See also* New York Performance Standards Consortium; New York State Regents Diploma; New York State Regents Exams
continuous-learning goal, 198–200
current system, 3–4, 177, 196, 197
districts and states, 201–203
external-facing and internal-facing, 213
federal government, 206–210, 213–214
importance, 196–197
incentivizing compliance, 208–210
OTL standards and indicators, 200–201, 203–206
reform proposal, 210–212
societal context, 193–196
supportive approach, 198–199
Adames, H. Y., 150, 152, 153
Adams, C. M., 201
Adaptive change, 187
Administrators. *See* Leadership
Advanced placement (AP) classes, 60
Advisory support, 41, 55, 85. *See also* Postgraduation planning and preparation
Afterschool support and activities, 56, 142, 162–163

Aggression response (vignette), 122
Ahmed, E., 140
Alienation, 37–38
Alim, H. S., 147
Allen, R. L., 43
Allensworth, E. M., 8, 11, 36, 89
All-level accountability. *See* Reciprocal accountability
Amanti, C., 14, 168
American Civil Liberties Union (ACLU), 137
American Psychological Association, 139
Ancess, J., 71
Andersen, S. L., 131
Anderson, C. M., 131
"Answer Sheet, The" (Strauss), 7
Antibias professional development, 56
Antiracism, 55–56, 155, 167–169, 187–188
Anyon, Y., 8, 42, 44
Arocho, J., 210, 211
Arredondo, M. I., 9, 42
Asmar, M., 137
"Assessing Habits of Mind" (Duckor & Perlstein), 72
Assessment. *See also* New York State Regents Exams
criterion-referenced, 25, 28
of English language proficiency, 170
formative, 10–11, 62, 77, 78, 118–119
of New York schools, 82, 83–84
performance-based, 68–69, 74f, 76, 81, 84–85, 86
Schools of Opportunity Criterion 4, 5f, 10–11
summative, 77, 78–79
Assignment to classes, 29
Astor, R. A., 38
Atteberry, A., 24
Attendance rates, 45
Auerbach, S., 14, 181
Ay, Y., 38

"Backwash effect," 28
Bae, S., 198, 200
Baker, E. L., 196
Ballard, P. J., 152, 153

Barlow, A., 85
Barnes, L.L.B., 198, 201
Barriers to learning, 2, 4, 38, 40, 187, 194
Bartholomew, A., 114
Bartolomé, L. I., 149, 151
Barton, P. E., 196
Bazzaz, D., 50
Becoming independent (vignette), 120
Behavioral and Emotional Screening System
    (BESS), 138, 139
Behavioral change and reform, 187
Bektas, F., 38
Bell, A., 62
Benbenishty, R., 38
Berg, J., 133, 140
Berkowitz, R., 38
Berliner, D. C., 197
Bernal, D. D., 153
Bernstein, Matt, 94–95, 98, 99, 100–101,
    103–105, 107
Berry, B., 93, 101, 194
Bertrand, M., 178
Best, M., 114
Bestul, L., 117
Bethune, L., 114
Biden administration, 208
Bike shop entrepreneur (vignette), 124
Black, D., 209, 211
Blasi, G., 201, 203, 206
Block scheduling, 41, 75, 83
Bowie, L., 50
Bowman, K. L., 210
Boyd, D., 11, 89
Braun, H., 198
Brazile, L., 189
Breakfast provision, 57
Briscoe, F., 177
Bronx River Watershed Alliance, 76
Brooks, Ivory, 184
Brown, A. L., 202
Brown-Banks, Carlina, 183
Brown v. Board of Education, 49
Brundin, J., 149
Bryk, A., 11, 89, 93
Bullying, 36, 42
Burns, D., 200, 202
Burns, J. R., 202
Burris, C. C., 1, 2, 8, 21, 24
Bush, K. A., 12, 131

Cammarota, J., 150
Campbell, E. Q., 2
Cantor, P., 1, 133, 140
Capper, C. A., 109, 110–111, 123
Cardichon, J., 202
Career planning. See Postgraduation
    planning and preparation
Carrola, P., 44

Carter, P., 13, 149
Carter, P. L., 3, 193, 200, 201
Carver-Thomas, D., 194
Casco Bay High School (CBHS)
    background, 91
    change process and pacing, 96–99
    crew students, 94
    Equity Summit, 97–98
    excellence and equity vision, 92–96
    professional interdependence, 101–104
    professional staff development, 89,
        99–101, 104
    school culture, 94, 106
    Schools of Opportunity Criterion 5, 11,
        89–91
    staff wellness, 105–106
    Strengthening Families, 114
    student demographics, 91
    teachers as leaders, 104–105
Catalano, T., 14, 161
Central Park East Elementary School and
    Central Park East Secondary School,
    70–71, 83
Chapelle, Dwane, 176–177, 180–184, 187,
    190
Chavez-Dueñas, N. Y., 150, 152, 153
Chen, G. A., 150, 152, 153
Children's Aid Community School, 85, 87
Choice enrollment policy, 159
Christensen Institute, 123
City, E. A., 188
City of Seattle, 188
Civil rights activism, 69–70
Clark Street Community School (CSCS)
    background and context, 109–111
    classroom practice, 126–128
    community partnerships, 114, 117–118
    designing for inclusive instruction, 123–126
    Equity Learning Walk, 100
    formative assessment, 118–119, 126
    foundational pillars, 112–115
    full integration approach, 115–117,
        123–126
    independence and interdependence goal,
        124, 125, 126
    interdisciplinary learning, 117–118
    overcoming low expectations, 121–123
    planning and vision, 111–112
    project-based learning, 112–114, 126
    restorative culture, 119–121
    Schools of Opportunity Criterion 6, 12,
        110–111
    student make-up, 110, 112, 115
Class disparities, 20
Classroom arrangements, 61
Closing the Opportunity Gap (Welner &
    Carter), 2
Coalition for Community Schools, 148

Coalition of Essential Schools, 71, 75
Çogaltay, N., 38
Cohen, J., 37, 38
Coherence, 82–83
Coleman, J. S., 2
Coleman report, 2
Collaborative planning, 102–103
Collection and reporting of resources and
    support, 201–202
Colorado Student Leadership Institute, 142
Comer, J. P., 142
Commins, N. L., 14, 172
Common Core curriculum standards, 3
Communities
    activism, 76, 92–93
    celebrations, 62–63
    classes, 142
    connecting to students, 53, 76, 85–86,
        141, 170–171
    empowering, 183
    input from, 201–202
    interdependence with schools, 117
    and locally based health care, 56–57, 133
    school partnerships, 39, 54, 85–86, 105,
        117–118, 142–143, 163, 188
Community schools, 142
Complaints, 201–202
Comprehensive accountability system,
    210–214
Conditional federal funding, 206–208,
    211–212
Conscientização, 150
Consistency, 28, 84, 126, 128
Cook, A., 85
Cook-Harvey, C. M., 198
Cookson, P., 194
COVID-19, 85, 135, 136, 139–140, 154,
    163, 164
Craig, S. E., 12, 131
Criterion 1: engaging curriculum for all, 5f,
    7–8. See also South Side High School
    (SSHS)
Criterion 2: healthy school climate, 5f, 8–9.
    See also Revere High School (RHS)
Criterion 3: more and better learning time,
    5f, 9–10. See also Pocomoke High
    School (PHS)
Criterion 4: variety of assessments, 5f,
    10–11. See also Fannie Lou Hamer
    Freedom High School (FLHFHS)
Criterion 5: teacher support, 5f, 11. See also
    Casco Bay High School (CBHS)
Criterion 6: students-with-disabilities
    support, 5f, 12. See also Clark Street
    Community School (CSCS)
Criterion 7: comprehensive student services,
    5f, 12. See also Dr. Martin Luther
    King, Jr., Early College (DMLK)

Criterion 8: culturally relevant curriculum,
    5f, 12–13. See also Dr. Martin Luther
    King, Jr., Early College (DMLK)
Criterion 9: support for language-minority
    students, 5f, 13–14. See also Lincoln
    High School (LHS)
Criterion 10: parent and community
    engagement, 5f, 14. See also Rainier
    Beach High School (RBHS)
Critical consciousness, 150
Critical thinking, 73, 78, 87
Culturally relevant curriculum. See
    Dr. Martin Luther King, Jr., Early
    College (DMLK)
Culturally Responsive Teaching and the
    Brain (Hammond), 125
"Culturally sustaining pedagogy," 147
Curriculum, 3, 25, 27, 75, 147, 149–152,
    155, 156

Daniel, J., 54, 142
Darling-Hammond, L., 1, 11, 71, 89, 93, 94, 97,
    102, 196, 198, 199, 200, 201, 202, 213
Darwin, M., 177
Data-use processes, 205
Davidson, K. L., 11
Davis, J. E., 44, 50
Dawson, P., 177
DeBray, E., 207, 210, 211
Dee, T., 177
Deescalating conflict, 141
Deficit-based views, 37, 38, 121–123, 151,
    153–154, 162
De Galarce, P. C., 12, 131
Dehumanizing curriculum, 149–152, 156
De Kadt, M., 75
Del Carmen Salazar, M., 149
Del Razo, J. L., 9
DeMatthews, D., 44
Deming, W. E., 198
Denver Board of Education, 141
Denver Health Clinic, 134
Denver Police Department, 141
Denver Public Schools, 155
Denver Scholarship Foundation, 142
DePaoli, J., 200
Detracking reform. See South Side High
    School (SSHS)
Dewey, J., 114
Diamond, C., 142, 148
Dickinson, J., 113
Differentiated instruction, 25, 26, 93, 98, 116
Diliberti, M., 140
District and state accountability, 200–206
District-level curriculum change, 154–155
"District power equalization," 208–209
Diversity, 29, 36, 60–61, 161
Do, V., 118

Dobbie, W., 2
Donohoo, J., 101, 118, 125
Doren, B., 113
Dorn, S., 196
Downing, B. J., 8, 42, 44
*Dreamkeepers* (Ladson-Billings), 187
Dr. Martin Luther King, Jr., Early College
    (DMLK)
    21st Century College Readiness
        Afterschool Programming, 142
    academic outcomes, 128
    Alternative Cooperative Education, 142
    background, 133
    Child Study Team meetings, 138
    community partnerships, 142–143
    curriculum, 148–151, 151–155, 156
    health and wellness, 136–140
    health crises context, 135–136
    holistic approach, 132–134, 137–138, 143
    Know Justice Know Peace initiative,
        154–155
    Minds Matter, 142
    physical environment, 134
    Place of Peace, 139
    political context, 148, 154
    professional staff development, 155
    radical healing framework, 152–153
    relationships prioritization, 134
    Safe2Tell, 137
    Saturday school, 163
    school culture, 140–142
    Schools of Opportunity Criteria 7 and 8,
        11, 12–13, 131–132, 146–147
    Strengthening Families, 114
    student agency, 148–149, 154
    student demographics, 133
    Whole Child Team, 137–138
Dryfoos, J., 142
Duckor, B., 71, 72, 78
Duke, D. L., 177

Eaton, S., 50
Eckerson, J., 169
Eckloff, T., 60
Eells, R., 101, 118, 125
Elementary and Secondary Education Act
    (ESEA), 206–207, 209, 211–212
Elliott, S. W., 196, 198
Ellspermann, J., 52
Elmore, R. F., 188, 198, 201
Elspermann, J., 52
Emergent bilinguals, 162
"Emergent multilinguals," 162
Employment opportunities, 173–174
English language arts (ELA), 27, 32–33
English language learners (ELLs), 14,
        67, 170–171. *See also* Lincoln High
        School (LHS)

English Language Proficiency Assessment
    (ELPA), 170
Enrichment, 50, 52–55
Environmental racism, 76
Environmental stewardship, 75–76
Epstein, J. L., 142
Equity and Excellence Commission (U.S.
    Dept. of Education), 209–210
Equity literacy, 95
Espinoza, D., 200
Every Student Succeeds Act (ESSA), 10–11,
    177, 198, 206
Exclusionary discipline, 38, 41–42
Exemptions to the New York State Regents
    Exams, 84
Expeditionary Learning (EL), 91, 100
Extended hours for student support, 9, 34,
    162–163
Extra-teaching responsibilities, 104–105

Falk, B., 71
Families. *See also* Rainier Beach High School
    (RBHS)
    engagement and advocacy, 14, 26, 33, 87,
        170–171, 180, 182
    input from, 183, 201–202
    resistance to change, 43–44
    school space for, 139
    support for, 85, 170–171, 172
Fannie Lou Hamer Freedom High School
    (FLHFHS)
    academic outcomes, 67, 81–82, 87
    accountability, 79–80f, 84–85
    Advisory, 85
    assessment, 76–81
    Bronx River study, 75–76
    collaborative spirit, 83–84
    community/school demographics, 67
    fishbowl activity, 98
    Graduation Portfolio, 78, 81
    habits-of-mind framework, 73, 74f
    history and legacy, 69–73
    Language Portfolio, 77
    park creation, 75–76
    portfolio and exhibition framework, 76–81
    project-based learning, 73, 75–76
    Rocking the Boat, 76
    school culture, 86–87
    Schools of Opportunity Criterion 4, 11,
        67, 68–69
Federal government, 135–136, 206–210, 211
Felton, P., 142
Female educators of color, 56
Fiarman, S. E., 188
Fisher, T. L., 113
Flanagan, C., 154
Flores, N., 14, 169
Floyd, George, 164

Food service, 57
Ford, D. Y., 50
Ford, T. G., 201
Formative Assessment for Maryland
    Education (FAME), 62
Forsyth, P. B., 198, 201
Foundation aid program, 211
Frank, K. A., 99
Frattura, E. M., 109, 110–111, 123
Freire, P., 150
Frelow, F., 194
French, B. H., 150, 152, 153
Freudenberg, N., 142, 148
Fritz, C., 142
Fryer, R. G., 2
Fullan, M., 213
Full integration design tenet, 116–117
Funding cuts for noncompliance with
    mandated standards, 202–203
Funding sources, 39, 45, 54, 189, 193,
    206–209, 211
"Funds of knowledge," 168–169
Furfaro, H., 50
Futterer, A., 135

Gallagher, A., 99
Galster, G. C., 194
Gandara, P., 50
Garbarino, J., 135
Garcia, Lourenço, 37, 39, 40–41, 43–44, 45
Gardner, M., 93, 97
Garrity, D. T., 21, 30
GED classes, 171
George, J., 194
George Floyd murder, 164–165
Gifted and talented programs, 50
Ginwright, S., 150, 151
Goessling, K. P., 135, 142, 149, 150, 153
Golberstein, E., 136, 139
Gold implementation level, 6
Goldman, S. E., 113
Gonzales, C., 200
González, N., 14, 168
Gooden, M. A., 44
Goodman, D., 178
Gorski, P., 11, 89, 95
Grading practices, 27–28, 188
Grading schools, 197
Graduation rates, 31–32, 45, 67, 81–82, 87,
    189
Grayson, Kimberly, 133, 137–138, 151–152,
    153, 155
Greene, J., 177
Green Valley Ranch (Denver), Colorado, 133
Griffith, M., 200
Grossman, P., 11, 89
Guaranteed tax base in school-finance
    systems, 211

Guffey, S., 37
Guo, S., 136

Habits of mind, 73, 74f, 78
Haertel, E., 196
Hamann, E. T., 14, 161
Hamer, Fannie Lou, 69–70
Hammond, Z., 125
Hargreaves, A., 198, 213
Harris, A., 39
Harrison, E. M., 113
Hart, H., 8, 36
Hattie, J. A. C., 101, 118, 125
Haydon, T., 112
Health and wellness curriculum, 32
Heifetz, R., 187
Hendry, G. D., 62
Heritage language, 168–169
Herman, R., 177
Hernández, L. E., 1
Heterogeneity goal, 29
Heterosexuality norm, 149
Higgins-D'Alessandro, A., 37
Hiring input, 182
History curriculum, 146, 151–152, 155
Hoachlander, G., 200
Hoagwood, K. E., 136
Hobson, C. J., 2
Hoffman, Matt, 56
Holistic approach. See Dr. Martin Luther
    King, Jr., Early College (DMLK)
Hopelessness, 122–123
Hopkins, D., 39
Houck, E. A., 207, 210, 211
House systems, 59–60, 83
Hout, M., 196, 198
Humanizing pedagogy, 132, 138
Hyler, M. E., 93, 97

IB (International Baccalaureate) Diploma
    Program. See International
    Baccalaureate (IB) Diploma Program
IDEA (Individuals with Disabilities
    Education Act), 12, 207
Ijadi-Maghsoodi, R., 136
Incentivizing compliance and federal
    funding, 208–210
Inclusion model, 12, 116–117
Individuals with Disabilities Education Act
    (IDEA), 12, 207
Ing, M., 11, 89
Innovation grant program, 211
Inquiry approach. See Project-based learning
Integrated Comprehensive System (ICS)
    model, 109, 110–111
Interdependence, 94, 101–104, 124,
    125–126
Interdisciplinary experiences, 92–93, 116–117

International Baccalaureate (IB) Diploma
    Program, 23, 28, 29–30, 31, 33, 180
Internet use. *See* Technology use
Ishimaru, A. M., 14, 178, 181, 189
Isolation, 37–38
Israel, M., 118

Jacobson, M., 177
Jefferson, A., 178
Jennings, M. E., 177
Jeong, G. K., 118
"Jobs to Be Done Theory," 123
Johannsen, J., 60
Johnson, A., 136
Johnson, P., 113
Johnson, R., 148
Johnson, S. M., 11, 89, 93
Johnson, William, 24

Kalogrides, D., 64
Kang-Yi, C. D., 135
Kantor, H., 194
Karadag, E., 38
Kataoka, S. H., 136
Kauffman, J. M., 114
*Keeping Track* (Oakes), 8
Kemp, J., 140
Kennedy, A. M., 112
Kersevich, S., 131
Kersevich, S. E., 12
Khalifa, M. A., 44, 177
Khojasteh, J., 198, 201
Kiely, M. T., 118
Kim, D. M., 131
Kini, T., 200
Kirkland, D., 150
Kirshner, B., 154, 178
Kleinert, H. L., 113
Kleinert, J. O., 113
"Know Justice Know Peace" podcast, 154–155
Koretz, D., 196, 197, 198
Koski, W. S., 201, 202, 203, 205, 206
Kozol, J., 50
Kraft, M., 89
Kuhfeld, M., 136
Kumashiro, K. K., 148, 149

LaCour, S. E., 2, 4, 24, 194
Ladd, H. F., 196
Ladson-Billings, G., 150, 187
Lai, K., 136
Lam, L., 198
Landrum, T. J., 114
Language-based clubs, 172–173
Language liaisons, 173
Language-minority students, 13–14, 159. *See
    also* Lincoln High School (LHS)
Lankford, H., 11, 89

Lash, T., 118
Las Razas Unidas, 172–173
Latino American history representation, 155
Leadership, 11, 39, 43–44, 45, 53, 93–94,
    102, 177, 180–184, 190
Learning partnerships, 117–118
Learning Policy Institute, 55
Lee, C. E., 118
Lee, J.-S., 60
Leithwood, K., 39
Leonard, L., 39
Lepine, J. A., Sr., 198, 201
Leung, M., 200
Leveling up, 25–26
Levin, S., 194
Levine, P., 154
Lewis, J. A., 150, 152, 153
Library hours, 162–163
Lincoln High School (LHS)
    Academic Resource Center, 163
    background and community context, 158,
        160–162
    Bilingual Career and Education Fair, 173
    bilingual/multilingual initiatives and
        opportunities, 173–174
    Club Day, 172–173
    communication with families, 166–167
    Connection Circle, 165–166
    Cultural Ambassadors, 172
    diversity and inequality, 163–168
    English language program, 170–172
    hertitage language program, 168–169
    Joven Noble Latino Leaders Club, 172
    language-based clubs, 172–173
    Learn to Dream scholarship, 171
    letters from the principal, 164–167
    Not Your Mother's PTA, 183
    professional staff development, 167–168,
        169, 173
    Schools of Opportunity Criterion 9, 14,
        159–160
    supporting opportunity, 162–163
    Susie Buffett Scholarship, 172
Lindstrom, L., 113
Linn, R. L., 196
Linsky, M., 187
Little, S., 42
Liu, G., 208, 211, 212
Liu, J., 136
Loeb, S., 11, 64, 89
Long, L., 112
Looping, 75, 83
López, F., 148
López, R. M., 9
Loukas, A., 9, 36, 37, 45
Lowe, R., 194
Low expectations, 21, 25–26, 33, 121–123
Lynch-Nichols, Rebecca, 93, 99, 102, 105, 107

Maa, W. C., 118
MacBlain, M., 112
MacBlain, S., 112
MacGregor, D., 114
Maier, A., 54, 142
Male educators of color, 55
Male privilege, 149, 154
Mann, H., 194
Mann, N., 70, 72, 77
Mann, Nancy, 70
Marion, S., 204
Martinez, M., 112
Maryland Food Bank, 54
Maryland Manual Online, 50
Massachusetts Dept. of Education, 42, 45
Masten, A. S., 58
Material exclusion, 189–190
Mathematics curriculum and support, 25, 27
Mathis, W. J., 177, 197
Maynard, R., 177
Mazzeo, C., 11, 89
McCabe, E., 37, 38
McCray, Susan, 94, 98, 101, 107
McLaughlin, M., 11, 89, 94, 102
McPartland, J., 2
Meier, D., 70–71, 83
Mental health and mental health care
    awareness, 136–137
    community-based, 56–57, 133
    Dr. Martin Luther King, Jr., Early College,
        136–140, 148–151, 155–156
    education, 136–137, 139
    and federal government, 135–136
    related to oppression, 135, 149–151,
        153–154, 155–156
    school-based provision, 12–13, 32, 57,
        85, 105–106, 133, 134, 136
    and Schools of Opportunity Criterion 8,
        12–13, 131–132
    traditional approach, 153–154
    urgent care access, 138
Mentoring, 52, 57–59, 103
Mercer, C., 198
Mertz, C., 60
Metro State University of Denver, 142
Michelli, N., 37, 38
Middaugh, E., 154
Miller, B. F., 136, 139
Mindfulness practice, 139
Minds Matter, 142
Miraftab, F., 189
Miramontes, O. B., 14, 172
Mississippi Freedom Democratic Party,
    69 70
Moll, L., 14, 168
Molnar, A., 148
Mommandi, W., 12
Mood, A. M., 2

Moore, H., 38
Morrison, B., 140
Mosley, D. V., 150, 152, 153
Multiage support, 59
Multilingual liaisons, 173
Multilingual students, 40–41
Multiple perspectives, 26–27
Mungal, A., 44
Murphy, J., 8, 24
Murray, C., 115
Musu-Gillette, L., 140
Mwavita, M., 198, 201

Nadeau, A., 14, 172
Naranjo, J., 115
National Association of Elementary
    Principals, 36
National Center for Education Statistics, 13,
    50, 194
National Education Policy Center, 1
National Museum of African American
    History and Culture, 151
National Research Council, 61
National School Climate Council, 9, 36, 37
National Scientific Council on the
    Developing Child, 58
Navalta, C. P., 131
NCLB (No Child Left Behind), 177, 196, 197
Negative school experiences, 121–123
Nellie Mae Education Foundation, 39
Neville, H. A., 150, 152, 153
Newman, R., 58
New York City alternative schools, 71
New York City Children's Aid Community
    Schools, 87
New York City Department of Parks, 75–76
New York City School Survey, 82, 83–84
New York City Summer Youth Employment
    Program (SYEP), 85–86
New York Performance Standards
    Consortium, 68, 77–78, 79–80f, 81,
    83, 84–85, 87
New York State Regents Diploma, 31–32,
    68–69, 71
New York State Regents Exams, 24, 26, 28,
    31, 68, 84
Nichols, S. L., 197
No Child Left Behind (NCLB), 177, 196, 197
Noncompetitive federal grants, 211
Noncompliance and funding, 203
Non-exclusionary discipline. See Restorative
    discipline
Nonrepresentation in curriculum, 149
Normalizing asking for help, 136–137

Oakes, J., 1, 3, 8, 9, 43, 54, 64, 142, 187,
    194, 200, 201, 203, 206
O'Day, J. A., 3

Okonofus, J. A., 60
Oleszweski, A. M., 177
Olsen, J. J., 198, 201
Olubiyi, O., 135
Opportunity gap, 2–4, 193, 194, 196
Opportunity-to-learn (OTL) indicators,
    203–205
Opportunity-to-learn (OTL) standards, 3,
    200–201, 201–202, 212
Osher, D., 133, 140
OTL (opportunity-to-learn) indicators,
    203–205
OTL (opportunity-to-learn) standards. See
    Opportunity-to-learn (OTL) standards
Oudekerk, B. A., 140
Outside-school reforms, 211
Ozer, E. J., 152, 153

Papay, J., 89
Parent and community engagement, 14, 87.
    See also Rainier Beach High School
    (RBHS)
Paris, D., 147
Paskey, J., 113
Patterson, A., 148
Pauline, M. E., 8, 42, 44
Paunesku, D., 60
Peer support, 94
Penuel, W. R., 11, 77, 99
Performance-based assessments (PBATs),
    68–69, 74f, 76, 81, 84–85, 86
Performance standards, 3. See also
    New York Performance Standards
    Consortium
Perlstein, D., 71, 72, 78
Persistence of tracking, 20
Personalized learning, 112–113
Philip, T. M., 202
Physical environment of school, 37, 134
Physical health and health care
    and Schools of Opportunity Criterion 7,
        12–13, 131–132
    supports for students, 12–13, 56–57, 85,
        134
    supports for teachers, 105–106
Pianta, R. C., 115
Pickeral, T., 37, 38
Pierce, Colin, 180–181
Pierce, Derek, 93, 102, 107
Pipher, M., 158
Pisciotta, L., 8, 42, 44
Pittenger, L., 199, 200, 202, 213
Place-based learning, 114
Plank, D. N., 199, 200
Plasencia, S., 1
Plumb, J. L., 12, 131
Pocomoke High School (PHS)
    adult-student relationships, 58–59

After School Academies, 56
AP Pathways, 60
Back to School Block Party, 62–63
Be the One, 58–59
Comic Con event, 53
community context, 49–50, 63
community involvement, 54, 62–63
enrichment, 54–55
Find Your One, 58–59
food service, 57
formative assessment, 62
"four tribes, one school" model, 59–60
health and wellness, 56–57
Intent Night, 57–58, 59
Leadership Education About Disabilities
    (LEAD), 53
lunch hour, 52–53
MADE MEN (Men Achieving Dreams
    Through Education), 55–56
pop-ups, 54
Principal's Advisory Group, 61
professional staff development, 56, 62
Project 100, 57–58
Project Lit, 54
representation and antiracist culture,
    55–56
school culture, 55–56, 60–61, 64, 82
Schools of Opportunity Criterion 3, 9–10,
    51–52, 63, 65
social and political challenges, 50–51,
    63, 65
Speak Up, 60–61
thrift stores, 57
Women Who RISE, 56
Worcester on Wheels, 54
young mothers support, 56
Your60, 10, 52–53
Podolsky, A., 198
Polcari, A., 131
Police abuse and violence, 154, 163, 164
Police-free school campaigns, 140–141
Politicized trauma, 149–150
Ponisciak, S., 11, 89
Portfolios, 71–73, 76–81, 87
Postgraduation planning and preparation,
    55, 57–58, 85–86, 142
Poverty, 2, 50, 67, 194
Powell, j. a., 189
Power, 181–182, 208–209
"Power equalizing," 208–209
Powers, J. D., 117, 135
Pratt Institute, 54
Price, D., 114
Prilleltensky, I., 150
Professional learning communities (PLCs),
    99, 102–103, 174
Professional staff development
    antibias/antiracism training, 56, 167–169

family communication, 173
instructional practices, 30–31, 39–40, 62
Progressive education, 71
Project-based learning, 61, 68, 73, 75–76, 86, 112–113
Public recognition events, 7
Puffer, M., 136

Race, 2, 8, 20, 44, 150, 179
Race to the Top, 207
Racism, 50, 63, 65, 69–70, 96, 135, 167–168, 187–188, 194. See also Antiracism
Rainier Beach High School (RBHS)
  academic outcomes, 189
  background and context, 179, 180, 189
  Building Leadership Team, 183–184
  "circling back," 185
  Community Cafe, 186
  equity and instructional improvement integration, 187–188
  families and community relationships, 180–184
  impact of reform, 189–190
  instructional rounds, 188
  "Loving Cities" project, 211
  Parent-Teacher-Student Association, 180
  reform approaches, 177–178
  school familial culture, 184–186
  Schools of Opportunity Criterion 10, 14, 176, 178–179
  SIG design team, 180–181
  Urban School Turnaround Initiative, 180
Rationing learning opportunities and resources, 20, 34
Ravitch, D., 196
Ray, M. J., 118
Rayne, Jenifer, 55–56
Rebell, M., 212
Reciprocal accountability, 196–197, 201, 205
Recruitment and onboarding, 83
Redding, S., 177
Reeves, D. B., 110
Reeves, J., 14, 161
Relationships
  adult-student, 53–54, 58–59
  collegial, 11, 94–95, 102
  and leadership practice, 184–185
  and restorative approach, 140, 141
  school-community, 39, 85–86, 142–143, 180–184
  and school culture, 8, 41, 46, 60–61, 81, 83, 184–186
  school-family, 184–186
  student-teacher, 37–38, 41, 43, 75, 125–126
Relevance of past, 70
Remedial work time, 53

Renée, M., 9, 178, 187
Resistance to reform, 21, 30, 33, 43–44
Resisting oppression, 152–154
Resource accountability, 3, 43, 200
Restorative discipline, 9, 36–37, 42, 104–105, 119–121, 140, 141, 188
Restorative Justice Coordinator, 141
Revere High School (RHS)
  advisory block, 41
  background and context, 35–38
  discipline policies, 41–43
  external partnerships, 39
  Freshman Academy, 41
  leadership change, 39
  multilingual student programs, 40–41, 45–46
  Newcomers Academy, 40–41, 45–46
  professional staff development, 39–40, 45–46
  relationship building, 41, 44–45
  resistance to reform, 43–45
  Schools of Opportunity Criterion 2, 9, 36–37
Richards, E., 50
Rigor, 33, 82, 92–93
Rincón-Gallardo, S., 213
Riser-Kositsky, M., 12
Ritter, G. W., 42
Roberts, J. E., 188
Robinson, K. J., 206, 207–208, 209, 210, 211, 212
Rockville Centre School District, 21–22
Rodela, K. C., 178
Rogers, J., 1, 201, 203, 206
Ron Clark Academy, 59
Rosa, J., 14, 169
Rosch, A., 8, 42, 44
Rose, T., 133, 140
Rothstein, R., 196
Rowan, B., 136
Ruíz, R., 13, 161
Ruzek, E., 136

Sadler, D. R., 9, 77
Safety, 36, 137, 164
San Antonio Independent School District v. Rodriguez, 206
Sanderson, K. A., 113
Santoro, Doris, 106
Saunders, M., 9
Scales, P. D., 112
Schachner, A., 1
Schlechty, P., 112
Schneider, J., 201
Scholarship opportunities, 173–174
School-centric approach to equal education, 194–195
School climate. See School culture

School culture. *See also* Revere High School
  (RHS)
  and academic achievement, 35–36, 37
  and affective outcomes, 37–38, 116, 166
  Casco Bay High School, 94
  dimensions of, 37
  Dr. Martin Luther King, Jr., Early College,
    140–142
  Fannie Lou Hamer Freedom High School,
    86–87
  Pocomoke High School, 64
  Rainier Beach High School, 184–185
School discipline, 8–9, 41–43, 46, 188. *See
  also* Restorative discipline
Schools-community partnerships, 39, 54,
    85–86, 105, 117–118, 142–143, 163,
    188
Schools of Opportunity Project
  about, 1–3
  application process, 6–7
  criteria for recognition, 4–6, 7–14
  high-quality education, 1
  high-quality teachers, 11
  holistic measurement, 2
  hope/optimism, 15
  review of application materials, 6
  self-assessment guide, 15
Schott Foundation, 211
Sciaraffa, M. A., 140
Scott, C., 202
Seattle, Washington, 179
Selvaraj, S., 142
Serna, I., 43
Sethi, J., 112
Shared decision-making, 181–182, 183,
    190
Sharratt, L., 39
Shavelson, R. J., 196
Shepard, L. A., 11, 77, 196, 197
Shields, P. M., 202
Shirley, D., 178, 213
Signs of Suicide presentation, 139
Silver implementation level, 6
Simplicity of data collection and analysis, 6
Sizer, Ted, 71
Skiba, R. J., 9, 42
Sleeter, C., 11, 89, 94, 96
Smith, C., 103
Smith, G. A., 114
Smith, M. S., 3, 207
Social inequities, 2, 20–21, 50, 70, 76, 135
Social justice, 91, 94, 95–96
Social studies, 32–33
"Social toxins," 135
Societal responsibility, 194
Soland, J., 136
Solorzano, D. G., 153
Southeast Community College, 171

South Side High School (SSHS)
  academic outcomes, 23–24, 31–32
  "double-up classes," 27
  early frameworks, 26–31
  early stages of reform, 25–26
  framework revisions, 32–34
  International Baccalaureate (IB) Diploma
    Program, 23, 28, 29–30, 31, 33
  math performance, 24
  Pathways program, 34
  professional staff development, 30–31
  resistance to reform, 30, 33
  Schools of Opportunity Criterion 1, 8, 20
  success indicators, 31–32
South Side Middle School, 25
Spanishes, 169
Spanish for Heritage Learners, 169
Special education. *See* Students with
    disabilities
Special needs students. *See* Students with
    disabilities
Spending Clause of the U.S. Constitution,
    206
Stanford Education Data Archive, 194
State school-financing system, 208, 210, 212
State tax laws, 210
Steinberg, Peter, 70
Steyer, L., 133, 140
Stosich, E. L., 198
Stratification and tracking, 20
Streaming, 7–8
Structural inequities, 2, 4, 38, 187
Stuart Wells, A., 43
Students. *See also* Students with disabilities
  and activism, 147, 155
  agency, 40–41, 64, 116, 148–149, 153, 154
  and choice, 52, 112–113, 116, 128–129
  engagement, 112, 117
  workload, 33
Students with disabilities, 12, 28–29, 31,
    32–34, 53, 57, 67, 207. *See also* Clark
    Street Community School (CSCS)
Success strategies for learners, 127–128t
Suiter, D., 83
Summative assessment, 77, 78–79
Summer reading, 103
Sun, M., 99
Supportive accountability approach,
    198–199
Suspensions, 41–42
Suvall, C., 140
Swick, D., 135
Symbolic inclusion, 189–190

Tarasawa, B., 136
Tashlik, P., 85
Tatum, B. D., 50
Teacher Academy of Maryland, 55–56

Teachers. *See also* Casco Bay High School
    (CBHS); Professional staff development
    collaboration, 40, 83, 118
    health care for, 105–106
    interdependence, 101–103, 118
    as leaders, 104–105
    minority representation, 55–56
    professional capacity, 199
    professional learning communities (PLCs),
        102–103, 174
    relationships with students, 37–38, 41,
        43, 54, 58–59, 75
    resistance from, 43, 44
    support for, 30–31, 44–45
    turnover, 90
Technology use, 39, 162, 164
Teicher, M. H., 131
Teitel, L., 188
Terrasi, S., 12, 131
Test, D. W., 114
Thapa, A., 37
Theoharis, G., 43, 44
Theokas, C., 1
Theory of action to achieve goals, 203–204
Thomson, K., 62
Thriving student (vignette), 113
Tijerina, E., 1
Title I, Elementary and Secondary Education
    Act, 209, 210, 211–212
Title IX, Elementary and Secondary
    Education Act, 207
Title VI, Elementary and Secondary
    Education Act, 207
Tracking and detracking, 7–8. *See also* South
    Side High School (SSHS)
Transformative practice, 139, 152–153
Transformative social-emotional academic
    learning (TSEAL), 139
Transportation services, 188
Trauma, 133–134, 135, 149–151
Tribe system, 59–60
Trigger enforcement mechanism, 202–203
Trujillo, T. M., 178, 197
"Turnaround reforms," 177–178
"Turnaround schools," 14, 177–178
Tutoring, 53, 163
Tyack, D. B., 206

Ullucci, K., 9
Universal acceleration, 21
Universal access, 1, 7, 34, 64, 93, 97–98,
    115–116
Universal design for learning (UDL), 62, 116
University of Maryland Eastern Shore, 55
Urgent mental health care access, 138
U.S. Dept. of Education, 12, 13, 208,
    209–210
U.S. Government Accountability Office, 50

Valladares, G., 8, 42, 44
Van Quaquebeke, N., 60
Vulnerability, 181

Walton, G. M., 60
Wang, K., 140
Ward, L., 148
Ware, J. K., 198, 201
Warikoo, N., 13, 149
Warren, M. R., 178
Warren, Richard, 55
Washington Building Leaders of Change, 188
*Washington Post,* 7
Wealth and election into advanced courses,
    25
Weinfield, F. D., 2
Well, K. B., 136
Well-being, 13, 32, 37, 46, 131, 149
Wellness care, 105, 136–137, 155–156. *See
    also* Mental health and mental health
    care; Physical health and health care
"Wellness Czar," 105
Welner, K. G., 1, 2, 3, 4, 8, 12, 13, 21, 24,
    43, 187, 193, 194, 200, 201, 214
Welsh, R. O., 42
Wen, H., 136, 139
West Farms, Bronx, New York, 67
*We Want to Do More Than Survive* (Love),
    103
Whiteness norms and privilege, 21, 148,
    149, 150, 154
Wiley, K. E., 8, 9, 37, 42, 44
Wilhoit, G., 199, 200, 202, 213
Williams, N. T., 9, 42
Wolff, J., 212
Worcester County, Maryland, 49–50
Work schedules, 41
Wraparound services, 12–13
Wyckoff, J., 11, 89

Yang, J. L., 8, 42, 44
Yang, M., 202
Yonezawa, S., 43
York, R. I., 2
Young mothers support, 56
Youngs, P., 99
Youniss, J., 154
Youth Ministries for Peace and Justice, 76

Zane, C., 113
Zeanah, C. H., 140
Zeanah, P. D., 140
Zehr, H., 140
Zeldin, S., 117
Zhang, A., 140
Zhang, J., 140
Zhang, L., 136
Zierer, K., 118, 125

# About the Contributors

**Dwane Chappelle** is Seattle's first director of the Department of Education and Early Learning (DEEL), serving since February 2016 when he was first confirmed to the role by Seattle City Council. Dr. Chappelle oversees the City of Seattle's efforts to partner with families and communities to achieve educational equity, close race-based opportunity gaps, and build a better future for Seattle students through strategic investments in education. Prior to becoming DEEL's director, Dr. Chappelle was principal of Rainier Beach High School, where the graduation rate increased by 25% under his leadership. Dr. Chappelle graduated from Grambling State University and earned his doctorate in educational leadership from Gonzaga University.

**Janet Eckerson** is an assistant professor of Spanish at the University of Nebraska at Kearney. From 2005 to 2019 she taught Spanish in Nebraska secondary schools. Her interests include second and heritage language pedagogy, language teacher preparation and professional learning, heritage language learners, and educational policy and practice impacting Latinx students in U.S. schools.

**Lourenço Garcia,** EdD, is a nationally recognized and award-winning educational leader with more than 27 years of teaching, research, leadership, and consulting experience. Under Dr. Garcia's leadership, Revere High School (Revere, MA) won several prestigious awards and honors, including the Schools of Opportunity National Award (Gold Medal, 2016) and the Best Urban High School in America (Gold Medal, 2014). Dr. Garcia is currently the assistant superintendent for Revere Public Schools.

**Matt Garcia** is a doctoral candidate in the School of Education at the University of Colorado Boulder. He is a graduate research assistant for the National Education Policy Center working on the Schools of Opportunity Recognition Program. Matt holds an MPA in public management and a BA in English, both from the University of New Mexico. Prior to graduate school, Matt oversaw private scholarships and internal grants at a community college foundation. His research interests lay at the intersection of social justice, policy, and market-based education reform.

**Kristen P. Goessling** is an assistant professor of human development and family studies at Penn State Brandywine and the principal investigator of the Philadelphia Participatory Research Collective. She is an interdisciplinary engaged scholar whose work aligns to create spaces of belonging where people build meaningful relationships, construct knowledge, and take action toward social change. Dr. Goessling uses participatory action research to investigate personal experiences of public policies with youth, students, and community members as co-researchers.

**Kimberly Grayson** is a powerhouse instructional leader and incredibly successful former principal. She is starting her 27th year in education as an Associate Dean of Regional Supports in the Leadership Division for Relay Graduate School of Education.

**Jill Gurtner** is the principal of Clark Street Community School (CSCS), in the Middleton Cross Plains Area School District in Wisconsin. She has been a public school educator at the high school level for over 30 years. Jill is driven by a passion to design and implement an educational system rooted in talent development for all learners that repays the educational debt owed to our most marginalized learners.

**Edmund T. Hamann** is a professor in the Department of Teaching, Learning and Teacher Education at the University of Nebraska–Lincoln, and a fellow of the American Educational Research Association (AERA). His primary scholarly interests are in three overlapping areas: (1) how transnational movement of students and families is responded to by schools (particularly movement between the U.S. and Latin America); (2) how educational policies are cultural productions transformed in their conversion to practice (particularly collaboration across tiers of the educational system, like state departments of education working with schools); and (3) how school reform is/is not responsive to various student populations (particularly transnationally mobile students and English language learners).

**Ann M. Ishimaru** (Japanese American yonsei/she/her) is the Bridge Family Associate Professor of Educational Foundations, Leadership & Policy at the University of Washington's College of Education and the director of the Just Ed Leadership Institute. Her scholarship seeks to cultivate Black, Indigenous, Latinx, Asian American, and Pacific Islander family-, community- and systems-based leadership to foster educational justice in P–12 schools and communities. In addition to numerous peer-reviewed articles in top educational research journals, she published *Just Schools: Building Equitable Collaborations with Families and Communities*, with Teachers College Press.

**Mark Larson** has been the principal at Lincoln High since 2015. Prior to that he was an associate principal, English teacher, and coach, also at Lincoln High. Mark received his bachelor's degree in secondary English education from Nebraska Wesleyan University and his master's in educational leadership from Doane College. Mark lives just a few blocks from Lincoln High with his wife, Ashley, their three kids (Lily, Sam, and Liam), and their dog (Tyson).

**Julie Fisher Mead** is a professor emerita in the Department of Educational Leadership & Policy Analysis at the University of Wisconsin–Madison. Dr. Mead researches and writes about topics related to the legal aspects of education. Dr. Mead's research centers on legal issues related to special education and legal issues raised by various forms of school choice.

**Linda Molner Kelley** served as codirector of the Schools of Opportunity project. As a former high school literacy and journalism teacher and as assistant dean of teacher education and partnerships and director for outreach and engagement at the University of Colorado Boulder, Linda developed a series of innovative K–16 school district and community partnerships. These included successful induction programs for novice teachers, job-embedded learning and research opportunities for experienced and master teachers, and campuswide support for university faculty and their students to engage in needs-based projects with local, national, and international communities.

**John Murphy** is the principal at South Side High School in Rockville Centre, New York. He has also served as the assistant principal and IB coordinator at South Side and has taught Theory of Knowledge and English for grades 7–12, including IB English. His research interests include differentiated instruction, multiple intelligence theory, and authentic assessment.

**Jeannie Oakes** is Presidential Professor Emeritus in Educational Equity at UCLA and is Senior Fellow in Residence at the Learning Policy Institute. She is past president of the American Educational Research Association. Oakes received a PhD in education from UCLA; an MA in American studies from California State University, Los Angeles; and a BA in English from San Diego State University.

**Jeff Palladino** has served the students of New York City for the past 25 years and has been the Principal of Fannie Lou Hamer Freedom High School since 2014. In 2016, he was invited to speak at the White House by the Barack Obama administration for the Reach Higher forum on higher education. He lives in Stamford, Connecticut, with his wife, Sandra, and children, Jason and Kelley.

**Derek Pierce** is the founding principal of Casco Bay High School in Portland, Maine, a lead school in the Expeditionary Learning Education network. Mr. Pierce was formerly a founding dean and later principal at Poland (Maine) Regional High School. He's proud to be the father of two Casco Bay alums (Siri and Liva) and the spouse of Anja Hanson, an academic adviser at Portland Adult Education.

**Jenifer Rayne** is a 4th-year principal of Pocomoke High School in Worcester County, Maryland. Under her leadership, this small, diverse high school has been recognized as a National School of Character and a Gold School of Opportunity. Jen Rayne's mission is to close opportunity gaps in K–12 Education.

**Kellie Rolstad** is associate professor of applied linguistics and language education at the University of Maryland. Professor Rolstad earned her PhD in education at UCLA, where she also earned degrees in linguistics (BA) and applied linguistics (MA). Dr. Rolstad previously served as associate professor of language and literacy and curriculum studies in the Mary Lou Fulton Graduate School of Education at Arizona State University. Before becoming a professor, she was a bilingual teacher for the Los Angeles Unified School District. Her research interests include the language of schooling, language diversity, alternative learning outcomes, and democratic education, and her work has appeared in *Bilingual Research Journal*, *Bilingual Review*, *Teachers College Record*, *Hispanic Journal of Behavioral Sciences*, *Educational Policy*, *Annual Review of Applied Linguistics*, *Educational Policy*, and in major edited collections.

**Lorrie A. Shepard,** PhD, is university distinguished professor at the University of Colorado Boulder in the research and evaluation methodology program. Her research focuses on psychometrics and the use and misuse of tests in educational settings. Her technical work has contributed to validity theory, standard-setting, and statistical models for detecting test bias. Her research studies on test use have addressed the identification of learning disabilities, readiness screening for kindergarten, grade retention, teacher testing, effects of high-stakes accountability testing, and most recently the use of classroom assessment to support teaching and learning.

**Kate Somerville** is a doctoral candidate in the School of Education at the University of Colorado Boulder. She works as a graduate research assistant at the National Education Policy Center for the Schools of Opportunity project and for the Research Hub for Youth Organizing and Education Policy. Kate holds an MA in teaching from Johns Hopkins University and a BA in public policy studies and political science from St. Mary's College of Maryland. Prior to starting at CU Boulder, Kate taught 2nd grade in Baltimore. Her research interests center around causes of student trauma and access to trauma-informed mental health support in segregated school environments.

**Michelle Renée Valladares** is associate director of the National Education Policy Center and faculty affiliate of the CU Boulder School of Education. She leads and partners in a series of projects that aim to increase educational opportunities for all students. Michelle has a PhD in education from the University of California, Los Angeles.

**Kevin Welner** is a professor of education policy at the University of Colorado Boulder School of Education and (by courtesy) at the School of Law. He's also the director of the National Education Policy Center. Welner's present research examines the use and misuse of research in policymaking and explores various issues concerning the intersection between education rights litigation and educational opportunity scholarship. He also continues to examine issues of tracking and detracking.

**Kathryn E. Wiley** is an assistant professor at Howard University and an expert in education policy with a focus on school discipline and climate. She uses multiple methods and a historical lens to understand contemporary education policies in the context of longstanding, racialized inequalities. She has a PhD in educational foundations, policy, and practice from the University of Colorado Boulder. She is from Dayton, Ohio, and is proud of her Sinclair Community College and Wright State University roots.

**Adam York** is a research associate with the National Education Policy Center. He supports partnerships and conducts research through the Research Hub for Youth Organizing, and manages other projects for the NEPC. He is also a faculty affiliate with the Center for Assessment, Design, Research and Evaluation (CADRE) and has taught courses at the University of Colorado Denver and University of Colorado Boulder in learning and human development, research methods, educational foundations, and policy. He earned his PhD in education and learning sciences from the University of Colorado Boulder, an MA in community counseling from Lewis and Clark College, and a BA in psychology from Colorado College.